GENERAL GORDON GRANGER

General Gordon Granger

The Savior of Chickamauga
and the Man Behind "Juneteenth"

ROBERT C. CONNER

CASEMATE
Philadelphia & Oxford

Published in the United States of America and Great Britain in 2013 by
CASEMATE PUBLISHERS
908 Darby Road, Havertown, PA 19083
and
10 Hythe Bridge Street, Oxford, OX1 2EW

Copyright 2013 © Robert C. Conner

ISBN 978-1-61200-185-2
Digital Edition: ISBN 978-1-61200-186-9

Cataloging-in-publication data is available from the Library of Congress
and the British Library.

10 9 8 7 6 5 4 3 2 1

Printed and bound in the United States of America.

For a complete list of Casemate titles please contact:

CASEMATE PUBLISHERS (US)
Telephone (610) 853-9131, Fax (610) 853-9146
E-mail: casemate@casematepublishing.com

CASEMATE PUBLISHERS (UK)
Telephone (01865) 241249, Fax (01865) 794449
E-mail: casemate-uk@casematepublishing.co.uk

Contents

For John Machell and Thomas Conner,
who are, like Granger, sons of upstate New York; and for
U.S. Army Sgt. Mary C. Conner.

Preface and
Acknowledgments

Much of this book was written in 2011–12, when I spent two seasons as site interpreter at Grant Cottage in upstate New York, where Ulysses S. Grant completed his memoirs before dying of cancer. It may seem odd for someone with a Grant connection to write the first biography of Granger, since the two men did not get along. Grant, as he made clear in those superbly written memoirs, had a low opinion of Granger, and as this book makes clear, had some legitimate reasons for that attitude. He was far from the only person to find Granger difficult to get along with.

While I continue to think Grant a mostly admirable man, writer and soldier, and an underrated president, his view of Granger should not be the last word. As a longtime newspaperman, I found Granger's story to be one of courage and achievement, and worth telling. Although obviously a lesser minor figure than his close contemporary Grant, there are numerous parallels in their careers, and Granger's memory well merits preserving.

I received generous help from Granger's great-grandson, Gordon Granger IV, who told me family lore and allowed me to visit his Virginia home and use unpublished letters from Granger to his wife in 1875–76, the last months of his life. Thanks also to Marylou Williams, who transcribed the letters for him, and to F. Champe Granger, great-great-granddaughter of the general. I wish to also thank the University of Virginia Alumni Association for helping me to get in touch with Gordon Granger IV, and Ancestry.com for pointing me in the right direction on this and other matters.

Many other Web sites such as the Library of Congress's have helped me unearth original sources and given me food for thought. Some, such as the Texas Historical Association's Handbook of Texas Online, are themselves worthy sources. Bill Thayer's website presents an impressive portal to Cullum's Register of West Point graduates. Google Books and other digitizers have made old treasures easily accessible, including my most often cited source, the multi-volume "War of the Rebellion: A Compilation of the Official Records of the Union and Confederate Armies," which I prefer to access through the eHistory site of Ohio State University.

Less objective sites, such as Bob Redman's aotc.net, which extravagantly praises the record of General George Thomas and the Army of the Cumberland, also have value. So, indeed, do lots of other sources, including roadside historical markers—my wife was rather impressed at seeing Granger's picture on one (with a good account of the Tullahoma campaign) that we stumbled across in the small town of Bell Buckle, Tennessee.

Various librarians have been helpful, including those at the Round Lake-Malta public library branch in upstate New York, which for $15 facilitated my borrowing an unpublished 1990 master's thesis on Granger by Robert W. Blackford from Southern Illinois University at Edwardsville. Also very helpful were Suzanne Christoff, associate director for special collections and archives at the U.S. Military Academy Library, West Point, Ann L. Gardner of the serials cataloging unit of the New York State Library in Albany, and the Margaret Reaney Memorial Library in St. Johnsville, NY.

Bette Bugni helped me access the impressive resources of the Sodus, NY village library, and provided me with information about the history of the schools in the town of Sodus. Wayne County Historian Peter Evans put me in touch with Bette, and was otherwise helpful, and the volunteer-run wayne.nygenweb.net told me about the grave site of Granger's mother. Hady Finch, a board member of Friends of Grant Cottage in upstate New York, provided me with the letter I quote from Private Benjamin Preston, courtesy of his descendant Patricia Bays. Royal B. Kinsley first brought to my attention the Civil War memoir of his ancestor, Rufus Kinsley.

My main helper in this project has been my wife of 29 years, Barbara J. Conner, whom I thank and cherish.

—ROBERT C. CONNER, 2013
Saratoga County, NY

Introduction

"Him that holds on to the end"

Gordon Granger was one of many otherwise obscure individuals whose lives were transformed and magnified by the Civil War, making a significant contribution to its vast history. His career and reputation suffered as a result of his failure to get along with superiors, including an even more obscure man in 1861 who soon became the Union's greatest general, Ulysses S. Grant.

Yet Granger fought all through the war, unlike many more famous commanders, and his leadership was consistently successful.

On September 20, 1863, he saved the Union Army of the Cumberland from catastrophic defeat at the Battle of Chickamauga. Two months later, he played a substantial role in its victory at Chattanooga. In 1864–65 he was a key player in the campaign to take Mobile, Alabama, first working with Admiral David Farragut to capture the bay forts; and eight months later leading a corps in the fight for the city and accepting its surrender. Two months after that, as commander of all U.S. troops in Texas, his actions sparked the "Juneteenth" celebrations of slavery's end which continue to this day.

W.H. McIntosh, who wrote an 1877 history of Granger's home county in upstate New York, doubtless exaggerated in declaring that "in the annals of local and general history, there is no soldier more patriotic, more capable, 1or more generally successful."[1] But the New York Times was scarcely less fulsome in its 1876 obituary, saying, "He was in every respect a great and distinguished officer. The story of his life is one of constant service and strict attention to duty."[2]

Granger's record of success as a combat officer is undeniable. Perhaps

1

unfortunately for his reputation and long-term career prospects, his combativeness was not confined to the battlefield but was an intrinsic part of his character.

Granger could be argumentative with any superior officer to the point of insubordination. His brutal honesty and lack of pretension were often perceived as confrontational rudeness.

The contemporary journalist William Shanks said, "Granger was a man equally courageous morally as physically, and pursued an object, or criticized a subject or person without the slightest regard to others' opinions. He never shirked a responsibility—in fact, would rather act without authority than not, as giving zest to the undertaking. Granger was almost always gruff, not only in his criticisms, but in his language, and never disliked a man without showing it."[3] What was seen by Granger's friends and associates as gruff good humor could come across to strangers as bad-tempered aggression. He seemed to relish his reputation as the blunt truth-teller, the rough soldier with no patience for playing the courtier. If it was in part a pose, still at some point the mask becomes the man. He also was a drinker, although, as with Grant—with whom he had many parallels and connections—there is no evidence that alcohol ever affected his combat performance.

Granger sometimes had cause to be stubborn, as when he sought to get decent supplies for his troops before going to the relief of Knoxville in 1863. This did not please an impatient Grant, who was soon to become commander of the entire U.S. Army. Grant had his reasons for disparaging Granger and two other senior generals in the Army of the Cumberland, George H. Thomas and William Rosecrans, as well as Granger's superior in the Mobile campaign, Edward Canby. But Grant's view of all four of these commanders tended to be skewed and overly negative.

At Chickamauga, the most important day of Granger's life, it was his friend Thomas J. Wood's obedience to Rosecrans' orders that nearly caused a catastrophe. It was Granger's reliance on his own judgment, despite what Rosecrans or any superior might have said, that saved the army. As the New York Times put it 30 years later, "Had it not been for [George] Thomas, with his staying power, and Granger, with his powers of insubordination, the Army of the Cumberland would have been shattered."[4]

That army, like the others in which Granger fought, has received less attention than the Army of the Potomac which battled Robert E. Lee in the east, Grant's Army of the Tennessee in the Mississippi Valley, or William T. Sherman's columns advancing remorselessly through the South in the war's last year. Yet Sherman's offensive into Georgia in 1864 was based out of Chattanooga, Tennessee, which had been hard won the year before by the Army of the Cumberland—in considerable part by soldiers under the command of Granger. Grant's very significant victories at Donelson, Shiloh and Vicksburg, and his subsequent rise to overall command, have led many historians to see the war in the west through his eyes. That is necessarily a one-sided view, neglecting the contributions of the Army of the Cumberland—which is not to deny the fact that Grant's role in the ultimate Union victory was as great as that of any other soldier.

Other factors have contributed to the neglect of Granger's reputation. His insistence on military discipline did not always endear him to volunteer troops, hence to modern historians. In his 1992 book on Chickamauga, Peter Cozzens says: "Neither Granger nor Steedman [a subordinate general] were attractive personalities. Granger's reputation as a martinet with a decidedly sadistic streak was well deserved."[5] This exaggerates the case for the prosecution, ignoring those occasions, such as the Knoxville campaign, when Granger risked his own career to stand up for his troops and protect them from unnecessary suffering. Many of those soldiers did come, if not to like him, then at least to respect his valuable qualities. Still, there is no denying Granger's contrarian, sometimes cynical streak, and his bad temper, which could result in arbitrary and excessive discipline—although he usually backtracked when the flare of rage had passed over.

A more balanced view is presented by Robert D. Hoffsommer, writing in a 1986 work: "A short, peppery, profane disciplinarian, Granger was not especially well liked by his troops. But he had what it takes to be a good soldier. A note he wrote to Rosecrans might well have been written for himself and Thomas at Chickamauga: 'The battle is neither to the swift nor to the strong but to him that holds on to the end.'"[6]

Granger's note adapts a biblical verse from Ecclesiastes. Hoffsommer's reference is to Granger's timely reinforcement and support which enabled George Thomas to become justly renowned as "The Rock of Chickamauga," after Rosecrans and other senior officers had fled the battlefield.

Granger's tenacity can be seen not just in battle but throughout the course of his career. By the time he died, his continuous service of over 30 years was distinctly unusual in the U.S. military. Some officers had been killed in the war, and many had turned in their commissions so that they could so as to join the Confederacy. Others, including Grant, Sherman, Rosecrans and George B. McClellan, had resigned before the war, rejoining the Army in 1861. Granger's West Point classmate Thomas Wood was one of those who resigned not long after the end of the Civil War, as did Grant (to become president) and Rosecrans. McClellan and others left the service after being shunted aside during the war.

Granger, by contrast, spent his whole adult life in the U.S. Army, while chafing sometimes at its peacetime dullness. He loved the prewar frontier life despite the lack of opportunity for promotion—at 39, when the Civil War started, he was still a first lieutenant. Back in that same Southwest in the 1870s, he held to the Army despite grave and growing health problems and a commanding general and president (Sherman and Grant) who remained unlikely to ease his way. By then he had a young family to support, and the economic depression that began in 1873 severely restricted other potential options for making a living.

Wood, who commanded a division under Granger at the Battle of Chattanooga, memorialized him at West Point after his death in 1876, writing for colleagues who would have known him personally or by reputation. Behind Granger's gruff exterior, said Wood, beat a kind heart in sympathy with the underdog. Granger, he said, was "cordial, sincere and genial. His manner was hearty and frank—at times, to the verge of brusqueness, which caused those not intimately acquainted with him to suppose him deficient in gentleness and proper consideration for the feeling of others; but this was a great mistake . . . for the mere tinsel of rank he had no respect. Wrong and injustice ever excited his indignation, and he never hesitated to give utterance to it. At the core his heart was tender and gentle; and his tender sympathy ever went out toward misfortune, sorrow and suffering."[7]

David S. Stanley, a younger officer who, like Wood, served under Granger in the Civil War, also had high praise for him in a postwar memorial written for fellow veterans. Shocked by his friend's early death, he recalled: "We, who have known him during the war, remembered him as a model of strength and manhood."[8] He also quoted a regimental colleague in the Mexican War who praised not only Granger's courage, but his kindness and consideration. Stanley also spoke highly of Granger in his own memoirs, which tend to be scathing about some other wartime colleagues.[9]

As a more modern historian, D. Reid Ross, puts it: "Granger's troops admired his bravery and had complete confidence in him. He was rough in manner, particularly toward new recruits, but had a tender heart. . . . His orders were brusque, his conversations to the point. To some he sounded harsh, if not arrogant."[10]

While the Civil War and its immediate aftermath was by far the most important part of Granger's career, his military service extended from fighting with distinction in Mexico under Winfield Scott in 1847, to negotiating peace with Apaches and fighting Comancheros in the 1870s as commander of the District of New Mexico.

After the Civil War, he continued to exasperate his military superiors. They perceived him cutting them out by dealing directly with President Andrew Johnson, with whom he had established a good relationship when Johnson was military governor of Tennessee. Grant thought, with reason, that Granger was angling to get out of tedious routine duties by seeking special favors from Johnson such as an assignment in Europe. Although he was not sent overseas, the president did employ him on more or less political missions that completely bypassed the normal chain of command. And Granger was happy to escape the unsympathetic supervision of Grant and Sherman, from whom he could expect little good. But his political links to the increasingly controversial Reconstruction policies of Johnson have not helped his historical reputation, and to some extent marked a retreat from the bold and effective positions for equal civil rights which he had affirmed in Texas on "Juneteenth."

They also further alienated him from Grant, who was aligning himself with the Radical Republicans against Johnson. Grant's friend and ally Sherman, who was to take over from him as head of the Army, was much less supportive of black rights, and according to a modern biographer "deeply opposed, on racist grounds, the fundamental purpose of Reconstruction."[11] That was never Granger's position, although he did not match Grant's growing radicalism, either. Granger's views probably remained closer to mainstream public opinion, and his actions from 1861 on throw considerable light on the swiftly changing attitudes in the United States toward slavery and black civil rights, over the course of the war and Reconstruction.

Also irritating the brass were Granger's absences from duty on medical leaves, although they seem to have been amply justified. While Grant's negative portrayal of Granger in his memoirs did not appear until both men were dead, Sherman published his own memoirs in 1875. Sherman included slighting references to Granger purportedly seeking a leave of absence in 1864 just before the onset of the Atlanta campaign. In reality, Granger was forced out by Grant and Sherman as commander of Fourth Corps in 1864, but was enabled to get back into the war at Mobile through the influence of Johnson. But in 1875, when Sherman was writing, Granger really had been out on a very long medical leave, which the commanding general probably found frustrating.

Granger had real health problems throughout his life, which worsened as he grew into middle age. He was on extended medical leave from 1873-75 after suffering severe eye and lung diseases—acute retinitis, loss of sight in his left eye, along with asthma and chronic bronchitis which involved repeated coughing up blood. These conditions were probably aggravated by the high desert climate of New Mexico. Perhaps Sherman's doubts about the genuineness of Granger's medical issues were alleviated by the two strokes the latter suffered after returning to active duty, the second of which killed him in Santa Fe on January 10, 1876. (Sherman also had to deal with a bizarre family aftermath.)

The writings of Grant, especially, and Sherman negatively affected the reputations of Granger and Thomas, both of whom died in their early 50s while on duty in the West, never writing any memoirs of their own. While plenty of his contemporaries lauded Granger, and he even got some kind words in the memoirs of Grant's protégé General Philip Sheridan, his reputation took another downward turn in the 20th century. A pro-Southern writer, Archibald Gracie IV, in 1911 bitterly and unfairly deprecated his role even at Chickamauga, and some modern historians have followed this negative lead. For a truer, more balanced view of Granger's life it is necessary to go back to the people who knew and appreciated him, sources from the 19th century like the *Cincinnati Gazette* reporter at Chattanooga who called him "brave, able, sensible, rough."[12]

Marshall Thatcher, who served in the regiment—the Second Michigan Cavalry—of which Granger was made colonel in 1861, says in his memoir: "With all his gruff ways, Gordon Granger at times revealed a strong character for justice, truth and mercy."[13] Along with his sometimes cynical remarks he could tell an aggrieved subordinate who sought justice, "I will do what is right, though the heavens fall." Granger often came on strong initially about some disciplinary matter, Thatcher says, and "there was not much love for the man at first among the officers and privates." They softened, however, when they saw what he did, that he would typically not carry out dire threats, and was in the end determined to be fair to the soldiers under his command.

Another such source is Lt. Colonel Joseph Fullerton, Granger's chief of staff at Chickamauga and Chattanooga, who wrote of him: "Gordon Granger was rough in manner, but he had a tender heart. He was not a respecter of persons. He was rather inclined to insubordination. This was especially so when he knew his superior officer to be wrong. Otherwise he was a splendid soldier. Rosecrans named him well when he wrote of him, 'Granger, great in battle.'"[14]

Critics may find Rosecrans unqualified to give that praise to the extent it is based on Granger's performance at Chickamauga, which the commanding general did not witness because he had fled the battlefield. But Rosecrans' overall war record was much better than Grant ever gave him credit for, and he also knew Granger as a capable subordinate in prior, less intense combats. Thomas, an excellent soldier also undervalued by Grant, also appreciated Granger's competence and leadership. Those qualities were urgently needed in the Civil War, which accounts for Granger's long active service in high rank despite his personality quirks and Grant's antipathy—which may date from some contact lost to history at West Point or in the Mexican War.

While this is the first biography of Granger, Robert W. Blackford, a graduate student at the University of Southern Illinois, wrote a 1990 master's thesis on his Civil War service. Noting Granger's lack of effective political patronage, Blackford says: "Part of this was due to his own personality, since socializing was not one of his strengths. Something of a rough character in his younger days, his service prior to the war [was] in the West, far from the drawing rooms of Eastern society. Out there he was [a] rough man in a rough world of small isolated units where results were everything . . .

"Outspoken and blunt, critical of blunders committed by others and possessed of a sense of humor which led to some ill advised actions, he could be his own worst enemy in working relationships. . . . Fearless in combat and crafty enough to match wits with the likes of [Gen. Nathan Bedford] Forrest, he survived the bullets and stratagems of the enemy to fall prey to the back room politics and personalities of his comrades. He is practically unheard of today."[15]

A century earlier, Thatcher was more fulsome in his praise, yet sounded a similar note: "The civil war in America developed few brighter military geniuses than General Gordon Granger, yet we have not, as a nation, begun to look upon him as among our heroes."[16]

It is of course the case that Granger's contribution to the Union cause was substantially below that of Grant, Sherman, Thomas or Sheridan, all of whom have deservedly had their share of biographers. But as Henry Boynton, a Medal of Honor winner and veteran of Chickamauga and Chattanooga, and one of the most vigorous defenders of the reputation of the Army of the Cumberland, said about Sherman and Grant: "It is not necessary to dim other records to brighten theirs."[17] Granger's story, like that of hundreds of other Civil War generals, has been scanted or, in his case, distorted. Yet he, like others more famous or obscure, rose to meet the major crisis of his life, the Civil War. His role in winning it, and on Juneteenth in establishing the meaning of that victory, deserves to be recognized and remembered.

NOTES

1. McIntosh, W. H. *History of Wayne County, New York*. (Philadelphia: Everts, Ensign, & Everts, 1877), 182–3.
2. *New York Times,* Jan. 12, 1876.
3. William F.G. Shanks, *Personal Recollections of Distinguished Generals* (1866), 271.
4. *The New York Times,* Nov. 26, 1893.
5. Peter Cozzens, *This Terrible Sound: The Battle of Chickamauga* (1992), 440.
6. *Historical Times Illustrated Encyclopedia of the Civil War* (Harper & Row, 1986), 319.
7. T.J. Wood, in *Seventh Annual Reunion of the Association of the Graduates of the United States Military Academy at West Point, New York* (1876), 66.
8. (David Stanley), *Reunion of the Society of the Army of the Cumberland*, Vol. 15 (Cincinnati: Robert Clarke & Co., 1883, 1884), 209. Stanley's name is not attached to the memorial, but on page 55 of Vol. 15 of the *Reunion* it is mentioned that he had agreed to write it. Stanley was still in the Army in 1883, so may have wished for some anonymity when wading into the controversies of Civil War history. In fact, at that time he was a colonel commanding the District of New Mexico, the exact positions Granger had held at the time of his death. Stanley was promoted to brigadier general the next year and retired in 1892.
9. Stanley, David S., ed. Samuel Fordyce. *An American General, The Memoirs of David Sloan Stanley*. Santa Barbara, Calif.: The Narrative Press, 2003. Stanley's memoirs are particularly and overly harsh toward Wood and Brig.-Gen. John Turchin.
10. D. Reid Ross, *Lincoln's Veteran Volunteers Win The War* (Albany, NY: SUNY Press, 2008), 154.
11. Michael Fellman, *Citizen Sherman.* New York: Random House (1995), 292.
12. *The Rebellion Record*, ed. Frank Moore Vol. 8 (1865), 233.
13. Marshall P. Thatcher, *A Hundred Battles in the West*, (1884), 275.
14. J.S. Fullerton, *The Reserve Corps at Chickamauga, The Century Illustrated Monthly Magazine* (1887), Vol. 33, 964.
15. Robert W. Blackford, *The Civil War Service of General Gordon Granger, U.S.A.,* unpublished master's thesis (Southern Illinois University, Edwardsville, 1990).
16. Thatcher, op. cit., 270.
17. Henry V. Boynton, *The Annual Address Delivered at the Twenty-third Reunion of the Society of the Army of the Cumberland* (1892).

1

Early Life and West Point

Gordon Granger, like many Americans of his day, came from an area that until very recently had been the frontier. He was born and raised in Wayne County, in far upstate New York, which had been claimed by the British until 1796 in a hangover from the Revolutionary War. It had also been the scene of fighting in the next war with the British, a few years before his birth. Gordon's father, Gaius Granger, was apparently a descendant of Launcelot Granger, who came from England to Massachusetts in the 17th century, marrying a woman named Johanna or Joanna. The family soon moved to near Hartford, Connecticut.

Gaius' parents were from New England, his father Elihu from Connecticut and his mother Apema (or Apama) from Massachusetts. They were among a number of Grangers who moved to Phelps, in rural Ontario County, west-central New York, between Rochester and Syracuse. Gaius was born in Phelps on September 20, 1797. Apema was the daughter of one Granger who married another. Her father, Aaron Granger, lived from 1736 to 1782. Aaron, the great-grandfather of Gordon, had served as a private in the American army during the Revolutionary War, fighting at Saratoga in 1777. Gordon Granger, whose mother died young, would spend much of his youth with his paternal grandparents. Elihu died in 1842, the year after his grandson went to West Point. Apema lived until 1853.

As a young man, Gaius Granger moved some miles north to a place called Joy in Wayne County, and he built the first house there, according to McIntosh's local history. Joy was named after Benjamin Joy of England, who owned much of the local land where other Grangers were moving to from Phelps. It is some seven miles south of Lake Ontario, and is in the town of

Sodus (a name of Indian origin). Like most of his neighbors, Gaius was a farmer, but they had to clear the unbroken forest that covered Sodus before they could plant crops. Gaius also quickly found use for the felled trees by building a saw mill, which was powered by Salmon Creek. He called his farm Oak Corners. (Many years later, Gaius' great-great grandson, Gordon Granger IV, would give the same name to his own farm in Virginia.)

Gaius married Catherine Taylor and Gordon was their eldest child, although the year of his birth is wrapped in obscurity and uncertainty. McIntosh gives it as 1818, which is much too early, and the standard date given by most modern sources is November 6, 1822. But Granger's grave marker in Kentucky cites a birth date of 1821, which accords with other evidence including his own application letter to West Point, as well as U.S. Census and Army data. There does not appear to be any hard evidence for the current consensus, and the actual date of his birth appears to be November 6, 1821.[1] He was almost certainly born at home, which seems to have been north-northwest of the hamlet of Joy.

Two younger sisters, Emeline and Catherine, followed. Both of them would outlive their brother and die, apparently unmarried, in the same part of upstate New York where they were born. Of the three full siblings, Gordon was the only one who married, and he delayed doing so until he was 47.

The ancestry of Catherine Taylor Granger is unrecorded, and her life was short. She died on April 17, 1825, at the age of 25, less than a month after the birth of her youngest child. She was laid to rest in the Johnson Burial Ground at Sodus Point, on the lake. Her tombstone, which calls her Cathrin, has a verse from the early 18th-century English hymn writer Isaac Watts:

> My flesh shall slumber in the ground,
> Till the last trumpets joyful sound,
> Then burst the chains with sweet surprise
> And in my Saviour's image rise.[2]

It seems reasonable to speculate that the loss of his mother when he was three years old permanently affected Granger, and contributed to the roughness of his adult character. On November 19, 1826, not long after his fifth birthday, he acquired an 18-year-old stepmother, Sara (Sally) Emery. His father's remarriage would produce 10 additional children. As a teen-ager, Granger would live with his grandparents in Phelps.

This was a remote northern countryside, good farming country in the gently rolling hills south of the lake plain, but also blanketed by heavy lake-effect snow through long winters. "All these settlements," says McIntosh about Sodus in the first decades of the century, "were made in the face of hardships innumerable, sickness frequent, and privations depressing and excessive."

By the 1890s, Joy would be described in another local history as "a pleasant rural hamlet, surrounded by good farms."[3] Those farms were converted to orchards in the 20th century, and with the advent of the automobile and the economic decline of upstate New York, Joy's store, church, school and businesses (which had included small manufacturers) went out of existence. (So did many stores and businesses in the village of Sodus, four miles to the northeast, although its old churches still function and the public library is thriving.) When Granger was living in Joy, the hamlet was in its infancy. The Presbyterian Church, for example, was not built until the decade after Granger left town; nor was the cemetery yet established. The Rural Union Cemetery is still functioning, surrounded now by orchards, behind where the church used to stand. Several Grangers are buried there, including a Gordon born in 1863, the year his namesake became famous at Chickamauga. There's a historical marker there, which is the only sign in the hamlet (if it still can be termed as such), apart from street markers. The casual visitor would not know he was in Joy.

A one-room school had been established in Joy by 1833, according to local historian Bette Bugni, which means Granger would have gone there. The white wooden building still stands on its rock foundation, on Main Street just north of Joy Road, in the shade of three maple trees. The one room is a large one, with big windows on three sides (not the north), and what appears to be a small attached outhouse in the back. The old school is now used as a community center for functions such as voting, but is not usually open and has no sign indicating its purpose or history. It's a quiet spot.

Education beyond the eighth grade would have had to be pursued elsewhere. The village of Sodus academy (or high school) did not open until 1855, thus would not have been available to Granger. So he went to school in Lyons, the Wayne County seat, which is south of Sodus and southeast of Joy. His grandparents were living in Phelps, a town just south of Lyons, and he could have commuted from their home to school.

The entire area remains remote and rural. Apple orchards predominate in modern Joy, and in the surrounding area can also be found cherries, corn, vegetables and grain crops, as well as undeveloped woodland. In Granger's childhood it was only a decade removed from being the wartime frontier. The first white settlers in Wayne County had arrived in 1789, and in Sodus in 1794. Territorial disputes with Britain (or Canada) had continued after the end of the Revolutionary War, and in 1812 a new war had flared up. In 1813, eight years before Granger was born, Sodus Point had been burned by British troops based in Canada across Lake Ontario. They made another attack on Wayne County in 1814, at Pultneyville.

The county is named after a general who fought the British in the previous generation's Revolutionary War, "Mad Anthony" Wayne. After that, Wayne fought Indians on the frontier—as did Granger in the 1850s (although by the 1870s the latter would be helping negotiate peace with the Apache chief Cochise).

The War of 1812 did not stop the development of Sodus. The first school commissioners were elected in 1813, in the middle of the war, with the town divided into 11 school districts. By the 1820s, as woods turned into farms and the Erie Canal was completed, the area was participating in upstate New York's rapid growth. Wayne County's population was listed at 1,410 in the 1800 U.S. Census, going up in subsequent decades to 6,575 in 1810, 20,309 in 1820, 33,643 in 1830, and 42,057 in 1840, the year before Granger left for West Point.

Granger's youth was a period of religious ferment, and the countryside participated in the Christian Great Awakening. The First Baptist Society of Sodus meeting house was built in the mid-1820s, and Episcopal and Presbyterian churches also were built in town that decade, with the Methodists following in the 1830s. Periodic revivals are noted in the local history. The area also played host to new sects, the Latter Day Saints and Shakers. The Shakers had a substantial settlement in Sodus in the 1820s and 1830s.

The West Baptist Church of Sodus held meetings in the 1830s and 1840s, but did not then get around to building a church. Joy is in the western part of town, and there were Grangers on the church roll, as there were some at other churches. Gaius' name does not show among the church members listed by McIntosh. He named one of his younger sons John Wesley, which could indicate the family was Methodist. Gaius did not play a prominent part in public affairs, although he served a year as one of two "overseers of the poor" in 1843–44, when his eldest son was at West Point.[4]

Granger, according to Army historian George Cullum, "had a good English education" before arriving at West Point.[5] But his progress at high school in Lyons had been retarded by the health problems which were to plague him through much of his life. According to a postwar memorial to Granger, apparently by David Stanley, presented at a military reunion in 1883, he had chronic bronchitis as a youth which delayed his entry into West Point. Meanwhile, "he taught school, as a boy, for one or two terms, not far from Phelps; spending most of his life with his grandfather, Elihu Granger, of Phelps."[6]

Actually, Granger seems to have taught for two years. It is possible that his health problems delayed his entry into West Point, but it may just have taken time to line up the backers needed for his application to the U.S. Military Academy. Ulysses S. Grant was admitted young to West Point, having just turned 17, and he didn't actually want to go but was required to by his pushy and ambitious father. Granger, for good or ill, had no such parental pressure. Granger's health issues, however, were very real, and perhaps should have argued against choosing a military career.

Before he was teaching in the Phelps area, he spent the 1839–40 school year as the teacher for District 16 at the one-room schoolhouse on Pre-Emption Road, on the eastern edge of the town of Sodus.[7] Teaching is in fact the only paid work he ever did apart from soldiering, so it's worth considering what it meant to him. Readers familiar with Laura Ingalls Wilder's novel *Farmer Boy* will recall the potential discipline problems that could be encountered by a teacher in a one-room rural schoolhouse in upstate New York. These were evidently difficulties which the 17-year-old Granger learned to handle, however, as he would—despite some bumps on the road—prove to be a good disciplinarian and leader in the Army.

Choosing to teach indicates that Granger did not want to follow in his father's footsteps by farming or running a sawmill, and health considerations may also have played a role in keeping him off the land. There were certainly enough younger siblings to farm the family's land, and enough opportunities elsewhere, both in booming upstate New York and across the already vast United States. A youth with an appetite for adventure might teach while waiting for his future to open up.

Teaching also indicates an interest in further education, but there was no means by which he could have afforded to pay for university. Fortunately, in West Point he found an alternative, excellent educational opportunity. Then, as now, the U.S. Military Academy at West Point paid all its students' expenses—if you could qualify to get in, and keep up with the work and the discipline once there.

By the 1850 census, Gaius Granger's farm was worth a substantial $3,400, yet like his son, he was not ready to settle down in the increasingly civilized and stable community he had known all his life. Instead, long after Gordon had left home, he upped stakes again and headed west to a new frontier, moving with his wife to Hillsdale, Michigan, in the 1850s. Gaius died in Hillsdale on August 20, 1863. His son was unable to attend the funeral, being just a month away from his momentous destiny at Chickamauga. Gaius' wife Sally moved back to Sodus, outliving her stepson and dying there in 1878.

As the eldest child, Gordon might have been expected to become a farmer by inheritance. But the situation was complicated by his mother's early death and the dozen younger siblings at home. So he went his own way. He matched his father's vigorous restlessness (a trait that was to be inherited in the next generation by his own son), adding to it his own ambition, curiosity and confidence, all channeled through the U.S. Army.

Granger had early shown an interest in military affairs, according to Collins Wells, a colonel in the local Riflemen militia. Wells was one of five people who sent letters in early January 1841 supporting Granger's application to the U.S. Military Academy. Granger, wrote Wells, was "a young man of pure morals an[d] exalted reputation" whom he had known since infancy. "He has performed military duty under me as a staff officer [and] is highly distinguished for perseverance and enterprise."

Appointments to West Point, the training academy for U.S. Army officers, are and were often arranged through congressional representatives, and McIntosh suggests U.S. Representative Theron Strong, a Democrat who later became a judge, played that role in Granger's case. There is, however, no letter from Strong in Granger's file, but curiously, one from the man who would be elected the next year as his successor, Bryam Green. Green, also a Democrat, had served in the state Assembly and Senate, though he had been out of office for 14 years. He was still probably Granger's most influential backer, and wrote: "I have been acquainted with Mr. Granger ever since he was a child. He is a young man of fine talents. His habits are moral, steady and uniform. His genius, for the study of mathematics, is far above par. His mind seems to be formed for investigation. If he should be successful in his application, I have no doubt, he will be an ornament to the school."

Also writing was Morton Eddy, another Democrat (all of which may help explain Granger's political leanings in later life). He said: "I am well acquainted with Mr. Granger and know him to be a young man of excellent talents of good moral character and has a well disciplined and cultivated mind."

Gamaliel Case, a Sodus farmer, said Granger was "a young man of candor with an enterprising and persevering mind." Another endorser—with an illegible signature—said the applicant was "a young man of good moral character" with a mind of "sound judgment and genius."

Granger himself wrote: "Petitioner wishes to be admitted as a cadet into the Military Academy West Point. His age in nineteen years. . . . His height is five feet nine inches." He signed off with an attempt at a traditional formal style: "If it is consistent to grant his request, your petitioner as in duty bound will ever pray."

He was conditionally accepted the next month, whereupon he and his father Gaius wrote back to say he would be going.

Gordon Granger was appointed to West Point in 1841 at the age of 19. He probably travelled by canal boat and possibly railroad east to Albany, and then south down the Hudson to the Revolutionary War fortress above the narrowing, bending river, 50 miles north of New York City. He became a cadet there on July 1.

Little remains from the West Point of Granger's day; it has been almost completely rebuilt and greatly expanded. Neither the motto, "Duty, Honor, Country" nor the Alma Mater, with its best-known lines, "And when our work is done, Our course on earth is run," had yet been written. Yet he would live up to them anyway, "steadfast in commitment to the profession of arms" (to borrow a phrase from a recent West Point speaker, Gen. Raymond Odierno), until he died at his Army post in far-off New Mexico.

At the academy, the first year's study was largely devoted to mathematics, along with French, military drill and "the school of the soldier." In the second year, rhetoric, geography and history were added to the mix, along with artillery instruction and "the school of the company." Drawing, "natural philosophy" and chemistry, with more artillery and a course on the duties of sergeants, came in year three. The fourth year included engineering, the science of war, mineralogy and geology, moral philosophy, political science, rhetoric, the duties of commissioned officers and the use of the sword.[8]

William Dutton, in the class behind Granger, wrote to his brother in June 1842 giving a slice of first-year West Point life: "We then march to the mess hall, & if one speaks, raises his hand, looks to the right or left (which is the case on all parade) we are reported indeed we are reported for everything. . . . When we arrive at the tables, the command is given 'take seats,' & then such a scrambling you never saw. . . . We have to eat as fast as we can, & before we get enough, the command is given 'Squad rise,' at dinner we have 'Roast Beef,' & boiled potato, & bread—no butter, at Tea, bread & butter &

tea. We have to drill twice a day, & a good many faint away. It is terrible, but I like the whole of it.... at taps at 10 every light must be out & after that the inspector happens in all times of night."[9]

According to Thomas Wood: "Granger achieved a military reputation second to none of his classmates of either side, in the late Civil War."[10] Those classmates included the Union generals William F. "Baldy" Smith and Fitz-John Porter, along with Wood himself. Granger would command Wood (after Thomas' departure) at Chickamauga and then at Chattanooga, where he also worked with Baldy Smith.

Also in the class was E. Kirby Smith. He became a Confederate general whose success in invading Kentucky prompted Granger's transfer there in the late summer of 1862. Smith wound up in command of the trans-Mississippi district, from which he fled to Mexico at the end of the war, leaving it to Granger to restore order in Texas and proclaim the end of slavery on "Juneteenth." Another future Confederate general, Dabney Maury, was in the next year's class. He would serve in Mexico and later Texas in the same regiment as Granger, and then oppose him in the Civil War's Mobile campaign. Granger in his first year at West Point would have encountered James "Pete" Longstreet, who graduated in 1842, and would fight against Granger in 1863–64 at Chickamauga and in East Tennessee.

Grant was five months younger than Granger but two years ahead of him at West Point. Granger may have resented the younger cadet's getting ahead of him, although he got along well enough with others in the same situation. They were both of humble origins, country boys from free states, unlike many of the West Point cadets. They were very different in appearance, though. Grant's features were handsome, more delicate than Granger's rough face, which could get rougher when he demonstrated his customary abrasiveness. Grant was fairly short, five feet eight inches or less. There is a painting of the Battle of Chattanooga, done about 15 years after the war by Thure de Thulstrup, which shows both of Grant's balky subordinates, Granger and George Thomas, towering over the commanding general.

Whatever the origins of the long antagonism between Granger and Grant, it seems likely to have started at West Point. It certainly was in place on Grant's part before the Battle of Chattanooga (as Philip Sheridan's memoirs attest), although the events there and immediately afterward reinforced Grant—to a considerable extent unfairly—in his negative predisposition. Grant, much more than Granger, could hold on to a grudge, and appears to have done so in this case.

Granger also met John Pope, another younger cadet who was ahead of him at West Point, graduating in 1842. Pope would become an important mentor to Granger's later career, as would another cadet much younger still, George McClellan, who graduated in 1846.

McClellan, who acquired a low opinion of Grant when he saw him under the influence of alcohol in 1853,[11] praised Granger during and after the Civil War. His friendship probably aided Granger's rise at the beginning of the war, though it contributed to the stalling of his later career, once McClellan had become anathema to the Republican Party while Grant was on track to become its standard bearer. Granger, like a great many Army officers and men, seems to have shared McClellan's generally conservative approach to slavery and other issues at the beginning of the war. Much more so than McClellan, however, Granger would prove ready and able to adapt to the changing policies of the Lincoln administration, competently executing important political functions. (He also proved a much better handler of intelligence than McClellan, who consistently and massively overestimated the Confederate army.)

Wood graduated fifth of the 40 members of the class of 1845, well ahead of his friend, who was 34th. Granger, Wood said, "was not what is usually termed a good student, he was not ambitious of academic honors." (The West Point annual record listed Granger as 35th out of 41. But Wood, who was in a position to know and was memorializing his friend for his fellow West Pointers, is likely to be more reliable in stating that Granger ranked 34th out of 40 graduates.)

Actually Granger's indifferent record at graduation represented an improvement over previous years. In 1842, after one year at the academy, he was ranked 58th out of 76 cadets then in the class—55th in mathematics and 56th in French. In conduct, he was ranked 152nd out of the total of 217 at the academy—five places ahead of Grant. Granger had 87 demerits.[12]

Cadets' demerits were judged more harshly as they proceeded through the academy. Each offense was given a certain number of demerits; thus absence from a roll call might be worth three, while disobeying an order or bringing liquor into barracks would each be accounted eight demerits. David Stanley's postwar memorial quotes a description of Granger as "of rather unshapely figure, and a little uncouth in his manner, but he went through the course at the academy creditably."[13]

The next year, 1843, Granger ranked 44th of the 49 remaining cadets, the other 27 having not made the grade. He was 39th in mathematics, 32nd in French, 60th in drawing (a subject that included some of those who dropped or flunked out, or who had to repeat the year), and 42nd in rhetoric, grammar and geography. His conduct record was worse, 195th out of 223, with 127 demerits. In 1844, he ranked 40th out of 41—34th in philosophy, 39th in chemistry and 50th in drawing. For conduct, he was 170th out of 211, with 133 demerits.

Despite any difficulties with the rigorous discipline and academic work, Granger hung in there until graduation, doing enough every year to keep moving up on schedule. In his last year, 1845, he ranked 27th in engineering, 24th in ethics, 38th in infantry tactics, 27th in artillery and 21st in mineralogy and geology. In conduct he was 174th out of 204, with 139 demerits. (No. 1 on the conduct roll that year was Thomas J. Jackson, the future "Stonewall" of Confederate fame, who was a year behind Granger and would soon be fighting with him in Mexico. Jackson had zero demerits, emulating his future commander Robert E. Lee.)

At West Point, Wood says, Granger did learn "the principles of military science as to be able to make a practical use and application of them in his subsequent widely diversified and active professional career." His time at the academy "was chiefly distinguished by the sturdy independence and manliness which formed so marked a feature of his matured and developed character."[14] Those attributes of character also included a lifelong obstreperousness and willingness to argue with superiors, which no doubt contributed to the racking up of demerits, dragging down his class standing.

NOTES

1. Granger's application packet is at the National Archives in Washington, D.C., although Suzanne Christoff, associate director for special collections and archives at the U.S. Military Academy Library at West Point, told me "they have been reproduced in a microfilm publication and, more recently, on Ancestry.com," which is where I found them.
2. Wayne County NYGenWeb site.
3. Cowles, G.W. and Smith, H.P,. *Landmarks of Wayne County, New York* (1895).
4. McIntosh, W. H. *History of Wayne County, New York.* (Philadelphia: Everts, Ensign, & Everts, 1877).
5. George Cullum, *Biographical Register of the Officers and Graduates of the United States Military Academy* Vol. 2 (1891 3rd ed.), 239.
6. David Stanley (see note to Chapter 1), *Reunion of the Society of the Army of the Cumberland*, Vol. 15 (1883), 209.

7. Interview with local historian Bette Bugni.
8. William Morton, foreword, *Cadet Life Before the Mexican War*, Bulletin No. 1, USMA Library, West Point (1945).
9. William Dutton, *Cadet Life Before the Mexican War,* op. cit., 12-13.
10. T.J. Wood, in *Seventh Annual Reunion of the Association of the Graduates of the United States Military Academy at West Point, New York* (1876), 55.
11. Thomas J. Rowland, *George B. McClellan and Civil War History* (1998), 60.
12. Granger's records are listed for each year of his attendance in the *Official Register of the Officers and Cadets of the U.S. Military Academy, West Point, New York,* at the USMA Library.
13. *Reunion of the Society of the Army of the Cumberland*, op. cit.
14. Wood, op. cit., 56.

2

Mexico and the Frontier

G ranger's relatively low graduation standing meant that at least initially he was destined for the infantry. He was appointed July 1 as brevet second lieutenant in the Second Infantry Regiment. Its headquarters had just been transferred to Detroit Barracks in Michigan, which is where Granger was assigned. Fort Wayne, named after the same general as Granger's home county in upstate New York, was being built at the barracks site on the Detroit River. Supervising its construction was Lt. Montgomery Meigs, who was to become quartermaster general during the Civil War.

According to a 1906 memoir by Friend Palmer, who was in Detroit in 1845, Granger was a "rough diamond," indeed "the roughest specimen of a West Point graduate I, or anyone else, ever saw . . . he was detailed to assume command of the quartermaster's and commissary departments. I was quartermaster and commissary clerk at the time and, of course, was in daily communication with Granger and we came to know each other well. He was all right, except that he was rough and uncouth, and got along well enough with the boys, but with the girls he was a back number."[1]

Palmer says Granger tried to court Louise Garland, a lieutenant-colonel's daughter, but lost out to another young officer, James "Pete" Longstreet, who became engaged to Louise and later married her. (Granger was to repeat that pattern more than a decade later when he unsuccessfully pursued Ellen Marcy, who would wind up marrying George McClellan.)

The U.S. Army when Granger entered it was only about 7,000 strong, but was about to greatly expand because of the Mexican War. It would contract after the war, but not down to the prewar level, then go through a similar but much larger expansion and contraction during and after the Civil War. Despite these vast fluctuations, which greatly affected an officer's rank and prospects for promotion, the Army was generally on an upward trend, and had about 25,000 soldiers at the time of Granger's death in 1876.

In 1845, the year of Granger's graduation from West Point, Texas was annexed by the United States. The new state had won its independence by rebelling from Mexico in 1836, and most of its citizens wanted to be part of the United States. Mexico did not clearly recognize Texas' independence[2] and strongly opposed U.S. annexation. Texas' southern and western borders with Mexico were in dispute, a dispute inherited by the U.S. government. That government—or at least the Polk administration—thought the United States' "Manifest Destiny" was to expand westward to the Pacific, taking over not just Texas but California and other territories then clearly part of Mexico. In July 1845, U.S. President James Polk sent Gen. Zachary Taylor and a small army to defend Texas. Diplomacy and implied threats got nowhere, and in 1846 Polk ordered Taylor into the disputed south Texas territory. On April 26 a contingent of U.S. Dragoons was attacked and captured by Mexican forces, with about 14 of the Americans being killed. This precipitated the U.S. declaration of war in May 1846.

The Mexicans declared war in July. In that month, after one year with the Second Infantry, Granger was transferred to the new Regiment of Mounted Riflemen. This regiment had been created by Congress in May to serve on the Oregon Trail. Granger was now stationed at Jefferson Barracks, St. Louis, Missouri, where the regiment was organized in October. It had its own distinctive, fancy uniform—trousers with black leg stripes bordered in yellow, a crimson sash, and gold eagles on the cap and belt.

It also sounds like Granger's kind of outfit, according to a brief history of the regiment written by one of its officers, Captain Charles Morton. Junior officers were readily given responsibility, and, according to an anonymous soldier quoted by Morton: "The officers were all gentlemen, brave and generous to a fault, strict disciplinarians, and looked well after the wants of their men, but the most cantankerous lot I ever met."[3] That exactly describes Granger's style as an officer throughout his career.

It was announced in November 1846 that the regiment would not serve on the Oregon Trail (it got there three years later). Instead, it would be diverted to the Mexican War. Soon the soldiers and horses departed by steamboat down the Mississippi to New Orleans, and thence by sailing schooner to Point Isabel, Texas, on the Gulf of Mexico near the Mexican border. Many of the horses were lost in a huge gale on the latter journey, and most of the remainder were transferred to the Second Dragoons.

Thus most of the Mounted Riflemen were not mounted in the Mexican War, but served as infantry soldiers. Morton says this "proved a blessing by saving the regiment from being left behind to escort trains for Taylor's army and chase guerrillas in the chaparral, and permitting it instead to participate in the campaign where it won such renown."[4] The reference is to Gen. Taylor's campaign on the war's northern front. Taylor's army had borne the brunt of the fighting, but now it was to be depleted and put on the defensive. The Army's general-in-chief, Winfield Scott, was building up a new invasion force for a different front, a seaborne landing and campaign into the middle of Mexico to capture the capital, Mexico City, and end the war by compelling the government to make peace and recognize American territorial gains. (Separate, relatively bloodless but significant campaigns had been undertaken by other U.S. generals, including the conquest of California and New Mexico.)

Scott had been a general since the War of 1812, in which he won the Battle of Chippewa and was wounded at Lundy's Lane. Although a Virginian, he would continue to serve as general-in-chief through the first months of the Civil War. Scott's campaign in Mexico would turn out to be the highlight of his career, strategically daring, hard fought and brilliantly successful. The Mounted Riflemen served all through it, engaged heavily in combat in all the major battles save one (Molino del Rey). They had been later than some getting into the war, but did as much as any to win its crucial campaign. Their fellow soldiers in Scott's army included many future commanders on both sides in the Civil War, such as Grant, Lee, McClellan, Jackson, Longstreet and George Meade. Most, including Granger, found it their most significant military education.

The Riflemen landed with the rest of Scott's army at Vera Cruz, Mexico, on March 9, 1847, and participated in the fighting there that month. For the most part, though, the infantry soldiers "battled with wind and sand, insects and thorny chapparal, hunger and thirst, such camp diseases as diarrhea, and all the other discomforts of camping out in the sand dunes."[5] Scott had fewer than 12,000 troops, a number that would grow significantly smaller as the army—including Granger—fought its way inland, along Hernando Cortes' old route to Mexico City. They were heavily outnumbered throughout the campaign.

Granger's lifelong fascination with artillery, which would later irritate Grant and provoke the scorn of some Civil War observers and historians, must have gotten a powerful boost at Vera Cruz. Scott did not want to storm the city, because of the losses it would incur, nor starve it out, because he was worried about the impending yéllow fever season on the Gulf Coast. So instead he bombarded it, and soon compelled its surrender. In 1864-65, when he and his fellow Mounted Rifleman Dabney Maury would oppose each as major-generals, Granger's artillery expertise would play a significant role in the Mobile campaign.

In Mexico, the 25-year-old Granger proved himself a formidable combat soldier. Stanley's SAC memorial—reliable because, like Wood's account, it was written by one who had served with Granger in wartime and for an audience of others who had done the same—says he "was in every battle, always distinguishing himself by his perfect coolness and indomitable courage. These qualities made him admired by the men of his regiment, who went cheerfully where he would lead.... At Cerro Gordo, Contreras, Cherubusco, and at the assault on Chapultepec, and at the Garita, he was conspicuous in his gallant conduct."[6]

The regiment suffered significant losses in the two-day battle of Cerro Gordo, helping capture the summit—from which the battle got its name—on April 18. The next month, during a pause in the campaign at Puebla, Granger was promoted to second lieutenant in the regular Army. In August, Scott's army was on the move again, approaching Mexico City from the south through spectacular mountain scenery.

The nineteenth and twentieth of August were probably the most important days of the campaign, and possibly of the Mexican War, when the battles of Contreras and Churubsco were fought—with Granger in the middle of both.

On the late afternoon of the 19th, an American contingent of fewer than 3,500 men, without artillery or cavalry, found itself exposed between two larger Mexican forces. The Americans, including the Mounted Riflemen, were commanded by Persifor Smith. "The situation was one which a bold and enterprising Mexican commander . . . might well have turned into a major American disaster—and Scott's army could not afford disasters."[7]

Helping stave off disaster were two second lieutenants of the Mounted Riflemen, Granger and John P. Hatch, who had much in common. They both came from the same part of upstate New York, were West Point classmates, and would go on to serve on the Western frontier in the 1850s and as Union generals in the Civil War. With five or six soldiers they seized an old ranch in front of the entrenchments and "were holding it against the fire of the

whole of [Mexican General Gabriel] Valencia's forces."[8] Granger and Hatch
had rejoined the main regiment by early morning, participating in the bayo-
net-charge attack that drove Valencia's force into headlong flight in 17 minutes.[9] Then Granger was in the follow-up victory of Churubusco where the
Riflemen helped take a stubbornly defended convent.

In-between the two engagements, General Scott came upon soldiers of
the regiment, and said: "Brave Rifles, veterans—You have been baptized in
fire and blood, and come out steel."[10] This was the basis of "Blood and Steel,"
which remains the motto of the Third Armored Cavalry, the modern successor regiment of the Mounted Riflemen.

For what the Army cited as his "gallant and meritorious conduct" at Contreras and Churubusco, Granger was brevetted first lieutenant (A brevet promotion was an honor but did not normally signify a real rank.) But, says an
anonymous fellow officer in the Mounted Rifles quoted in Stanley's SAC
memorial, ". . . he did not fight for brevets or for glory. He went into a battle
for the pure love of the thing. But in his private life he was even tempered,
affectionate, unselfish, and most considerate of the feelings of others. No act
of cruelty was ever perpetrated by him on any man under his command, and
while he was considered at times an 'Odd Dick,' he was of the stuff that real
soldiers are made of. When he died there was a real sorrow among the surviving officers of the old Mounted Rifles."[11]

As the army advanced after the battles, another young officer, Lt. D.H.
Hill, indicated in his journal that the behavior of the non-regular troops toward the civilian population was at times reprehensible: "The vile Volunteers
& raw levies have been here & the inhabitants have fled to escape from these
savages."[12] Granger probably had the same reaction, learning lessons about
the importance of military discipline and army-civilian relations that he
would apply as a Civil War general—when he would find himself opposing
Confederate Lieutenant-General D. H. Hill at Chickamauga. He also had
the chance to observe and discuss Scott's occasional tactics of armistice and
proclamations, and their effects on operations. Ultimately, no armistice held
until Mexico City was conquered, which happened in the next stage of the
campaign.

On September 13, the Riflemen were in a support role of the troops attacking the fortress of Chapultepec, storming several batteries there and on
the causeways leading into the center of Mexico City, where, the next morning, it was a member of the regiment who raised the U.S. flag above the Mexican national palace.[13] The divisional commander, Maj.-Gen. John Quitman,

was with the regiment in this advance, and reported: "After the taking of the batteries at Chapultepec, in which portions of this corps took an active part, this efficient and splendid regiment were employed as sharp-shooters in the advance, through the arches of the aqueduct, where their services were invaluable. My only concern was to restrain their daring impetuosity."[14]

For his "gallant and meritorious conduct" in the battle, Granger received another brevet promotion, this time to captain.[15] He would not attain that rank in the regular Army until the Civil War, but his outstanding combat record in Mexico had been officially recognized.

Regarding the commanding general's reference—long remembered with pride in the regiment—to "fire and blood," the U.S. casualty rate in the Mexican War, and that of the Riflemen, was not low compared to the relatively small size of the forces engaged. "Approximately the regiment lost in Mexico four officers and 40 men killed; 13 officers and 180 men wounded, many of the latter dying and could be properly rated as killed; one officer, and 202 men died; 141 men were discharged for disability, largely from wounds."[16] (The one officer and 202 men who "died" were presumably the victims of diseases such as yellow fever, dysentery and typhoid.) While the war looms far smaller in U.S. history and memory than the vast civil conflict which was to follow, the fighting in Mexico was hard and Granger lost friends and many comrades there.

It was also a brilliantly successful campaign and war for the outnumbered U.S. Army, whose victories vastly expanded the territory of the United States. The successful junior officers there who became generals in the Civil War were to use that military education with devastating effect against each other's armies.

Mopping-up operations morphed into a guerrilla war that went into the new year of 1848, providing further education for future Civil War commanders. This conflict involved not only military operations against insurgents, but also the maintenance of discipline within the Army and the punishment of American wrongdoers: Two teamsters were hanged in Jalapa for murdering a Mexican boy, and an Eighth Infantry soldier was hanged for murdering Mexican women. "Such actions went far in keeping the friendship of the local inhabitants and weakening the position of the guerrillas."[17] A peace agreement was reached early in 1848, and was ratified in March by the U.S. Congress and in May by the Mexican government.

The Riflemen remained in Mexico until the summer of 1848, when they headed back to New Orleans and then up the Mississippi River to Jefferson

Barracks in Missouri. While in Mexico, "the men of the regiment retained a keen taste for ripe tomatoes, green corn, and Mexican girls; and up to the very day the regiment paraded on the plaza to march for Vera Cruz and home, the dear little Mexican girls hung about these big six-foot men . . . and these same big fellows, who climbed the hill at Cerro Gordo, made the seventeen-minutes' dash at Contreras, and were among the stormers at Chapultepec, and charged the Belise gate—and all this without 'turning a hair'—bawled like babies when parting from these little women."[18] The regiment sailed from Vera Cruz on July 7.[19]

Granger went on recruiting service later that year, but returned in time to make the epic 2,000-mile journey to the Pacific coast of Oregon. The Riflemen set out May 10, 1849, and it took them more than six months to get there. There were, of course, no railroads yet on this route, and no easy way to get to the West Coast.

The trek through the vast, barren, mountainous frontier wilderness was in its way as hazardous and deadly as the recent war. They went "through a country without roads and often without wood, water or grass," says Morton's regimental history. " . . . Cholera raged in the stream of emigrants allured by visions of gold to the new Eldorado in California, and fabulous stories were inflaming the minds and turning the heads of the soldiers. Unlimited wealth could be picked up for the trouble! The death rate was appalling. Excepting Fort Kearney and the fur trading station, Laramie, there was not a house between Leavenworth and the Columbia [River]. On reaching the latter the horses were too much worn down to march, and the mules [had] to haul loads over the Cascade Range. Men were dismounted and the horses driven by details at easy stages. An enormous raft was constructed and the baggage put aboard to float down, while the command marched on foot. The detachment on the raft let it get into the terrific current of the rapids, it became unmanageable and was dashed to pieces against the boulders. All but one were drowned and the entire cargo was lost."[20]

Stanley says it was "the longest march ever attempted in this country up to that time . . . a trip of seven months' weary plodding along."[21]

They built Fort Vancouver at the site of an old fur trading post, in Washington state on the northern side of the Columbia River, near Portland, Oregon. Granger was stationed there and about 75 miles east at Fort Dalles, on the other side of the Cascade Mountains. There was "disagreeable service, but not much fighting"[22] until 1851, when the Riflemen went back to Missouri—starting this time by ship, from the West Coast. Granger took the opportunity to indulge his restless nature by getting a year's leave of absence to visit Europe, a leave which took up most of 1851. He returned that winter, getting delayed in December by bad weather at Newport, Kentucky, then going down the Ohio and Mississippi rivers to New Orleans, from where he probably got a boat to Texas. He returned to the Mounted Rifles in Texas in early 1852, being promoted to first lieutenant in the regular Army on May 24. He is often referred to by his brevet rank of captain in these years, long before his actual promotion to that rank in 1861.

While the Mounted Rifles had not yet been officially designated as cavalry, in effect they functioned as such on the Texas and New Mexico frontier, where Granger spent the next eight years.

From 1852 to 1858, Stanley's SAC memorial says, "Granger was constantly engaged in frontier scouting, when frontier service meant wide awake business; the hostile Comanches and Lipans at that time infested Texas all the way to the coast, appearing within a few miles of Corpus Christi, and almost in the suburbs of San Antonio. To follow, to intercept, and rout this wily foe, always cunning, and, when caught, always dangerous, was a most exciting life. The writer has heard General Granger speak of it as the happiest period of his service; frequently he was engaged in fierce combats with the savages, and the romance and adventure of the life suited his active nature."[23]

The Lipans were an Apache tribe, and it was conflicts with these two fierce Indian peoples, the Comanche and Apache, that would dominate Granger's professional concerns on the frontier, both now in the 1850s and at the tail-end end of his career in the 1870s. Both were warlike peoples who raided deep into Mexico. The Comanches had been especially successful in Texas, including in conflicts with Apaches and in capturing slaves, mostly Indian and Mexican, many of whose women and children were assimilated into the tribe.[24] But Comanche power and survival were being challenged by the new Anglo settlers in Texas and their new protectors, the U. S. Army, as well as by drought, disease and hunger. Over-grazing and over–hunting, along with competition from livestock, were causing the bison herds to decline. While Texas' overall population increased from 140,000 in 1847 to over 600,000 in 1860,[25] the Comanche population was in steep decline, falling to about 10,000 in the middle of the 1850s. But that did not make the desperate survivors inclined to peacefully accept their fate. And it turned out that the numbers of Indians and bison would both increase in the 1860s (due to more rainfall, and Anglos being distracted by the Civil War), leading to new Comanche raids and warfare.

While Granger was in Texas in the 1850s, Comanche reservations were established, but they would not last, because many of the Indians and Texans maintained their mutual hostility and raiding, each seemingly bent on extermination of the other.

Granger was serving mostly in South Texas, moving around a lot. In a few months of 1852 he went from Fort Ewell to Fort Inge to Fort Merrill, doing tasks including scouting and escorting the commanding general of the department.[26] These forts were tiny, recently established and soon to be abandoned. Conditions were primitive. At Ewell, "The buildings had been constructed by troop labor of soft adobe, which was not strong enough to support a roof without bracing. Most buildings were covered with canvas. Attempts to grow kitchen gardens for food were unsuccessful due to lack of rainfall. Food and clothing were sometimes at a premium, and troops were often sick. For two years after July 1852 every officer and man was sick on the average of once every three months. Scurvy was frequent. Many soldiers deserted the fort and went to Mexico."[27]

1853 saw him stationed by the Rio Grande at Fort McIntosh and Ringgold Barracks, and on June 18 "being engaged in the Pursuit and Destruction of a Band of 15 hostile Indians, at Golondrina Pass,"[28] Texas. Sometimes the soldiers pursued bandits instead.

Next he was transferred to Fort Inge, a small South Texas frontier post near the Nueces River, built to protect the western mail route from Indian raids. "The missions of the soldiers included security patrols for the construction of the San Antonio-El Paso military road, escorts for supply trains and mail, protection for frontier settlements from bandits and Indian raiders, and guarding the international boundary with Mexico. The fort was a typical one-company, fifty-man post for most of its history. For a brief period in 1854 it was the regimental headquarters for the United States Mounted Rifles Regiment with a garrison of 200. One staff inspector reported that Fort Inge . . . is in 'a state of constant warfare and constant service.'"[29]

It was the Apaches who threatened the stage coaches on the San Antonio-El Paso road, according to a blunt 1927 history: "During the operation of this stage company these hostile savages frequently prevented the carrying out of a regular schedule, stopping the stages, pillaging its contents, and killing its occupants."[30]

Back scouting and at Fort Merrill in 1854-55, he then moved to Corpus Christi, was conducting recruits into the state, and in 1856 was stationed at San Antonio and farther south at Fort McIntosh on the Rio Grande. Out scouting that April 13, he engaged in a skirmish with the Lipan Indians on the Nueces River.[31]

Still, it was not all fighting. "In garrison, Granger was a jovial companion, and while he liked to live well"—and undoubtedly participated in the hard-drinking barracks life—"he could always adapt himself to the situation. He was a splendid shot, and an enthusiastic hunter"[32] known for providing game for himself and his troops on the trail. It was still a mostly wild and empty country, especially as Granger's service took him farther west, across the Texas border into the New Mexico Territory.

Stanley also served on the frontier in the early 1850s, and says in his memoirs[33] that Granger "was very much in love with Miss Sally Strother of Louisville." She was expected to inherit a considerable fortune, and so "Granger's motives were suspected." But she wound up marrying a German baron instead, which led Capt. John Pope to chaff Granger, causing him to be "upset." Pope called Granger by the nickname "Count," Stanley says, which perhaps indicates his Army colleagues thought Granger had a tendency to put on airs and seek social advancement. Possibly Granger had met Miss Strother during his 1851-52 leave of absence.

Later in the decade, possibly while on recruiting service in the East, Granger met Ellen Marcy, daughter of an Army officer. He was a "rival in love" to George McClellan, according to a biography of the latter.[34] Nor were they the only young officers courting Ellen Marcy, who was engaged for a time to A.P. Hill. McClellan and Hill would become, respectively, Union and Confederate generals in the Civil War. Before that war started, McClellan had resigned from the Army and become a railroad executive, marrying Ellen in 1860.

Granger would eventually marry a doctor's daughter from Kentucky, but not until four years after the end of the Civil War.

Pope, under whom Granger would serve with Stanley early in the Civil War, also served with them on the frontier in the 1850s. And when Granger commanded the District of New Mexico in the 1870s, he reported to Pope at Fort Leavenworth, Kansas, and got on with him. In the 1850s, Granger, Pope and Stanley "were on intimate terms," says Peter Cozzens in his biography of Pope. "They were of a kind: gruff, bombastic and foul-mouthed; direct in their speech and decisive in their actions."

It is not known whether Granger had any reservations about the government policies which placed him in conflict with Mexicans and Indians. Grant, who also fought in the Mexican War, claimed in his memoirs to have been strongly opposed to it in principle. Some politicians opposed it at the time, including one-term U.S. Rep. Abraham Lincoln. But most Americans, probably including Granger, thought U.S. westward expansion was an irresistible and inevitable force, and that the Army's role was to minimize its costs, especially to the American settlers.

Pope had a pro-Indian reputation after the Civil War, and by the 1870s Granger was prepared to negotiate with Cochise and prepare the way for peace with the Apaches. Even in the late 1850s, when Granger was a junior officer in New Mexico, the Army was not always hostile to the Indians. A federal Indian agent, Dr. Steck, was providing supplies to starving Chiricahua and Mimbre Apache.[35] And the Army was trying to protect Mescalero Apache from Mexican attacks,[36] even pursuing murderous Mexican raiders and capturing 35 of them.

On the pre-eminent issue of slavery, Granger's views were radicalized over the course of the Civil War, as were those of most Americans loyal to the Union, including Grant, Lincoln and the Virginian George Thomas.

After more than a year on recruiting service, in 1858 Granger escorted recruits into New Mexico, and was stationed at Fort Craig. In 1858-9 he escorted the commanding officer of the Department of New Mexico (a post Granger himself was to hold in the 1870s). For a few months he was stationed much farther west, at Fort Defiance, over what later became the Arizona line. He then returned to Fort Craig, a remote but large military post in south-central New Mexico, on the old Spanish colonial trail from Mexico City to Santa Fe.

Granger was away on sick leave from late March 1860 until April 1861. The U.S. Census on June 13 found him in New York City (lower Manhattan), a city to which he would also tend to gravitate after the Civil War. On September 30 he was in Great Barrington, Mass., an area in the Berkshire Mountains which was and is a popular summer resort, from where he reported back to the regiment on his continuing disability. What exactly it was is unclear, but probably involved a recurrence of his youthful bronchial troubles. He would not have been given this leave without cause, and there is a long documented history of his lung problems, other ailments and general bad health which would eventually lead to a premature death. However, that doesn't mean he was above stretching out the leave. That's what his superior officers—with reason—thought he was doing on occasion in the late 1860s because of a reluctance to return to normal peacetime duties as a colonel, having served as a major-general in the Civil War.

Granger turned 39 on November 6, 1860, and was still a first lieutenant. This was a slow promotion track even for the peacetime Army—although he had seen precious little peaceful service. He was wearing out his health for small reward, and must have given some thought to leaving the service, which was a very common practice for prewar officers.

Ironically, though, the very lack of promotion may have been a disincentive to quit. Grant, who had left the Army in 1854, did not resign his commission until just after being promoted captain, and so had the prestige in civilian life of being known as Captain Sam Grant. Not that this did anything to further Grant's prospects; he had a very difficult time supporting his family as a civilian in the 1850s.

Granger as yet had no family of his own, which left him more freedom but without much to show for his life. Yet even as he contemplated his prospects, all America was being swept up in a great political crisis—one that Granger, at leisure, must have observed closely. Its military implications were grimly obvious, along with the unprecedented opportunities that could soon be present for every soldier. That would have been a reason to extend his leave. Anyone could see that if war came, the major theaters of operations would be a long way from New Mexico.

NOTES

1. Friend Palmer, *Early Days in Detroit* (Hunt & June, Detroit, 1906), 409.
2. John S.D. Eisenhower, *Agent of Destiny: the Life and Times of General Winfield Scott* (New York, The Free Press, 1997), 214–15.
3. Charles Morton, *The Third Regiment of Cavalry*, in *The Army of the United States* (ed. Rodenbough and Haskin, Maynard, Merrill & Co., New York, 1896), 194. The Mounted Riflemen became the Third Regiment of Cavalry in 1861, which in modern times has become the Third Armored Cavalry.
4. Ibid., 195.
5. Robert Selph Henry, *The Story of the Mexican War* (New York, Frederick Ungar Publishing, 1950), 266.
6. (David Stanley), *Reunion of the Society of the Army of the Cumberland*, Vol. 15 (Cincinnati, Robert Clarke & Co., 1884), 211.
7. Henry, op.cit., 334.
8. Stanley, op. cit., 211.
9. K. Jack Bauer, *The Mexican War*, (New York, Macmillan Publishing, 1974), 295.
10. W. B. Lane, *The Regiment of Mounted Riflemen*, or *From Puebla to the City of Mexico*, in *United Service: A Monthly Review of Military and Naval Affairs*, Vol. 1 (LR. Hamersly & Co., Philadelphia, 1895), 303. Morton (op. cit.) has Scott saying these words

in Mexico City after the final big battles of the campaign, as does Bauer (op.cit.). However, the detailed and sourced account of Lane, an eyewitness, is credible. Scott may well have addressed the regiment in these terms on more than one occasion.

11. Stanley, op. cit., 211–12.
12. (Ed.) George Smith and Charles Judah, *Chronicles of the Gringos* (Univ. of New Mexico Press, 1968), 240.
13. Lane, op. cit., 310.
14. Ibid., 312–13.
15. *Cullum's Register*, Vol. 2, 237.
16. Morton, op. cit., 198.
17. Bauer, op. cit., 334.
18. Lane, op. cit.
19. Morton, op. cit., 198.
20. Ibid., 198–99.
21. Stanley, op. cit., 212.
22. Morton, op. cit.
23. Stanley, op. cit., 213.
24. Pekka Hammalainen, *The Comanche Empire* (New Haven, Yale University Press, 2008), 252–9.
25. Ibid., 305.
26. *Cullum's Register*, Vol. 2, 237. Also, regimental records in Returns from Military Posts.
27. Art Leatherwood, *Fort Ewell, Handbook of Texas Online*, Texas State Historical Association.
28. *Cullum's Register*, op. cit.
29. Thomas T. Smith, *Fort Inge, Handbook of Texas Online*, Texas State Historical Association.
30. Carl Coke Rister, *The Southwestern Frontier* (Cleveland: Arthur H. Clark Co., 1928) 35.
31. *Cullum's Register*, op. cit.
32. Stanley, op. cit., 212.
33. *An American General: The Memoirs of David Sloan Stanley* (ed. Fordyce, Santa Barbara, Calif., The Narrative Press, 2003), 72.
34. H.J. Eckenrode and Bryan Conrad, *George B. McClellan: The Man Who Saved the Union* (University of North Carolina Press, 1941), 21
35. Scott Rushforth, *Ethnographic Overview and Assessment of Chiricahua National Monument and Fort Bowie National Historic Site*, (National Park Service, Denver, CO, 2010), 238.
36. Morris E. and Catherine H. Opler, *Mescalero Apache History in the Southwest*, January 1950 New Mexico Historical Review, 10.

3
Civil War

When Fort Sumter in Charleston harbor was attacked by the Confederates on April 12, 1861, inaugurating the Civil War, Granger was still on sick leave in New York City. He immediately reported for duty.[1]

A considerable number of military officers from the South, such as Winfield Scott, George Thomas and David Farragut, remained loyal to the Union. But there were also a few from the North like John Pemberton, Bushrod Johnson and Archibald Gracie III—often with Southern wives or other connections—who became Confederate generals. Granger had no such intimate connections, and had been alarmed at the stirrings of secessionist sentiment in the southwest for over a year before it actually resulted in disunion. While his views on slavery and secession were probably in line with those of George McClellan and many other relatively conservative loyal officers, there is no reason to think he ever contemplated disloyalty or quailed from fighting against his old friends and comrades who joined the Confederacy.

It was as an illegitimate rebellion that the war was seen by most Northerners. Even before the fighting began, Lincoln's First Inaugural Address had stressed slavery as the prime cause of the conflict, but neither he nor most other Northerners then envisaged a war for emancipation. That did not mean Union soldiers thought of themselves as fighting simply for the government or abstract principles. The new president summoned up "the mystic chords of memory" and "the better angels of our nature" that were needed to bind the country together; in 1862 he put the issue this way: "We shall nobly save, or meanly lose, the last best hope of earth."[2]

Despite his sometimes cynical nature, Granger shared the patriotism that swept the North as so eloquently encouraged by the words by Lincoln. And as the war went on, with his military role sometimes taking on a political dimension, he would faithfully follow the changing policies on slavery of the president he never met.

Granger first served as a mustering officer in Ohio, signing up civilian volunteers and re-enlisting recruits for three-year terms, as well as organizing and training them. The appointment seems to have been arranged by his friend McClellan, who was now back in the army as a major-general commanding the state's militia, and on May 3 was named commander of the Department of the Ohio in the Regular Army.

"I appointed him [Granger] division inspector," McClellan wrote in his memoirs, "and repeatedly applied for him as a member of my staff; but these requests were constantly refused, and he was not permitted to retain the post of inspector. During the short time he was with me he rendered remarkable services."[3] McClellan, himself a superb organizer and trainer of volunteer soldiers, recognized similar qualities in Granger, as would other soldiers throughout the Civil War.

On May 5 Granger at last got a Regular Army promotion, to captain (still technically with the Mounted Rifles, although he was not serving with them). Around this time Jacob Cox, a volunteer general from Ohio, came across him at a recruiting camp near Columbus. "Captain Gordon Granger," Cox wrote in his memoirs, "of the regular army came to muster the re-enlisted regiments into the three years' service, and as he stood at the right of the Fourth Ohio, looking down the line of a thousand stalwart men, all in their Garibaldi shirts (for we had not yet received our uniforms), he turned to me and exclaimed: 'My God! that such men should be food for powder!' It certainly was a display of manliness and intelligence such as had hardly ever been seen in the ranks of an army."[4]

Granger was known for making somewhat grim pronouncements like this, but his "food for powder" line also indicates an imaginative sympathy with the volunteers, which would help him lead such men effectively in combat.

Cox also gives a good account of Granger's realistic appraisal of the coming conflict, and his positive effect on the troops: "Granger had been in the Southwest when the secession movement began, had seen the formation of military companies everywhere, and the incessant drilling which had been going on all winter, whilst we, in a strange condition of political paralysis, had been doing nothing. His information was eagerly sought by us all, and he lost no opportunity of impressing upon us the fact that the South was nearly six months ahead of us in organization and preparation. He did not conceal his belief that we were likely to find the war a much longer and more serious piece of business than was commonly expected, and that unless we pushed hard our drilling and instruction we should find ourselves at a disadvantage in our earlier encounters. What he said had a good effect in making officers and men take more willingly to the laborious routine of the parade ground and the regimental school; for such opinions as his soon ran through the camp, and they were commented upon by the enlisted men quite as earnestly as among the officers."[5]

Granger was ordered to bring 200 recruits to Fort Leavenworth, Kansas, northwest of Kansas City near Missouri's western border, which he accomplished on June 1. They were supposedly en route to New Mexico, but did not get there because of the gathering storm in Missouri.

Missouri was a slave state which had not seceded and ultimately did not secede—at least according to the national government—but was bitterly divided. Lincoln had only gotten 10 percent of the vote in the 1860 presidential election and the state went for Stephen Douglas.

The state's governor, Claiborne Jackson, and many others favored secession, and four months later, in October 1861, would set up a government-in-exile in the southwestern part of the state which was recognized by Jefferson Davis' Confederate government in Richmond. One faction of Missourians favored neutrality, some sincerely while others, including Jackson, as an initial tactical ploy. The unionists were split between abolitionists and those favoring or at least accepting the retention of slavery. And Missouri was the front line of the incipient war in the West.

This could not be ignored at Fort Leavenworth.

"A force of rebels amounting to five hundred collected at Liberty, three miles from Liberty Landing, below Fort Leavenworth, and on the opposite side of the Missouri River," says Stanley's SAC memorial. "Taking a steamboat, with three hundred men, Major [William E.] Prince landed at Liberty Landing, and surprised the rebel force in the town of Liberty just at daybreak. The rebels grabbed their guns, and made a rush for an enclosure surrounded by a very high board fence. . . . Granger saw in an instant the necessity for prompt action, and shouting in his immense voice, 'run against the fence, men,' he led the way, and three hundred men simultaneously striking the fence, down it went, almost in the faces of the astounded Confederates, who, at [Captain] Granger's loud command, laid down their guns without firing a shot, just at the moment they thought to commence a fight."[6]

Soon enough the real fighting would commence.

In June Granger was appointed acting assistant adjutant-general on the staff of Major Samuel Sturgis, and left with him on an expedition south against Confederate forces. They linked up with General Nathaniel Lyon on July 5 south of Kansas City, joining Lyon's federal army pursuing Governor Jackson and Confederate General Sterling Price into the southwestern part of the state.

Lyon's offensive would culminate in the first major battle in the west. Meanwhile in the east, where the world's attention was focused, the Union cause suffered a grievous blow on July 21 when the Confederates routed a Union army under General Irwin McDowell along a stream called Bull Run near Manassas, Virginia. This was the war's first major battle, and among other things demonstrated that Granger had been right to tell Cox in Ohio that the North was in for a long, hard struggle.

Sturgis commanded one of four brigades in Lyon's army, which had in total fewer than 6,000 men. Unusually for the Civil War, the Union force was heavily outnumbered. Price's Confederates had been reinforced by General Benjamin McCulloch, and their joint army was at least 12,000 strong. Major General John Fremont, the Union commander of the Department of the West, was concentrating troops in eastern Missouri and the Mississippi Valley, and decided he could not spare reinforcements for Lyon's campaign despite the latter's urgent requests.

Nevertheless, Lyon moved out of Springfield on the offensive on August 1, apparently not realizing how strong the Confederates were. His forces had the better of a skirmish the next day at Dug Spring (or Springs), in which Granger participated. Sturgis, Stanley says, commanded Lyon's right wing, and Granger "was a sheet anchor to our little, and very raw and undisciplined force."[7]

Only about four Union soldiers were killed at Dug Spring, the Confederate cavalry suffering heavier losses and being driven from the field. However, as would be the case throughout the war, many casualties were not caused by battle. A number of the inexperienced troops were apparently on the verge of death from drinking stagnant spring water, according to the Union officer Thomas Knox: "I passed scores of men who had fallen from utter exhaustion," Knox said. "Many were delirious, and begged piteously for water in ever so small a quantity. Several died from excessive heat, and others were for a long time unfit for duty. Reaching the spring which gave its name to the locality, I was fortunate in finding only the advance of the command. With considerable effort I succeeded in obtaining a pint cupful of water, and thus allayed my immediate thirst.

". . . As the main portion of the column came up, the crowd around the spring-house became so dense that those once inside could not get out. The building was lifted and thrown away from the spring, but this only served to increase the confusion. Officers found it impossible to maintain discipline. When the men caught sight of the crowd at the spring, the lines were instantly broken. At the spring, officers and men were mingled without regard to rank, all struggling for the same object. A few of the former, who had been fortunate in commencing the day with full canteens, attempted to bring order out of chaos, but found the effort useless. No command was heeded."[8] Such scenes must have impressed on a junior officer like Granger the need for discipline, as well as the need to provide for an army's supplies.

Realizing now he was badly outnumbered, Lyon withdrew to Springfield, and the Confederates advanced to Wilson's Creek, 10 miles southwest of the town. Rather than waiting to be attacked—which could be expected soon— or retreating without a fight with the enemy in pursuit, Lyon determined on a surprise attack. It would be a pincer movement, with Union Colonel Franz Sigel operating in the Confederate rear. The twin assaults were launched early on the morning of August 10.

Both attacks were at first successful, but Sigel was soon driven from the field and Lyon's main force was hard pressed.

Granger, although on Sturgis' staff, was serving as an aide to Lyon at the beginning of the battle. He had the opportunity to take the initiative in combat and help out the artillery at crucial points, as was noted gratefully in the official reports of artillery Captain James Totten and Lieutenant John DuBois.

Granger was bringing an order from Lyon to DuBois on what became known as "Bloody Ridge" to move his battery to the right, when they observed Union troops in retreat to the north and Confederates under Colonel James McIntosh advancing through a cornfield. Granger countermanded Lyon's order and told the battery to fire on McIntosh's troops, forcing them to withdraw.

Lyon was killed at about 9:30 a.m. The next senior officer, Brig.-Gen. Thomas Sweeny, was wounded, and Sturgis assumed command. In this emergency, Granger the staff captain plunged himself wholeheartedly into the combat. By all accounts, his performance was superb.

Sturgis, in his official report, says his subordinate "rendered such excellent aid in various ways, that a full mention of those services would render this report too voluminous for an official statement. Suffice it to say that he appeared to be almost ubiquitous—now sighting a gun of DuBois' battery, and before the smoke had cleared away sighting one of Totten's; at one moment reconnoitering the enemy, and the next either bringing up re-enforcements or rallying some broken line. To whatever part of the field I might direct my attention, there would I find Captain Granger, hard at work at some important service; his energy and industry seemed inexhaustible."[9]

Late in the battle, when a section of the Union line was, in Sturgis' words, "in imminent danger of being overwhelmed by superior numbers," Granger rushed to bring up reserves. He directed their artillery "upon the enemy's right flank, and poured into it a murderous volley, killing or wounding nearly every man within 60 or 70 yards. From this moment a perfect rout took place throughout the rebel front, while ours, on the right flank, continued to pour a galling fire into their disorganized masses."[10]

Captain Frederick Steele of the Second U.S. Infantry describes the same incident in his report: "Captain Granger came up to me, and we discovered that the enemy were about to renew the attack upon us. Captain Granger rushed to the rear and collected several hundred volunteers of different regiments, while we held the enemy in check, and formed them on our left. We then advanced upon the enemy, and drove them off the field, and never saw one of them afterwards. After collecting our wounded we retired slowly from the field."[11] (Steele and Granger would serve together in Alabama and Texas in 1865, when both were major generals.)

Knox, who after being wounded left the Army to become one of the war's most controversial journalists, presents an engaging picture of Granger's battlefield demeanor, leadership and tactics: "Though himself somewhat excited, he was constantly urging the raw soldiers to keep cool and not throw away a shot. Wherever there was a weak place in our line, he was among the first to discover it and devise a plan for making it good. On one occasion, he found a gap between two regiments, and noticed that the Rebels were preparing to take advantage of it. Without a moment's delay, he transferred three companies of infantry to the spot, managing to keep them concealed behind a small ridge."

Granger told the soldiers to lie in the long grass and keep their heads down: "I'll tell you when to fire." He stayed concealed too, but with his eye on the advancing Confederates. He warned his troops to hold their fire, letting the rebels come closer, and to shoot low when they did engage, and finally gave the order for them to so with the words, "Give them hell." The rebels broke and ran. "There, boys; you've done well," Granger said. "Damn the scoundrels; they won't come here again." Says Knox: "With this, the captain hastened to some other quarter."[12]

Knox saw Granger as "a strange compound of coolness and excitement. While his judgment was of the best, and his resources were ready for all emergencies, a by-stander would have thought him heated almost to frenzy. The warmth of his blood gave him a wonderful energy and rendered him ubiquitous; his skill and decision made his services of the highest importance."

Yet another tribute to Granger came after the war from William Wherry, a Union officer and aide to Lyon. Granger, "noted for his daring and intrepidity," brought up and directed DuBois' battery, "which created a perfect rout along the whole front" of the Confederate right. Nevertheless, despite repulsing a number of Rebel attacks, the weight of enemy numbers plus the death of General Lyon persuaded the remaining Union commanders to retreat. As the battle ended, Wherry says, "Granger and others urged remaining on the ground," but were overruled.[13] That pattern of personal courage, focusing on artillery, bringing up the reserves, and determination to hold Union ground, would be repeated at Chickamauga and other battles.

Union casualties at Wilson's Creek—killed, wounded, captured and missing—were about 1,300, somewhat higher than Confederate. And the national army was forced to abandon Springfield and retreat to Rolla in central Missouri, where it could be supplied by rail. The defeat, closely following Bull Run, was another blow to Union morale. The Confederates advanced northwards and won a small victory at Lexington the next month, but were unable to consolidate their gains in Missouri.

That rebel failure was in no small part due to those Union troops who held the line at Wilson's Creek, preventing the defeat from becoming a rout. Granger was prominent among them. His performance was noted in the report to Washington from Fremont, the commanding general in the West, who said Granger was "distinguished for active and conspicuous gallantry, and for highly valuable services in reconnoitering the enemy, assisting in the service of the batteries, and in rallying and inspiring confidence amongst the troops."[14]

Still a captain while pushing 40, Granger had nonetheless played a major, positive role in a significant battle. His ability was now recognized, and he found the path to repeated promotion wide open. The Union's vast new army of civilians needed to be trained and led, while a large number of the small prewar corps of officers had resigned to join the enemy. At last, what he had to offer would be needed, appreciated and used. The trickier part, as Granger would discover later in the war, would be retaining high command. Demonstrating success on the battlefield, avoiding grievous errors and exercising sound political judgment would not necessarily be enough, especially if he failed to play his cards right in internal Army politics.

Granger was brevetted major "for gallant and meritorious conduct" at Wilson's Creek, and on September 1 he was given command of the St. Louis Arsenal, which earlier that year had been at the center of the struggle for control between the forces of Union and Secession. On the 20th he received there an order from Brigadier-General Justus McKinstry regarding an issue that would continue to reverberate through the border states in the coming years. Granger was told there would be delivered "into your custody certain runaway negro slaves who have been heretofore apprehended and committed to the military prison. I desire they be employed at police duty and such other labor as you may choose until they are reclaimed by their masters, who upon proof of their ownership and that they are loyal to the United States will be entitled to receive them back into their service."[15]

McKinstry's order might seem to conflict with the views of his abolitionist superior, Fremont. But earlier that month, Lincoln had repudiated an order of Fremont's freeing the slaves of disloyal owners, so there is no question he would have supported McKinstry in defending the "rights" of Unionist slave-holders at that time. Lincoln was determined to retain the support of white Unionists in Missouri and other border states to keep them out of the Confederacy—and to uphold existing law. Granger would repeatedly have to grapple with these issues, especially when he served in Kentucky in late 1862. Presumably, he obeyed McKinstry's order. But as the war went on, his policies and actions, unlike McClellan's, would closely follow Lincoln's evolution toward abolition.

On September 2,[16] Granger was appointed colonel of the Second Michigan Cavalry by the governor of that state, Austin Blair. It does not seem to have been a political appointment, but one made at the recommendation of Fremont or his staff, because the regiment was going to be deployed in Missouri. That fall in Michigan it was still being recruited, and was mustered in at Grand Rapids, while Granger stayed at the St. Louis Arsenal. He seems to have gotten the appointment because of his performance at Wilson's Creek, and the recognition by Blair and others that the green volunteer troops would benefit from the leadership of a combat-hardened professional soldier, who had spent much of his career as a cavalryman on the Western frontier.

Granger assumed command of the 1,163 officers and men of the Second Michigan Cavalry Regiment when they arrived in mid-November at Benton Barracks in St. Louis. The volunteers needed to be turned into soldiers, and Granger was the man to do it.

Marshall Thatcher's memoir of the Second Cavalry says the new colonel's "military genius soon asserted itself by many severe lessons to the volunteer officers and men of this regiment. He brought them up to the full standard of regulars within a period of three months."[17] Granger's tough discipline started at the top. He compelled the resignation of the lieutenant-colonel for drunkenness,[18] and conducted daily drills for all the new regiment's officers. In doing the latter, "more or less amusement was caused by the awkwardness of some who were not as well drilled as most of their men," as demonstrated by falling off their horses. The only ones daring to laugh, though, were private soldiers "who kept at a respectful distance," because "a frown from 'Old Granger,' as he was sometimes called, would kill further than an old flint lock."[19]

Granger, Thatcher says, "though a gruff appearing man, had succeeded in winning the respect of his regiment by his strict attention to all the details of making a well disciplined body of soldiers out of a mass of awkward men from every walk in life." Granger's reputation as a stern disciplinarian would last through the rest of his career, but most of the soldiers under his command seem to have grown respect for him—indeed, like Thatcher, to the point of admiration.

When officers in the regiment were put forward for promotion, wrote Stephen Z. Starr in his three-volume history of Union cavalry, Granger put them before a rigorous examining board which "seemed more like a trial than an examination." Anyone losing—or selling—a weapon "will have double its value deducted from his pay," he ordered.[20]

While another cavalry regiment at Benton Barracks in St. Louis, the 2nd Iowa, crowded into poorly ventilated quarters, had sixty men die of sickness in as many days, the 2nd Michigan suffered no such losses. Granger had issued orders with detailed instructions for maintaining cleanliness and good ventilation, which protected the health and lives of his men. One biography of "Little Phil" Sheridan, who would become the next colonel of the 2nd Michigan, says of Granger: "His discipline was severe, but it made the regiment efficient beyond almost any other body of troopers then in the service."[21]

Granger seems to have borne some resemblance in character to a fictional regular Army officer, John Carter. This is the anti-hero of *Miss Ravenel's Conversion from Secession to Loyalty*, a novel by Union veteran John W. DeForest. Carter "was a terror to his whole brigade. . . . He knew his business so well, he was so invariably right in his fault-findings, he was so familiar with the labyrinth of regulations and general orders through which almost all others groped with many stumbling, and he was so conscientiously and gravely outraged by offences against discipline, that he was necessarily a dreadful personage. . . . But while he was thus feared, he was also greatly respected; and a word of praise from him was cherished by officer or soldier as a medal of honor."[22]

In February 1862 the 2nd Michigan was assigned by Fremont's successor, Major General Henry Halleck, to the newly created Army of the Mississippi under John Pope, who in May 1861 had been promoted from captain to brigadier general. Pope would prove his worth in the coming campaign, which involved little fighting but much maneuver and was highly successful. However, his subsequent failure in the east at Second Bull Run shows that speedy promotion did not necessarily help a Civil War officer's career—or, more significantly, the soldiers who fought and died under his command.

Pope's army, as its name implied, was now aimed south down the Mississippi River; controlling the "Father of Waters" was the Union's key military goal in the west.

A scene recorded by Thatcher illustrates how Granger often treated superior officers. As his troops were parading in St. Louis, Granger brusquely called Pope's attention to them: "Pope, look here!"

"Well, what of it?" responded the general.

"What of it? You damned fool. You never saw a better looking regiment nor a better drilled regiment in your life!"[23]

Granger was to do good service in the upcoming campaign, which Pope recognized in his *Military Memoirs*, but his subordinate's rude manner clearly rankled, even if this commanding officer chose not to make an issue of it.

"Granger was a man of brains and courage," Pope writes, "but I think a coarser-grained man, both in looks and in manners, I never saw. . . . His broad, flat face, and rugged, angular features and an expression which he always wore on his face, half insolent and half familiar, indicated pretty clearly his character and disposition and did not endear him to those brought into relations with him. His manner was not only blunt to a degree, but well nigh intolerable to strangers. He was, however, a man of great force of character and of undoubted courage, a valuable soldier in battle and a good counselor in campaign. The trouble with him was, that he could not help severely criticizing, indeed abusing, those to whom he professed friendship and to whom he really seemed to be attached."[24]

Whatever his reservations about Granger's personality, Pope recognized his military ability. The 2nd Cavalry steamed south on the Mississippi from St. Louis on February 21, 1862, landing at Commerce, Missouri, where the rest of Pope's army of about 20,000 almost entirely green troops was coming in from St. Louis, Cincinnati and Cairo, Illinois, which sat at the confluence of the Mississippi and Ohio rivers. Col. Granger's command immediately expanded to include other cavalry regiments. Pope gave him the Third Brigade, at first consisting of two Michigan cavalry regiments, the 2nd and 3rd. Another regiment, the 7th Illinois, was soon added to what became Granger's cavalry division. Although small for a division, Pope's initiative to organize a separate cavalry command represented an advance in military thinking which quickly became the norm.

The army's objective was 30 miles south, the Confederate positions at two big bends in the Mississippi River near the corners of Kentucky and Tennessee and the border of Missouri, at New Madrid and Island No. 10. Pope credits four officers including Granger with helping organize his army, so that before the end of the month "we marched south with a well-equipped force, ready to do and capable of doing the work before it."[25]

The march route avoided following a bend in the river, but the wet winter weather and flooded road through the Great Mingo Swamp made for hard going. As Pope said in his report, "Incredible labor and exposure, wading through the swamps, and in many places dragging wagons and artillery by hand."[26] The floods also seem to have deterred the Confederates from advancing to meet them—or as Pope speculated accurately, they did not believe the invaders would be able to come this way. But come the Union soldiers did, repairing the corduroy road—made of logs and sand and in very poor shape—as they went, using the typical Yankee ingenuity and energy that were to play such a major role in military successes throughout the war in the west and Deep South.

Those western victories had already begun. In January, George Thomas won the Battle of Mill Springs in eastern Kentucky. In February, Grant captured two forts on the Tennessee and Cumberland rivers in west Tennessee, the latter, Donelson, after a battle that compelled the surrender of the Confederate army. As the Army of the Mississippi moved south, the long Confederate line to its east across Kentucky had collapsed, and most of Tennessee, too, including Nashville, was falling into Union hands. Among the posts abandoned by the Confederate commander, Albert Sidney Johnston, was the Mississippi River fortress of Columbus, Kentucky, which had been styled "the Gibraltar of the West" (after the British island south of Spain which guarded entry to the Mediterranean).

That would leave New Madrid, Missouri as the northernmost Confederate outpost on the Mississippi. The cavalry led Pope's advance, successfully skirmishing on March 1 and capturing three guns and some prisoners.[27] The army arrived at New Madrid on March 3, "and at once drove in the pickets and outposts of the enemy and closely invested the place," Pope reported. It was to take another 10 days before he could begin an artillery bombardment, because he had to send word back to Cairo for cannon.

Granger's 2nd Michigan Cavalry helped capture Point Pleasant, 12 miles southwest of New Madrid where the river could be blocked to prevent Confederate reinforcements coming up. According to Second Division commander Brig. General Schuyler Hamilton (a grandson of Alexander Hamilton), the 2nd Cavalry displayed a "cool and soldierly bearing. . . . From their ranks the first blood was drawn on that day." The campaign was, however, notable for its lack of casualties as well as its complete success.

Granger received command of detachments from two other regiments, and on March 6 Hamilton reported that Granger "pressed the enemy on our left vigorously, driving in his skirmishers, but was unable, from want of heavy artillery, to make any serious impression, on account of the heavy fire of the enemy's gunboats and the exposed character of the position, without undue exposure of our troops."[28]

When the siege guns arrived, Granger as usual was involved with firing them (a preoccupation which in future battles would attract some high-level criticism). His troops, though, appreciated his involvement, as had the artillery officers at Wilson's Creek.

Granger, wrote Thatcher, "gave us an exhibition of his skill as an officer in charge of siege works. The perfect composure with which he went along the line of heavy guns, touching a gun now and then to raise or lower the range, while shot and shell from the enemy forts plowed the ground all about him, often covering him with clouds of dirt, without so much as drawing from him an indication that he saw or heard anything but his own work, drew from all his men deep though silent admiration; and all the harsh things seen in him or felt in ourselves were buried forever."[29]

The bombardment caused the Confederates to evacuate New Madrid on the night of March 13, retreating to Island No. 10, which Pope's army now besieged in operations involving setting up artillery and digging a canal, with plans for the Navy to run past the Confederate batteries and ferry the besiegers across the river, so they could cut off the garrison and attack from the rear.

While Thatcher may have exaggerated in describing Granger as "Pope's right hand man and chief counselor during that short and brilliant campaign" to capture New Madrid and Island No. 10, Granger was relied on by his commander and assumed growing responsibility. His command was expanded to a Cavalry Division with four regiments—the 7th Illinois and 2nd Iowa in addition to the 2nd and 3rd Michigan—in two brigades. And effective March 26, there was named a new brigadier-general of volunteers, Gordon Granger.

NOTES

1. David Stanley (see note to Chapter 1), *Reunion of the Society of the Army of the Cumberland*, Vol. 15 (1883), 213. Also George Cullum, *Biographical Register of the Officers and Graduates of the United States Military Academy* Vol. 2 (1891 3rd ed.), 238-9, and T.J. Wood, *in Seventh Annual Reunion of the Association of the Graduates of the United States Military Academy at West Point, New York* (1876), 57.
2. In Lincoln's Dec. 1 message to Congress.
3. George B. McClellan, *McClellan's Own Story* (Charles L. Webster & Co., 1887), 44.
4. Jacob Cox, *Military Reminisces of the Civil War* (Vol. 1, Scribner's, 1900), 33.
5. Ibid.
6. Stanley, op. cit., 213.
7. Ibid., 214.
8. Thomas Knox, *Camp-Fire and Cotton-Field* (Blelock and Company, New York, 1865), 64-66.
9. *The War of the Rebellion: a Compilation of the Official Records of the Union and Confederate Armies* [abbreviated as *OR* in subsequent references]. Volume 3, Part 1, 69.
10. Ibid., 68.
11. Ibid., 79.
12. Knox, op. cit., 77–8.
13. William M. Wherry, *Wilson's Creek and the Death of Lyon*, in *Battles and Leaders of the Civil War* (ed. Johnson and Buell, 1887) Vol. 1, 291.
14. *OR*, op. cit., 55.
15. *OR*, Series 2, Vol. 1, *Military Treatment of Captured and Fugitive Slaves*.
16. *Cullum's Register*, op. cit., 238.

17. Marshall P. Thatcher, *A Hundred Battles in the West. St. Louis to Atlanta, 1861–1865. The Second Michigan Cavalry* (Detroit, 1884), 270–1.

18. Ibid., 276.

19. Ibid., 30.

20. Stephen Z. Starr, *The Union Cavalry in the Civil War*, Vol. 1 (Louisiana State University Press, 1979), 198.

21. Frank Burr and Richard Hinton, *The Life of Gen. Philip H. Sheridan* (Hurst & Co., New York, 1890), 46.

22. J.W. De Forest, *Miss Ravenel's Conversion from Secession to Loyalty* (1867, 1939), 211.

23. Thatcher, op. cit., 32.

24. John Pope, *The Military Memoirs of General John Pope* (ed. Cozzens and Girardi, Univ. of North Carolina Press, 1998) ,103.

25. Ibid., 47.

26. *OR*, Vol. 8, Pt. 1, 81.

27. Starr, op. cit., 58.

28. *OR*, Additions and Corrections, Series 1, Vol. 8, 103

29. Thatcher, op. cit., 37.

4

General Granger

On the morning of April 6, 1862, Major General Pope, still besieging Island No. 10 in the Mississippi (so-named for being the tenth island downriver from Cairo), sent Brigadier General Granger on a reconnaissance, search and destroy mission aboard the gunboat *Carondelet*. On the night of April 4 the *Carondelet*, captained by Henry Walke, had become the first U.S. vessel to run past the Confederate batteries on the island. On April 6, the ship went "steaming down the river in the midst of a heavy fire from the enemy's batteries along the shore," according to Pope's report. On the 20-mile return leg, the naval guns "silenced the enemy's batteries opposite Point Pleasant, and a small infantry force, under Capt. L.H. Marshall, landed and spiked the guns."[1]

There were ten Rebel batteries firing at the gunboat, five on the island and five on the mainland.[2] This expedition does not seem an obvious command for the head of the army's cavalry division, and Granger's presence is a sign both of Pope's confidence in him and his own determination to engage in all the aspects of the campaign, no matter the potential danger or whether they had anything to do with cavalry. He was one of Pope's most trusted advisers in a successful campaign, and if it was going to be won by artillerymen or sailors, then Granger wanted to participate in their exploits. The war in the west, where the rivers were potential highways of Union advance, demanded army-naval cooperation. Granger became adept at this, especially in the war's last year in Mobile Bay.

At Island No. 10 the army and brownwater navy jointly pressed their attack on April 7, bombarding the Rebel positions while using the newly dug canal to bypass the island's defenses and ferry the troops, including Granger's cavalry, across the river into Kentucky—from where the 2nd Iowa Cavalry moved on to capture a Rebel camp and 200 prisoners. The Confederates evacuated to Tiptonville, Tennessee, where they surrendered on April 8. About 4,500 Rebels were captured, and Granger assisted in processing them. Union combat losses in the campaign were very small, about 32 killed, wounded and missing. More died of smallpox.

The lack of effective Confederate resistance was in part due to demoralization because of Fort Donelson and other ongoing disasters in the western theater. These culminated in the Battle of Shiloh, fought on April 6–7, at which Albert Sidney Johnston's grand counteroffensive failed to crush the Union invaders, and instead Johnston himself was killed and his army forced to retreat. Shiloh, the largest battle of the war to that point, largely overshadowed the Army of the Mississippi's campaign, although Pope's report took a just pride in what his soldiers had accomplished:

"We have crossed this great river, the banks of which were lined with batteries and defended by 7,000 men. We have pursued and captured the whole force of the enemy and all his supplies and material of war. . . . Such results bespeak efficiency, good conduct, high discipline, and soldierly deportment of the best character far more conclusively than they can be exhibited in pitched battle or the storming of fortified places. Patience, willing labor, endurance of hardship and privation for long periods, cheerful and prompt obedience, order and discipline, bravery and spirit, are the qualities which these operations have developed in the forces under my command, and which assure for them a brilliant and successful career in arms.'[3]

Perhaps the commanding general would have been better off had his victory involved a longer campaign giving him more combat experience. It was enough that summer to win Pope promotion and transfer to the east, but there he was decisively defeated in late August at Second Bull Run by Robert. E. Lee's Army of Northern Virginia.

Still, Pope's Army of the Mississippi had performed with boldness, vigor and efficiency; and Granger was one of the primary subordinates he relied on for field performance and counsel. He had earned his commander's confidence and the general's star on his shoulder.

Not long after the victory, Pope's army re-embarked on steamboats, going up the Mississippi and down the Tennessee rivers to Hamburg, Tennessee, south of the Shiloh battlefield. It was now part of a large, combined army of which Henry Halleck had taken personal command. Despite the victory at Shiloh, Grant had come under criticism for allowing his troops to be surprised on April 6, and some thought that only the timely arrival of Don Carlos Buell's divisions had prevented a disaster. Halleck would now advance slowly and cautiously toward the strategic railroad junction of Corinth, Mississippi.

Granger's four-regiment cavalry division landed at Hamburg on April 23, and according to his later report "immediately commenced a series of scoutings and reconnaissances." As on the march to New Madrid, rainfall and flooding were a constant problem. "In many instances," he wrote, "the very unusual service to mounted men of building roads and bridges, earthworks for batteries, rifle pits, and lying in the trenches as infantry have likewise been undergone without a single murmur."[4]

Granger, says Blackford, "used his troops relentlessly, employing them not only as cavalry but as combat engineers in the construction of roads. His unit's rate of advance was so great that he and his men were pulled back from forward positions by Halleck, whose conduct of the operation was in such stark contrast to the dash displayed by Granger and Pope."[5] Those bridges and corduroy roads had to be built through swamp and tangled brush. And when wagons couldn't get through, the cavalry acted as Pope's supply train.

And then there were the Confederates. Granger reported that "almost every day brought with it some sharp skirmish with a vigilant enemy." Halleck's all too deliberate offensive did not involve much combat, but Pope was probably his most aggressive subordinate (Grant being sidelined as second-in-command without direct control of troops). Granger's cavalry in the advance of the army's left wing saw a good deal of what fighting there was. Operating in partial independence of each other, his regiments were constantly driving back Confederate pickets and keeping the Union advance going.

Halleck's slowness, and his slighting of Grant, tend to be the focus of historians, but this was a significant campaign, conducted by a Union army of about 100,000. The railroad center of Corinth—where the east-west Memphis & Charleston Railroad crossed the north-south Mobile & Ohio—was a major strategic objective, and its capture would help split the Confederacy, the dismemberment of which was a Union goal partly achieved in 1862 and completed in the following years.

Pressing south from Hamburg, Granger's cavalry fought several skirmishes in late April and early May. His division was leading the Union advance and fending off Confederate efforts to outflank its left, pressing on to Farmington, Mississippi, a few miles east of Corinth. On May 9 a counterattack launched by Confederate General P.G.T. Beauregard drove Federal troops away from Farmington, and this only reinforced Halleck's caution.

Granger's report details multiple small actions undertaken by his regiments, sometimes several on the same day. That was the case on May 8, for example, which "was the day of our first occupation of Farmington, and subsequent events warrant me in saying that these constant movements of large bodies of my command upon our extreme left throughout the day effectually prevented the enemy from consummating his plan of a flank movement."[6] Possibly Granger here exaggerates the effect of his soldiers' work, since it seems unlikely that the outnumbered Beauregard expected to do much more than delay Halleck's advance. Pope's cavalry division spent two weeks fighting around Farmington before permanently occupying it on May 17, a day after Granger had led a personal reconnaissance.

Austin Blair, the governor of Michigan, was visiting his state's regiments at the front in May, and Granger wrote him a letter recommending the appointment of 31-year-old Philip Sheridan as colonel of the 2nd Michigan Cavalry. Like Granger at the time of his own appointment to the 2nd Michigan colonelcy, Sheridan was a staff captain—in his case on Halleck's staff—and a West Point-educated career soldier. Blair had reservations about the harsh discipline imposed on his volunteer troops by Granger and other Regular Army officers, but he also respected the original colonel of the 2nd Michigan. The governor accepted Granger's advice and on May 25 appointed Sheridan colonel.[7]

On May 28, Granger sent Colonel Washington Elliott south with a raiding party of two regiments, Elliott's own 2nd Iowa and Sheridan's 2nd Michigan, on a mission to destroy supplies and railroad tracks behind enemy lines. They travelled light and lived off the country, sometimes being supplied by civilians who thought they were Rebels. They skirmished with Confederate cavalry before capturing Booneville, close to 30 miles south of Corinth. There Elliott captured and paroled more than 2,000 sick or wounded prisoners, and destroyed 26 railroad cars along with much track and military stores before withdrawing. By this time Beauregard had already determined to abandon Corinth, which he did on May 30, causing Elliott to speed his own withdrawal back to Union lines.

Blackford says "The competent showing of Federal cavalry in the west, as demonstrated by Granger's operations," is in part attributable to his corps commander. "While Union horsemen in the east were employed in small detachments as helpmates to the infantry, as guards, escorts, dispatch riders and scouts, Pope deployed his troopers in strength as a swift, concentrated striking force." Granger no doubt fully supported this deployment of cavalry, which would become standard throughout the army. He proved an effective instrument of Pope's policy, having trained and welded his men into an effective fighting force.

Granger himself led the May 30 pursuit of Beauregard's retreating army,[8] capturing 200 wounded after skirmishing with the Confederates, with one 30-man detachment of the 2nd Iowa capturing 50 prisoners. Granger came through Booneville on June 2, and the next day advanced further south toward Baldwin. He was praised in the report of an infantry division commander, Major General William Rosecrans, who lauded "the signal ability in which he handled the cavalry."[9]

Sheridan on June 4 reconnoitered toward Beauregard's new base at Tupelo, and engaged in a successful skirmish two days later. On June 10 (the day before Rosecrans succeeded Pope as commander of the Army of the Mississippi), Sheridan's 2nd Michigan took Baldwin.

The "Army of the Mississippi" was in effect a corps in Halleck's larger army, as was Buell's "Army of the Ohio" before it was detached. And the performance of Pope's cavalry, i.e. Granger's command, was markedly superior to the cavalry in Buell's corps, including its increasingly significant reconnaissance functions.[10] Granger reported losses from April 24 to June 6 of 12 killed, 83 wounded and 32 missing in his four regiments. Disease in the increasingly sultry Deep South weather took a greater toll.

Washington Elliott was promoted to brigadier general in June and named Pope's chief of staff, leaving Sheridan to command his brigade consisting of the 2nd Michigan and 2nd Iowa. That meant the young colonel was now leading half of Granger's cavalry division.

General Pope departed for Virginia on June 26, having already been succeeded by Rosecrans. "Goodbye Pope, your grave is made," was Granger's typically mordant and metaphorically prophetic farewell, as reported in Stanley's memoirs.

At this time General Buell's Army of the Ohio was sent east toward Chattanooga, Tennessee, repairing the railroad as it went. Unfortunately, guerrillas and Rebel cavalry kept destroying the tracks behind him, and progress was excruciatingly slow. On July 23 the Confederate army at Tupelo, now under Braxton Bragg, began moving to Chattanooga by rail via Mobile. Confederate cavalry, having marched there directly, was already raiding Union supply lines to the north. Nathan Bedford Forrest captured the communications hub of Murfreesboro, Tennessee, along with over 1,200 Union prisoners, while Colonel John Hunt Morgan was wreaking havoc in Kentucky.

Like Pope, Halleck, too, was summoned east in July to become general-in-chief of the Union armies, another indication that the Lincoln administration was impressed by the military successes in the west. This meant that Rosecrans and Granger were now serving under Grant. Granger, despite his ornery nature and disregard for "the tinsel of rank," had a productive relationship with both Pope and Rosecrans, as he would with his future commanders in the later years of the war—Horatio Wright, George Thomas, John Schofield and Edward Canby—but not with the most important of them, Grant. And the Ohio native and Illinois resident was on his way to becoming the army's pre-eminent leader. Grant, according to Sheridan's memoirs, already in 1862 "did not fancy" Granger.[11] Sheridan does not say why, whether, for example, there was some personal clash dating to that period; or, as discussed previously, whether the roots of the antagonism go back a couple of decades. But in 1862, Grant seems to have wanted to replace Granger as Sheridan's mentor—which he would succeed in doing later in the war.

The partial dispersal of the Union army did not go unnoticed by the Confederates, who were preparing to go on the offensive on several fronts of the war, while Grant went on the defensive as the Union army's strength in Mississippi was reduced.

On July 1, Sheridan's brigade drove off a Confederate attack south of Booneville, successfully counterattacking in three places the superior Rebel force (according to Sheridan's account).[12] His performance was so impressive that Granger and four other generals, including Rosecrans, Elliott and Alexander Asboth, on July 30 urged Halleck, now in Washington, to promote him to brigadier-general. This was accomplished, even though Sheridan had been a colonel for barely two months. More than a year later, after fighting in three other substantial battles, Major General Sheridan would command a division under Granger at the Battle of Missionary Ridge, and in the subsequent campaign in East Tennessee. In 1864 he resumed his meteoric rise as Grant's chief of cavalry in the east, winning the Shenandoah Valley campaign and ultimately cutting off Lee at Appomattox in 1865. Granger's early furtherance of Sheridan's career was one of his significant contributions to the Union war effort.

Sheridan, meantime, had mixed feelings about Granger. He was grateful for his patronage, and very aware of his qualities both difficult and admirable.

What Sheridan most objected to, he writes in the memoirs, was Granger's "uncontrollable propensity to interfere with and direct the minor matters relating to the command, the details for which those under him were alone responsible. Ill-judged meddling in this respect often led to differences between us, only temporary it is true, but most harassing to the subordinate, since I was compelled by the circumstances of the situation not only invariably to yield my own judgment, but many a time had to play peacemaker—smoothing down ruffled feelings, that I knew had been excited by Granger's freaky and spasmodic efforts to correct personally some trifling fault that ought to have been left to a regimental or company commander to remedy. Yet with all these small blemishes Granger had many good qualities, and his big heart was so full of generous impulses and good motives as to far outbalance his shortcomings; and notwithstanding the friction and occasional acerbity of our official intercourse, we maintained friendly relations till his death."[13]

While much of this description rings true, it is amusing to see Sheridan—whose reputation for ill temper was at least as deserved as Granger's—refer to "smoothing down ruffled feelings." In fact, the two men shared a cavalryman's swagger, courage and confidence, along with sound military instincts. More to the point, Granger can hardly be blamed for micromanaging a brand new regimental colonel and brigade commander. When he saw how well Sheridan was doing, he let him proceed without undue interference, and Sheridan very likely learned more than he admitted from his energetic and more experienced superior.

Rosecrans noted Sheridan's victory at Booneville and separate actions of the 3rd Michigan and 7th Illinois cavalry regiments, issuing a general order on July 2 complimenting Granger "for the signal services the cavalry under his command have been and still are rendering to this army." However, the order, issued through Elliott (who remained chief of staff but would soon head east to join Pope), went on to say, "and trusts that increasing ambition, care, watchfulness and zeal for instruction, discipline, and order may add more to its efficiency and renown."[14] That kicker gave the compliment to Granger a decidedly backhanded flavor, and indicates that Rosecrans, a pious Roman Catholic, had some reservations about the conduct of his cavalrymen and their commander.

But like most military men who got to know Granger in the Civil War, Rosecrans came to respect him, and quickly entrusted him with more responsibility. Granger's cavalry division had expanded to seven regiments, and now Brig. General Asboth went on a leave of absence and his Fifth Division of infantry was combined with the cavalry under Granger. He now had charge of six (later seven) infantry and seven cavalry regiments, along with three artillery batteries and siege guns. This was more than a brigadier's command, and Granger was in line for another promotion.

On July 29, Sheridan reported to Granger "reliable information" that "the enemy have been and still are moving in large numbers to Chattanooga"[15] (which Buell's army would never reach). The source of this accurate information was letters found after two cavalry regiments, the 2nd Iowa and 7th Kansas, drove the enemy out of Ripley on July 28. This proved to be a significant report, one of many generated by Granger's forces, demonstrating the potential of cavalry to collect intelligence while it was constantly moving, fighting minor engagements and going behind enemy lines. Granger told Rosecrans, who informed Grant the same day, and Grant told Halleck on July 30. Sheridan's information was an indication of the initiative shifting to the Confederates, who were planning to launch a two-pronged invasion of Kentucky, while the Union forces were bogged down in a hot and hostile country.

Granger had already been reporting on Bragg's movements, and continued through August to make regular reports about the Confederate shift in operations from Mississippi to Tennessee and Kentucky. But the Confederates were also planning offensives in other areas, including Mississippi under Generals Sterling Price and Earl Van Dorn, who had crossed their forces from Arkansas. In September Rosecrans' troops would win the Battle of Iuka, and in October they would defeat a determined effort to recapture Corinth itself.

Before those events, however, Granger had left the theater, being sent to help meet the new Confederate threat to the northeast. But he still had plenty to deal with before he left Mississippi, and complained to Rosecrans that he needed more cavalrymen with better weapons. Rosecrans amplified these complaints while repeatedly passing them on to the War Department, which did not make him more popular with his superiors. Nor was Buell's popularity in that quarter helped by similar complaints about insufficient cavalry forces that were being worn down by hard service—which does not mean he, Rosecrans and Granger were wrong.

The Union army also had to deal with a particularly troublesome form of the Confederate resurgence: increased guerrilla activity. The Partisan Ranger Act had been passed on April 21 by the Confederate Congress, and according to a modern historian, it "spawned widespread popular resistance outside traditional military boundaries. Such irregulars merged with what would today be termed civilian non-combatants into auxiliary men-in-arms force multipliers to Confederates, pestilential threats in Union military eyes."[16]

On August 11, Granger got a message from Rosecrans which said: "General Grant says he has information that 800 to 1,000 conscripts and guerrillas rendezvousing about Ripley are raiding up toward Pocahontas . . . burning cotton, &c. Can you verify that and if possible cut off and capture a large number of them? 'Sharp' is the word."[17]

Granger responded immediately, prompting Rosecrans to get back to Grant: "I have just received the following from General Granger in reply to my dispatch predicated on yours of today: 'I have already captured the guerrilla party referred to. . . . It consisted of 17 instead of 800.' In reply to my advice he says: 'Sharp is our name, game, and practice.' It seems so."[18]

All the Union armies in the occupied South were frustrated by the hostility of the white inhabitants, sometimes expressed in sniper fire and other attacks by guerrillas who spent most of their time in civilian pursuits. These activities were seen as murderous by outraged Union soldiers, including Granger, but ruthless tactics were increasingly being adopted by both sides, with or without official sanction.

The 7th Kansas Cavalry was troublesome in this regard. Composed largely of abolitionist Jayhawkers, its march through Tennessee to join Granger's division had been "marked by robbery, theft, pillage and outrages upon the peaceful inhabitants," according to Halleck, even including rape.[19] It and the 2nd Iowa also engaged in some pillaging when they captured Ripley, west of Booneville, on July 28.

When Granger was on more neutral turf, as in the border states of Missouri and Kentucky (to where he would soon be headed), he was concerned to restrain his troops so as not to alienate the civilian population. But the bulk of the white population of Mississippi was inveterately hostile to the Union cause.

On August 28 Granger wrote a lengthy message to Rosecrans' chief of staff, Lt. Colonel Henry G. Kennett, reporting on Sheridan's August 26 engagement west of Rienzi, when his picket post was overrun but he rallied the troops and counterattacked effectively, driving the Confederates into headlong retreat. Sheridan's own report says he was attacked "by a large force of the enemy, say 700 to 800." Sheridan says the rebels were commanded by a "Colonel Falkner," but adds, "It was understood that they were guerrillas."[20]

While Granger had not long before disciplined soldiers for unauthorized picking of apples, now he was calling for a more rigorous mode of warfare, with the use of tactics that presaged what Sheridan and Sherman would be doing two years later.

"There is no doubt but what every man in this State who has a gun is a guerrilla, and would shoot any of us down whenever he thought it safe to murder us without risking his own neck," Granger wrote. "Two things are most necessary and important: First, there must be some definite and fixed policy on our part to combat and break up this most infernal guerrilla system of theirs; it is bound soon to waste our entire army away and for no equivalent. We must push every man, woman, and child before us or put every man to death found in our lines. We have in fact soon to come to a war of subjugation, and the sooner the better."

Referring to Sheridan's pursuit of guerrillas, Granger reported, "Orders were given to take no prisoners."[21] Actually, Colonel Edward Hatch, commanding the 2nd Iowa under Sheridan, did report taking eight prisoners in the successful engagement. Sheridan's report, immediately after referring to guerrillas, says: "Unfortunately 11 prisoners were brought in."[22] This does imply that Granger and Sheridan were expecting surrendering guerrillas to be shot. While Confederates had adopted the same ruthless policies, e.g. hanging bridge burners who were expecting a Union army advance into east Tennessee, Granger's order to kill prisoners on the spot, with no trial or effort to ascertain guilt, is impossible to justify as a matter of morality. It falls into a pattern of intemperate, occasionally vicious words and actions directed sometimes at his own troops, sometimes at the enemy, generally reconsidered and corrected upon calmer reflection. Such lapses in judgment, however, may have contributed to the distrust toward Granger felt by some of his colleagues and superiors to the detriment of his career—although Sheridan's identical attitude does not seem to have retarded his advance.

Granger's message to Kennett closed on another bleak note, referring to the overrunning of Sheridan's picket post which started the engagement, and "the running away of Captain Eaton, 2nd Iowa Cavalry, at the head of his men, instead of patrolling the country as he was ordered to do. He is being tried on charges which will cost him his life if proven. Of course you can't blame Sheridan for the willful neglect and cowardice of one of his officers."

The fortunes of war were shifting. In Virginia, Lee had driven McClellan down the Peninsula before turning on Pope and thoroughly defeating him August 28–30 at Second Bull Run. With both McClellan's army and

Pope's defeated, Lee turned his sights north to an invasion of Maryland.

Also at this time, two Confederate armies invaded Kentucky, confirming the intelligence that had been provided by Granger's forces. The first, commanded by Major General Edmund Kirby Smith, obliterated a force under Union Major General William "Bull" Nelson at Richmond, in east-central Kentucky, on August 30. Smith then captured Lexington, to the north, on September 2, and the next day, moving west, occupied Frankfort, the state capital. The larger Confederate army, moving up from Chattanooga, was commanded by Braxton Bragg. This two-pronged invasion threatened to undo the great Union victories that had been won in the West in the first months of 1862.

So on September 2nd Halleck ordered Grant to send Granger's division "to Louisville, Ky., with all possible dispatch." Louisville is west of Frankfort, at the northern boundary of the state on the Ohio River. Rosecrans plaintively asked Grant the same day: "You will not send Granger's cavalry, will you?"[23] By the next day, he was reconciled to losing Granger, but asked Grant to delay the transfer so as not to endanger an Army hospital and supplies.

Two days later, on September 4 Rosecrans passed on the order that "Granger will proceed with the infantry division now under his command, the Second Michigan Cavalry, Colonel [sic] P.H. Sheridan commanding, Hescock's battery and Barnett's battery, to Louisville, Ky., and report for orders to Major General H.G. Wright."[24] So Grant was leaving most of "Granger's cavalry" with Rosecrans, and sending Granger himself with a mostly infantry force to Kentucky.

Rosecrans' general order to Granger also demanded "the utmost secrecy and dispatch, covering his front while so doing by the two cavalry regiments he leaves behind." Granger had to address Rosecrans' concerns about coverage of his front, so it took two days for him to depart north.

"In ordering Granger to Louisville," says a 20th-century historian, "Halleck was playing cards well, for the small, well trained division would be a good nucleus for new organizations ... names like Gordon Granger and Phil Sheridan would stimulate morale."[25]

The troops marched back to Corinth, went by rail to Columbus, Kentucky, then steamed up the Ohio River. Granger had arranged for Sheridan to go, too, as the latter relates in his memoirs (telling how Grant was much sorrier to lose Sheridan than Granger). While Sheridan's command for the moment had been reduced, he rightly expected to find more troops to lead into battle where the crisis was gathering. His commander may have been thinking along similar lines, but it was Sheridan who would soon be fighting at Perryville and Stones River, while Granger, after the immediate crisis passed, found himself shunted off into a senior role that took him away from the fighting and into a more political world. It had been a year since Granger himself had seen serious combat, and another year would pass before he got to command troops in a major battle. But he was promoted anyway that fall to major general of volunteers, effective September 17, because his responsibilities were rapidly expanding.

He spent September scrambling from place to place organizing troops—as he testified in February 1863 as a defense witness at a court of inquiry examining the conduct of Major General Buell, whose Army of the Ohio had been rushed north to meet the Confederate threat in Kentucky. Following Buell's relief in October, Secretary of War Edwin Stanton ordered a court of inquiry to investigate his conduct of the Kentucky campaign. The commission's report in 1863 largely exonerated Buell, but he did not return to active service.

Granger arrived in Major General Horatio Wright's Department of the Ohio—which included almost all of Kentucky—on September 13, 1862, commanding four regiments of infantry, one of cavalry and two batteries of light artillery. Sheridan was sent to Louisville on September 14, while Granger proceeded to Covington, Kentucky, across the Ohio River from Cincinnati, to command "some eight or nine regiments more."[26] In early September the national government feared a Confederate threat not merely to Kentucky but to Cincinnati. Kirby Smith got to within eight miles of Cincinnati, but pulled back at Granger's approach. Granger was organizing and deploying the incoming Federal forces, and gathering intelligence. As Bragg's army approached Louisville, southwest of Covington down the Ohio River, Granger's troops—now about sixteen regiments—were moved there by river and rail to defend against what was seen by him and others as the more imminent threat.

Granger arrived about September 17[27] in Louisville, where he was second in command to Nelson, whom Granger was ordered by Wright to assist. Nelson was still recovering from wounds received at Richmond. On that day Bragg captured Munfordville—south of Louisville in the middle of the state—along with 4,000 Union troops under John Wilder. But the influx of Federal reinforcements was stabilizing the situation, Kentuckians were not rising in support of the Confederates, and Bragg declined to do battle with Buell's Army of the Ohio to prevent it from reaching Louisville. Nor did

Buell, short on supplies, want to fight a battle at this time.

Granger and his regiments got to Louisville first. He worked "night and day" to strengthen its defenses, organizing the construction of trenches and fortifications, manning them with his and Nelson's troops, of whom there were a total of about 36,000, many of whom lacked training, along with four to five thousand civilian volunteers including "squirrel hunters." Only two of seven artillery batteries were in good condition and manned by skilled troops. Of the others, Granger testified, "I had something to do to get the guns and harness into condition, and the men were so ignorant that they did not know how to unlimber or limber up. . . . We were in hopes, in case we were attacked, to hold on to the trenches and suburbs if possible, to enable General Buell's army to come up and attack them in their rear, and it was seriously contemplated by General Nelson to burn the city as fast as they drove him from it."[28]

Granger helped build two pontoon bridges in case Louisville needed to be evacuated, while sending supplies, cavalry and engineers to ease the way in for Buell's army. He also unsuccessfully urged Nelson to bluff the Rebels. Granger's rejected plan was to pretend to retreat north across the Ohio River, but instead secretly move the army of Louisville south of the city to link up with Buell, and conduct a joint offensive against Bragg.[29]

Meanwhile, Granger was constantly gathering and evaluating intelligence about the two invading Rebel armies, and communicating with other Union commanders. Buell, as Granger testified at the latter's court of inquiry, "had spies out, so had I, and sometimes I communicated with him two or three times a day and he with me. We had information from prisoners, spies, and deserters who were coming in; besides we had men in our employ who visited their camps, who would go and stay three or four days at a time."[30]

Granger also noted that he had begun tracking Bragg's movements while he was still in Mississippi. It is worth quoting him at some length, as the testimony shows the importance he rightly attached to intelligence work, and what that consisted of in this important campaign:

"I will add that I supposed I was the first officer that reported the movements of [Bragg's] army from the time it left Tupelo. I was then in position to know more, being at the time in command of the advance guard of the whole army of Corinth, from 25 to 40 miles in front of Corinth. Through spies and deserters, while at Booneville, Blackland, Rienzi and Baldwyn [sic], I was the first to learn that that army was moving in the direction of Chattanooga, and so reported in through General Rosecrans to the commander-in-chief. I took great pains to ascertain the number of troops, dates of departure, composition of the army, and its destination. The movements of the rebel army and the approximate numbers I reported from day to day in the months of July and August last."[31]

This suggests that Granger was reporting on Bragg's movements well before Sheridan's report of July 29, and indeed he testified that he was aware of Bragg's move from Tupelo on July 8, and of the departure of 4,000 cavalry in June.[32] Bragg's advance arrived at Chattanooga around July 18, he told the court, leaving only relatively small forces under Generals Price and Van Dorn in Mississippi.

Buell arrived in Louisville on or shortly after September 25 and assumed command. The arrival of his army greatly reduced the immediate threat to the city, although work continued on digging trenches to protect it, which were mostly completed by September 28.

At the court of inquiry in February 1863, Granger's testimony stretched out for several days and was supportive of the cautious strategy of Buell. He also demonstrated a detailed grasp of the logistics and other military aspects of the complex campaign, along with the geography of Kentucky and Tennessee. As usual he paid no regard to army politics. Buell had been repudiated by the country's military and political leadership, yet Granger forthrightly defended his judgment.

On September 27 General Wright asked Buell to send Granger and his division back to Covington, along with Sheridan. Two days later, with Granger still in Louisville, Nelson was shot dead there by a subordinate brigadier— or rather, an exceedingly insubordinate one—Jefferson C. Davis, after an argument. The next day, the War Department attempted to remove Buell and replace him with George Thomas, but Thomas declined the appointment because of the ongoing campaign. Granger, meanwhile, attended Nelson's funeral at Calvary Episcopal Church. Davis was never prosecuted for murder, and continued to serve in the army through the Civil War and beyond.

Granger did depart at the beginning of October for Covington, where he declared martial law, but Sheridan stayed with Buell. Halleck, in Washington, was still concerned about a threat to Cincinnati, but in Kentucky the campaign's momentum had shifted.

On October 8, Buell's army encountered elements of Bragg's force at Perryville, south of Frankfort. It was an odd battle as some 16,000 Confederates unknowingly faced over 40,000 Federals; however when the Rebels attacked the Federal left, an acoustic shadow prevented Buell and most of his army from even realizing a battle was on. After about 4,200 Federal and

3,400 Rebel casualties, the Confederates vacated the field, and in fact the entire state of Kentucky, having been disappointed at the lack of recruits and support they found there.

Buell's failure to realize what was going on at Perryville, along with his dilatory subsequent pursuit, confirmed Washington's already low opinion of his military capacity. Yet, as Granger was to point out at the court of inquiry, Buell's strategy had been reasonably successful: "There is no doubt, although Bragg made a successful raid into Kentucky, that he certainly lost ten times more than he accomplished," Granger said. "I suppose the round trip cost him not less than 20,000 men, besides the wear and tear and destruction of his material of war. It is true, at the same time, it put us to a great deal of inconvenience and set us back in our operations, but I do not see how it advanced him. I think he would have done better to have remained in front of General Buell."

Horatio Wright had meantime declared that Granger's command would serve "as a nucleus about which to form an army of the new troops raised in the states of the department." (Wright's department, headquartered in Cincinnati, included Ohio, Indiana, Illinois, Michigan, Wisconsin, western Virginia and most of Kentucky.) On October 8, the same date as the Battle of Perryville, Granger was put in command of the new "Army of Kentucky," still under Wright. This army would eventually amount to about 26 regiments in three divisions commanded by brigadier generals. But Granger had only about 15,000 troops when he moved south toward the Kentucky capital of Frankfort soon after the Confederate retreat. By October 25 he was established at Lexington (where in 1876 he would be buried), and there, ensconced in Kirby Smith's former headquarters, he commanded the Central District of Kentucky that winter. Most of his men were new soldiers. Readying them for the demands of war was one of Granger's primary responsibilities for which he was well qualified.

Meanwhile, the armies of Bragg and Kirby Smith had linked up to retreat toward the Cumberland Gap and eastern Tennessee, followed cautiously by Buell, who had difficulty penetrating Bragg's cavalry screen. Buell, after breaking off the pursuit to move west toward Nashville, was relieved in late October and replaced by Rosecrans. The Army of the Ohio soon became the Army of the Cumberland. Bragg's army moved to Murfreesboro in central Tennessee.

After failing to find significant numbers of volunteers in Kentucky, the Confederates had resorted to conscription and much worse. Granger testified at the Buell court of inquiry that Kirby Smith commanded the rearguard of the Confederate retreat. Granger interviewed many civilians along the route in Kentucky "who said that he murdered a great many; there were sixteen Union men hung at Rockcastle River, which Smith has the credit of doing." When his West Point classmate Kirby Smith had invaded Kentucky, Granger's informants told him that "he met the people with smiles and affability and gave them more protection than they wanted; but after he failed in being able to obtain recruits he turned his troops upon them through his disappointment at finding that he was to be driven from the state."[33]

Kirby Smith's actions, like Granger's take-no-prisoners order in Mississippi, demonstrate the increasing ruthlessness of the war. This was especially so on the Confederate side in border states like Kentucky and Missouri, where the guerrillas William Quantrill and Bill Anderson were beginning to build their murderous reputations. These events also proved the value of winning and retaining public support. In Mississippi, where the white population was overwhelmingly pro-Confederate, Granger had proposed severe measures against guerrillas and the population supporting them. But in Kentucky and east Tennessee he took care not to alienate the civilian population, which while mostly Unionist was more often than not opposed to abolishing slavery.

Three months later, President Lincoln and Halleck would issue a pamphlet outlining a new code for the laws of civilized warfare, primarily written by a Columbia College professor, Francis Lieber. It grappled with such newly urgent issues as slave emancipation, guerrilla activity and the status of noncombatants, answering questions that had been raised by Granger and other soldiers in the field, and giving them direction.

On September 22, 1862, Lincoln had announced he would issue an Emancipation Proclamation freeing slaves in Confederate-controlled states—which would not include Kentucky and, as it turned out when the proclamation was issued in the new year, did not include Tennessee either. Lincoln acted in September soon after the Army of the Potomac under McClellan had won a partial victory at Antietam, forcing Lee to retreat from Maryland back to Virginia.

McClellan was nonetheless replaced in November, and his successor, Ambrose Burnside, was defeated in December by Lee at the Battle of Fredericksburg. In the west later that month, Grant's campaign in the Mississippi Valley suffered reverses. He was forced to retreat after Confederate cavalry under Van Dorn destroyed his supply base at Holly Springs; and more cavalry

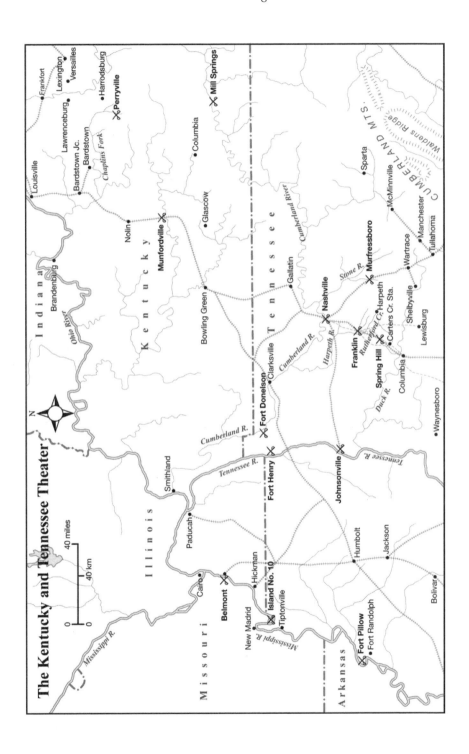

under Nathan Bedford Forrest tore up his line of communications in western Tennessee. Not knowing of Grant's withdrawal, a force under Sherman went ahead and launched an attack at Chickasaw Bayou, north of Vicksburg, only to meet with a severe repulse. While on its way to recross the Tennessee River, Forrest's cavalry nearly became trapped between two Federal infantry brigades at Parker's Crossroads, but escaped after Forrest's famous (perhaps apocryphal) command, "Charge them both ways!"

Despite blunting the Confederate invasions in both Maryland and Tennessee that autumn, Union prospects still appeared highly dubious. The Rebel offensives could be discouraged, but a Federal one into Southern territory—save Farragut's naval conquest of New Orleans the previous April—had yet to fully succeed. And the Lincoln administration remained anxious to reassure Kentucky unionists who opposed abolition.

On November 18 Granger sent a message from Lexington to Wright in Cincinnati which began: "I am daily annoyed and harassed by the many complaints made to me by Union men of this part of Kentucky, of the abduction of their negroes, by officers and men in this army. . . . Already a Colonel of one of our Regiments has been indicted under the laws of Kentucky for abduction of negroes."[34] Runaway slaves were crowding and creating problems in military camps, Granger continued, and some officers were protecting them from their owners, even when the owners were unionists, which "gives the greatest discouragement to our friends and supporters."

Granger's position sounds inhumane to modern ears, and his language is undeniably harsh. He refers at one point to "worthless negroes," and describes complaints made by members of the 10th Kentucky Cavalry in these terms: ". . . that while they were fighting to protect their property, under the constitution and laws of the country, some of the men in other regiments of their own Army, were taking and secreting such property from them."

Part of the problem was Granger's fiery temper, which often led him into unwise communications. But the message also indicates a conservative approach to the slavery issue, similar to that of his friend McClellan. Perhaps Granger was brooding about McClellan's dismissal by Lincoln earlier that month, but if so he soon proved that unlike Little Mac, he was able to change with the times and follow administration policy. And to be fair to Granger, that policy remained ambiguous.

As Granger pointed out to Wright, the Kentuckians had a good case under the law and the Constitution, and the Union and army needed to retain their support. It was a real and serious problem that he addressed. Lincoln himself had reversed the edicts of abolitionist generals like Fremont, and, in discussing the controversy said in an August 1861 letter: "I think to lose Kentucky is nearly the same as to lose the whole game." The state was the birthplace of Lincoln, who had never liked slavery. But Confederate President Jefferson Davis also was born in Kentucky, and the existence of slavery there, at least until the war itself started to change attitudes, had been mainly uncontroversial among the white population.

A year later, Lincoln wrote: "If I could save the Union without freeing any slave I would do it, and if I could save it by freeing all the slaves I would do it; and if I could save it by freeing some and leaving others alone I would also do that."[35] Most Kentuckians, including most Unionists in the state, had sought to stay neutral in the war's first year, and, as would soon be demonstrated, the threat of the state legislature voting to secede remained real. Securing their continued allegiance to the Union was a necessary task for army commanders. Granger had the difficult job of finding or creating constructive common ground between those of his soldiers who were abolitionists and others who were not, including the majority of Union-supporting white Kentuckians who opposed freeing the slaves. Wright passed Granger's complaint to Halleck in Washington with a request for a clarification of policy, but got back an evasive reply.

Nor was it just a matter of relations with the people and government of Kentucky. Granger's own troops were divided on how to handle the issue, with abolitionists on one side and defenders of slavery on the other. This was a potential threat to military discipline, made worse by Granger's own uncertainty as to what policy he was supposed to enforce.

Even troops from the North, who had no love of slavery, were often unsympathetic to the abolitionist position, sometimes supporting instead another of the Lincoln administration's positions, encouraging freed slaves to emigrate to Africa or elsewhere. In a letter the next year to his wife from Tennessee, Benjamin C. Preston of the 92nd Ohio Infantry endorsed confiscating Rebel "property" including slaves, "and put them to the best use they can, and as soon as the war is over rid them from among us which will be done . . . the negroes are not going to be allowed to run among us as many suppose . . . a parcel of southern sympathizers have been going to you and make you believe this war is all for the negroes, but it is not. It is our country . . ."[36] While Preston was not directly under Granger's command, he was in the same army and would fight beside Granger's corps at Missionary Ridge in November 1863.[37]

On December 8, 1862, a public meeting was held in Lexington where complaints were aired about alleged Army violations of Kentucky law relating to slavery. A protest resolution was passed, which Granger passed on to Wright on December 12. Wright wrote back two days later. The text of the resolution does not survive, but according to Wright's paraphrase it contained "certain interrogatories addressed to you [i.e. Granger], which are, in substance, as follows, viz: Does the military claim or intend to assert supremacy over the civil power in the Union State of Kentucky; if so, why, and to what extent? Whether the forcible detention of certain slaves belonging to Union Citizens of Kentucky within the lines of Regiments under your command was authorized, and whether the same will hereafter be sanctioned or authorized, and, if so, under what law, and for what purpose? Also requesting you to furnish the names of slaves so detained, and the regiment in which each is detained."[38]

The citizens meeting had designated a three-man committee to which Granger wrote a letter on December 11, the day before he referred the matter to Wright. In it he defended the army, saying it would comply with both state and Federal law, and urging the citizens to go through military channels and not to stir up trouble: "Such meetings can be easily influenced and controlled by a few designing and bad men … to the great damage of our cause. Heretofore, many, who were once honest and loyal Citizens, have been so led astray by the machinations and duplicity of disloyal men at such, that they have joined hands with them in their traitorous designs against the Government. For this reason such meetings are much to be regretted."[39]

On the same date, December 11, Granger got a message from a subordinate brigadier-general, Quincy Gillmore, whose October 22 "contraband order" had been severely criticized by abolitionists. Gillmore, commanding the Second Division, had by that order barred "contrabands"—runaway slaves—from his lines, "except under such restrictions as will place them within direct and entire control from these headquarters."[40] While Granger and Wright supported their brigadier, Gillmore felt it necessary on December 11 to state: "I have never, that I know of, by any order of mine, hindered any slave of his liberty in any way, shape, or form, and do not remember to have ordered but one to be sent beyond the lines."[41] (His critics no doubt noticed that the last part of that sentence seems to contradict the first.)

Wright's December 14 message told Granger to tell complainers that the army would follow the laws of the state unless they conflicted with Federal law, and would support the (military) governor in maintaining law and order, but would not hunt down runaway slaves.

While the actions and language of Granger and his fellow generals are open to criticism, the reality and seriousness of the problems they were trying to address are illustrated by an extraordinary December 30 message from Granger's commander Wright to General-in-Chief Halleck in Washington: "I have information, on which I am inclined to rely, that in case the President issues his proclamation of emancipation on the 1st proximo, the Legislature of Kentucky, which meets on Monday next, will legislate the State out of the Union, and that the Governor's message will favor such action; also that the court of appeals has a disloyal majority, and will reverse all judgments of loyal inferior courts against rebels. I propose, first, to so dispose the force I have as to have several Northern regiments in the vicinity of Frankfort; second, to arrest all members of the Legislature voting for ordinance of secession, and all State officers favoring it; or, third, to arrest any members of the Legislature who, by their speeches or other acts, recommend the secession of the State; I prefer the second proposition; fourth, to arrest the reputed disloyal members of court of appeals on first indication of disloyalty, or, if thought best, on arrest of the Legislature."[42]

Such extraordinary actions would not have been unprecedented. The year before, Lincoln's suspension of habeas corpus had enabled him to have the army arrest Maryland state legislators suspected of Confederate leanings on their way to a meeting where they planned to vote the state out of the Union. The war's outcome was still very much in doubt at the end of 1862, and Kentucky's secession, if permitted, might have had almost as disastrous a military consequence as Maryland's would have had the year before.

Meanwhile, Wright had Granger station "three–four reliable regiments" near Frankfort, the state capital.[43] It was a potential crisis, although in the event Wright's fears proved exaggerated—perhaps because the news of Rosecrans' success with Bragg at the Battle of Stones River influenced the views of Kentucky politicians in the new year. Still, it shows the very difficult political environment in which Granger was working.

Blackford notes Granger's "grasp of political realities," how he avoided antagonizing Unionist slave-owners when their support was vital "and yet, later in the war, relied on black troops and protested their use as laborers by the Confederates when they were prisoners of war. He was, in fact, the complete opportunist on the slavery question and, as such, a useful agent of Lincoln's changeable policy."[44] In Kentucky that winter, he helped keep a lid on the crisis, preventing it from blowing up into a full-scale distraction and threat to the Union war effort.

Despite the lack of Rebel recruits for Bragg's and Kirby Smith's armies that fall, plenty of Kentuckians were outright supporters of the Confederacy. They included a volunteer cavalryman whose often exaggerated exploits were especially popular with the ladies of the South, and whose legend lived on in postwar "Lost Cause" mythology: John Hunt Morgan. Granger, the successful professional soldier, is buried in Lexington Cemetery under a pillared marker accounting some of his career. Morgan's posthumous fame was greater than his military accomplishments, and a large equestrian statue of him was unveiled in 1911 which still stands in downtown Lexington.

Morgan, still a colonel for most of 1862, had raided Kentucky in July with two regiments, and then turned on Buell's supply lines in Tennessee. There, despite his aura of chivalrous romance, he gave the order "no quarter" and led by example in killing Federal soldiers who were trying to surrender.[45]

His successes encouraged Kirby Smith and Bragg to invade the Bluegrass state, and Morgan, too, came back, following Smith into Lexington on September 5. When the Confederate infantry retreated after Perryville in October, Morgan resumed the offensive, first in Kentucky and then near Nashville. In December he was promoted to brigadier general and defeated part of the Army of the Cumberland at Hartsville. Then he conducted another damaging raid into Kentucky between Louisville and Nashville. Wright told Granger to reinforce Munfordville, and Granger relayed intelligence about the raid. But it was a detachment of the Army of the Cumberland which ineffectively pursued Morgan out of the state and back to Tennessee in the new year.

Granger's military responsibilities included reacting to raids and the threats of raids, and to guerrilla or associated activities, such as breaking up bands of Confederate deserters who were reported in November to be terrorizing Union men in Bath County, east of Lexington.

Thanks in part to Granger's initiative and direction, cavalry raids were no longer strictly a Confederate prerogative. On November 25, he and Wright met with Brigadier-General Samuel Carter, an east Tennessee native and former naval officer who had switched to the army after declaring his loyalty when the war came. On December 10 Wright authorized Carter to lead a raid with 1,200 cavalry into eastern Tennessee. This would be, according to the pre-eminent historian of the U.S. cavalry in the war, "the first long-distance raid staged by the Union cavalry," and "the idea of the Carter raid came from General Granger."[46] Its main purpose was to disrupt Confederate communications, especially the East Tennessee & Virginia Railroad. It also was a pre-emptive strike, designed to make it more difficult for the Confederates to launch new raids or invasions of Kentucky through the Cumberland Gap.

Granger of course was a veteran cavalryman, and he worked closely with his much less experienced subordinate Carter in Lexington until December 20 to make preparations. He suggested that supplies go initially on wagons and then be transferred to mules, the better to traverse the rough, wilderness mountain country through which the raiders would go. There turned out to be fewer than a thousand of them, which left Granger only about 500 cavalry in Kentucky.

Still, the hard-pressed cavalry of Granger's "Army of Kentucky" was able to conduct other successful operations. Wright reported to Halleck that on December 28 about 250 cavalrymen surprised a camp of 350 Confederates at Elk Fork, over the Tennessee line on the road to Knoxville, killing 30, wounding 17 and capturing 51, without the loss of a man; and that in a separate surprise attack southeast of Lexington in Powell County, Kentucky, about 150 U.S. horse soldiers routed a larger guerrilla force, capturing 12.[47] The Kentucky regiments that won these skirmishes had been dispatched by Granger.

Carter's raid also was successful. As Wright reported to Halleck on January 7, 1863, Carter's troops destroyed two railroad bridges and 10 miles of track. "Five hundred and fifty rebels were killed, wounded and taken prisoners. Seven hundred stand of arms and a large amount of flour, salt, and other rebel stores, also a locomotive and two cars, were captured and destroyed," Wright said. Many of the paroled prisoners, according to Carter, said they were happy to be out of the war.

"Great credit is also due to Major-General Granger," Wright concluded, "under whose immediate supervision the expedition was fitted out, and whose long cavalry experience was a guarantee that nothing tending to its success would be neglected or forgotten."[48] Halleck sent back an enthusiastic reply congratulating Carter's force, which suffered fewer than 200 casualties.

Meanwhile, Rosecrans' main army had advanced from Nashville and fought one of the war's major battles with Bragg from December 31 to January 2 at Stones River, outside Murfreesboro, Tennessee. At first the Rebels had hammered in the Federal right, pushing it back over a mile. But then the Federals held on, with Sheridan's division fighting gallantly toward the center, and George Thomas implacably holding the center itself. On New Year's Day both armies warily contemplated each other, and then on January 2 Bragg launched an ill-advised attack against Rosecrans' left, which had the effect of throwing away his earlier tactical advantage while compelling the Confederate army to withdraw back to more secure lines at Tullahoma to nurse its many casualties. The Federals had achieved a success, if only by again blunting a Confederate attack rather than initiating a successful one of their own.

Both Morgan's raid and Carter's were launched in advance of this battle, but neither had any significant impact on it. Still, Carter's raid showed that the Union Army was capable of effectively using the raiding tactic, as it would with increased strategic effectiveness later in the war. Carter's raid damaged Confederate communications and put further pressure on their economy, and the lost Rebel soldiers and supplies could not easily be replaced. The raid also increased the morale of Union supporters, who were a majority in east Tennessee, possibly stimulating them to join the army or engage in their own guerrilla operations.

But Carter's experience also convinced Granger and Wright that it was not feasible that winter to launch a larger-scale invasion through the rough, wet and mountainous wilderness of east Tennessee, despite Lincoln's long-standing desire that the army liberate this Union-loyal area. Liberation would have to come from the west, and the sensible military decision was made to send Granger to support Rosecrans in central Tennessee.

———

On January 20, 1863, the Army of Kentucky—with about 18 regiments of infantry, four of cavalry and four artillery batteries but only amounting to about 14,000 soldiers—was attached to Rosecrans' Army of the Cumberland. Granger was ordered to proceed via Louisville to Nashville, leaving Gillmore in command of central Kentucky. "As was most judicious," says Thomas Wood, "he was brought nearer to the front, being transferred to the State of Tennessee, and placed in command at Franklin."[49]

They travelled by boat on the Ohio, Tennessee and Cumberland rivers toward Nashville. Passing on February 3 near the site of Grant's victory at Donelson the year before, the six gunboats accompanying the flotilla engaged in repelling a Confederate cavalry attack on the Union fort at Dover, Tennessee—which was supposedly well within Union lines.[50]

Franklin, which Granger's advance forces occupied in February, was at the right flank of Rosecrans' long front, and vulnerable to attack by Confederate cavalry—well led and more numerous than the Federal mounted soldiers. The town is about 20 miles south of Nashville and 35 miles west of Murfreesboro, where Rosecrans and the main body of the Army of the Cumberland faced Bragg at Shelbyville, Tullahoma and along the west-flowing Duck River. Granger guarded the army's right flank, responsible for preventing Rebel cavalry from getting beyond it and behind Rosecrans' army.

Granger's command suffered an early reverse in March when a brigade under Colonel John Coburn (a lawyer and politician before the war) was sent by Brig. General Charles Gilbert to reconnoiter and gather forage south of Franklin. According to a history of the Army of the Cumberland by one of its veterans, Henry M. Cist, Coburn's cavalry skirmished with the enemy on March 4, and the Confederates retreated to Spring Hill. That night, Coburn told Gilbert he was confronted by a superior force and suggested withdrawal, but Gilbert told him to advance.[51] Another version of these events, by Starr, has Coburn advancing without waiting for Gilbert's reply and without adequate reconnaissance and prudence. Granger later faulted him for "not approaching the enemy with sufficient caution."[52]

Attacked on the 5th of March at Thompson's Station by larger Confederate forces led by Generals Earl Van Dorn and Nathan Bedford Forrest, Coburn and most of his troops surrendered. Union losses were 48 killed, 247 wounded and 1,152 taken prisoner[53] —or even higher by some accounts. Confederate casualties were perhaps 200. Stanley's memoirs put most of the blame on Gilbert. Rosecrans' report blamed Coburn and Gilbert but not Granger.

Granger sent Brig. General Absalom Baird's brigade by rail to reinforce Franklin, and assumed personal command there, moving his headquarters and preparing to go on the offensive.

But Granger's health was not good. He suffered from recurring bouts of illness throughout his life, but sickness was hardly a rarity among Civil War soldiers; indeed, far more died from disease than from combat. A medical history of Union generals cites two occasions in the war, in March 1862 and January 1864, when Granger was too sick for duty.[54] His health also was poor in March 1863, leading Rosecrans on March 7 to communicate instead with his subordinate, Baird, because "I want General Granger to sleep and get well."[55]

Fortunately, Rosecrans knew, trusted and valued him (even though the army commander's chief of staff James Garfield was critical of Granger's movements at this time). Granger and Rosecrans were back in communication the next day.

Granger had resisted Rosecrans' pressure to go on the offensive, because he was outnumbered. But support was being deployed, including a division under Sheridan, who reported back to Granger's command on March 8. Also reporting to him was Colonel Robert Minty's cavalry brigade, and he was at least coordinating with other troops, including those under two brigadier-generals, Green Clay Smith and James Steedman. Sheridan raided Confederate camps at Unionville, capturing 70 prisoners, and Steedman captured 100 of Van Dorn's troops at Chapel Hill. Steedman, a brave, energetic volunteer officer, was stationed at Triune, between Franklin and Murfreesboro. "Since neither Granger nor Van Dorn reported formally on their operations of the next few days," Starr's history notes, "the exact course of events is somewhat unclear, although it can be deduced from a number of dispatches and subsidiary reports."[56]

Granger advanced south from Franklin toward Van Dorn at Spring Hill, a few miles south of Thompson's Station, on March 10. The Union troops drove the Confederates about 5 miles farther south beyond Rutherford Creek near Columbia, before pulling back the next day because they had difficulty getting infantry and artillery over the rising creek. The Confederates retreated, only to return.

Van Dorn was back in the Spring Hill area by March 22, as Granger informed Rosecrans. The Confederates also could strike in Granger's rear north of Franklin, as Forrest did at Brentwood on March 25. This resulted in another Union defeat, making March 1863 Granger's least successful month of the Civil War. Forrest captured two infantry garrisons, which put up precious little resistance. Granger sent Clay Smith's cavalry in pursuit, which did engage Forrest and inflicted some casualties, with control over Forrest's captured Union soldiers and wagons going back and forth in the skirmish. Still, Forrest got away with several hundred prisoners, several times more than his own total losses.

Rosecrans' instructions at this time were for Granger to react to enemy movements, "make him extend his line, and weaken his center, while you secure our line of communication, even if you have to rest in front of Nashville. If we can draw in some of his force, and catch it, it will be well."[57] Granger also was training and drilling his troops, most of whom were inexperienced, and overseeing the construction of fortifications. Those included Fort

Granger at Franklin, which was attacked and successfully defended twice in the next few months under his command.

Fort Granger replaced a much smaller and inferior fort. It was built between March and May, with laborers often working 24 hours a day. Constructed of packed dirt supported by rough timbers, it took in almost 12 acres, housing up to 8,000 troops and 24 artillery pieces. The next year, when Granger was serving in Alabama, the earthen fort named after him played a major role in the Battle of Franklin, an important Union defensive victory against Confederate General John B. Hood's invading army.

Granger was also continually gathering and reporting intelligence, although the local white people were much more likely to help the Confederates than him. He had a little over 10,000 men ready for combat, and fewer cavalry than the Confederates should they choose to concentrate against him. And Spring Hill, south of Granger's headquarters at Franklin, was where the Confederate cavalry leaders Van Dorn and then Forrest most often had their headquarters. Van Dorn's tenure in central Tennessee was short-lived, however, as on May 7 he was shot and killed by a civilian, apparently a jealous husband.

Granger's cavalry background helped give him a feel for intelligence, and he would take information wherever he could get it, including from his colleagues and commander. A typical April 5 report to Rosecrans concludes: "Have you any news? Very respectfully, G. Granger, Major-General."

In south-central Tennessee, to a much greater degree than mostly Unionist Kentucky, the secessionist views of the local white inhabitants and their guerrilla activity were a boon to the Confederate army. Accordingly, Granger's policy shifted from conciliation back to the sterner attitude he had been developing in Mississippi in 1862. The best evidence for this is a message written later in the year by a subordinate brigade commander, Colonel Daniel McCook, who had advanced south to Columbia:

"Some such decided measures as you adopted at Franklin must be adopted here and at Pulaski to break the necks of the rebels," wrote McCook on August 29. "As far as your influence extended their conduct was perfectly refreshing, but south of Duck River they are impudent and defiant; they must be 'Grangerized.' Mrs. Hunter, on Carter's Creek, should be sent south—she and daughter; says she helped to burn the bridges before and will do it again. All the families you sent from Franklin should be sent south of the Tennessee [River]; they spread wide dissatisfaction."[58]

According to Henry J. Aten's history of an infantry regiment then under Granger's command, "The whole country between Nashville and the army at the front was infested with guerrilla bands. These bands were largely, if not wholly, composed of citizens, who, during the day, while apparently attending to their usual avocations in a quiet and lawful manner, learned the position of troops, where a picket might be shot, or foragers or stragglers murdered with little to risk to themselves."[59] Then they might come out after dark, and proceed to pick off—kill—the Union troops, before resuming their apparently law-abiding daytime lives. Aten describes burning the property of one suspected guerrilla leader, and makes it clear he personally would have supported harsher measures.

On April 7 Granger reported to Rosecrans that Van Dorn was back at Spring Hill, and he speculated that the Confederate general either meant to attack him or to go around the army's right flank and head for Kentucky. Rosecrans telegraphed back suggesting Granger combine with Gen. David S. Stanley's cavalry to attack Van Dorn. Granger agreed, suggesting Stanley's force move toward him via Triune, which Rosecrans ordered. Stanley reported to Granger April 9 and came under his command.

Granger's intelligence proved accurate. He placed troops at various defensive positions around Franklin, including Stanley's cavalry "four miles out on the Murfreesborough road, to guard the ford at Hughes's Mill," according to the contemporary historian John Fitch.[60]

Van Dorn and Forrest did attack Franklin and its incomplete fortifications on April 10, beginning with a night attack shortly after midnight. It was easily repulsed. That morning Granger got a misleading report from Brig. General James Morgan indicating another attack on Brentwood, and dispatched his cavalry to defend against the nonexistent threat. But he still had enough forces at Franklin to repel additional Confederate attacks, even getting to indulge his favorite pastime of directing effective artillery fire, forcing the enemy back.

Van Dorn sent Forrest "around to gain Granger's rear by a road crossing the Harpeth three miles east of the town, known as the Nicholl Mill Road. It was in anticipation of this movement that General Granger had placed General Stanley in the position he held."[61] After an inconclusive skirmish with Stanley's flank attack—which Granger was unable to reinforce in time because he'd sent away his cavalry reserve—the Confederates retreated south to Spring Hill. Fitch says the Confederates suffered about 300 casualties, including 80 prisoners, as opposed to only 37 on the Union side. Confederate figures put the casualty figures as more even, but it's undeniable that Van Dorn's attack did not accomplish its purpose.

Stanley, although under Granger's orders, made his own decision to attack at Franklin. Rosecrans now gave him command of two cavalry divisions, although Stanley would come back under Granger's command in the upcoming Tullahoma campaign.

On April 27, Granger dispatched the 6th Kentucky Cavalry on a night move "to surprise and capture the Texas Legion," as he reported to Rosecrans. Attacking at daybreak about eight miles south of Franklin on Carter Creek Pike, they "made prisoners of the entire force, consisting of 9 commissioned officers and 112 men, 300 horses and mules, 8 wagons" plus all their arms and equipment, "without the loss of a man on our part. Several rebels were killed and wounded." Granger told his commander that "this daring feat . . . was made almost under the eyes of Van Dorn, within 1 mile of his main body."[62] The Confederates pursued the raiders north for five miles without inflicting any damage. On April 30, Granger reported that the Confederates had "moved their stores and baggage back 20 miles behind Shelbyville," which is about 25 miles south and a little west of Murfreesboro.

But despite these new successes of an increasingly confident cavalry, the Army of the Cumberland had made precious little offensive progress since January, and Rosecrans was coming under increasing pressure from Washington to move. On June 8, he appointed Granger head of the Army of the Cumberland's Reserve Corps, with three divisions. On the same date, Rosecrans asked his subordinate generals what they thought about an advance. Almost all of them, including Granger and even Sheridan, advocated caution. Granger reported that Bragg's army had not been significantly reduced to counter Grant at Vicksburg, and the pressing need was to "double or treble our cavalry."

Forrest had attacked Franklin on June 4. Granger was now based southeast of there in Triune, preparing for Rosecrans' summer campaign. He quickly sent reinforcements to Franklin, most of them cavalry including his old regiment the 2nd Michigan, which drove off the Rebels. (Always sensitive to artillery issues, Granger's report is critical of the way the defenders under Col. J.P. Baird handled their cannon.) Baird reported casualties of no more than 10, while capturing 28 Confederates and killing or wounding a like number.

Forrest, the most dangerous of Confederate cavalry commanders, attacked Triune itself a week later, and was again driven off. In the latter engagement, Confederate losses were almost 100 including 23 killed; Union losses included six killed.

These encounters showed the increasing effectiveness of Granger's forces. Rosecrans had spent months petitioning Washington for cavalry reinforcements, which did not endear him to an impatient and cost-conscious War Department. While Edwin Stanton and Halleck implied that Rosecrans' army had been idle since January, to the extent it had been active Granger was often involved. (Just as the year before, in Halleck's slow movement on Corinth, Granger's troops were in the advance and engaged in more combat than most.) Despite the deficiencies of Union cavalry and prior Confederate superiority in that arm, Granger's cavalry background and expertise were proving very helpful to the army. That would continue to be the case later in June, when Rosecrans finally took the offensive. By then, the Army of the Cumberland commander had managed to build up Union cavalry and mounted infantry forces to match the Confederates in number. And as they would soon demonstrate at Shelbyville, the cavalry under Granger's command could fight as well or better as any.

Granger launched Rosecrans' Tullahoma campaign on June 23, advancing his Reserve Corps and Stanley's cavalry (again under his command) south from Murfreesboro toward Shelbyville, which is northwest of Tullahoma. This move was a feint by Rosecrans, whose main thrust would be made by Thomas going through Hoover's Gap around Bragg's right flank to Manchester, northeast of Tullahoma. Major Generals Alexander McCook and Thomas Crittenden also were moving south and east.

Granger and Stanley played their full part in this successful maneuver. Rosecrans' targets were several "gaps" that would let his divisions pass through the increasingly hilly terrain of south-central Tennessee.

Granger's Reserve Corps was now over 20,000 strong, with half as many cavalry attached. He moved east from Triune to Salem, sending General Robert Mitchell's cavalry division south where it skirmished at Rover. This drew Confederate General Joseph Wheeler's cavalry to the Rebel army's left, western flank, weakening Confederate defenses to the east, which helped Thomas take Hoover's Gap the next day. Granger sent feed wagons with the infantry to provide some forage for horses in the war-ravaged country.

Reconnaissance and intelligence from Granger's command showed much of Bragg's army at Shelbyville, which was where Rosecrans wanted him and where Granger's offensive was aimed. Hoover's Gap was the crucial victory of the campaign, but Granger's feint continued to distract Bragg from taking measures to counter Thomas' advance.

Granger sent cavalry under Colonel Robert Minty on June 25 to Fosterville, where he clashed with Confederates near Guy's Gap before withdrawing. Granger reported that day to Rosecrans that Bragg's main force was at Shelbyville. On June 26 Granger visited Liberty Gap and reported to Rosecrans that the enemy appeared to be retreating from there and Guy's Gap "in the direction of Shelbyville or elsewhere." Stanley, ordered to "feel the enemy" the next day, found Guy's Gap held only by cavalry, who after a couple of hours skirmishing showed signs of retreating. Stanley suggested an attack, and Granger, as he stated in his report, "then ordered General Stanley to bring up his cavalry and clear the gap at once."[63]

Stanley did so, and the Union cavalry drove through the gap toward Shelbyville, where Wheeler's Confederates made a stand with artillery three miles north of town. Granger was now convinced that the Confederates were looking to retreat, and "although the orders I had received did not contemplate an advance beyond the gap . . . I rapidly pushed the cavalry force of my command forward."[64] The dismounted cavalry supported by infantry drove Wheeler back into Shelbyville, where he made another stand with artillery. Union artillery countered the Rebel fire, and the position was broken by a Union cavalry charge directed by Minty (accompanied by Stanley), which drove the Confederates into headlong flight and left Granger in possession of Shelbyville.

General Wheeler himself escaped from Shelbyville by swimming across the Duck River. His force's rout was so rapid that Forrest could not find a way to support him. Granger reported his troops had captured between 400 and 500 prisoners, and "the country north of Duck River is, I think, entirely clear and safe." Stanley estimated Confederate casualties at Shelbyville as at least a thousand.

Meanwhile, Thomas and Rosecrans were to the east in Manchester, threatening Bragg's rear communications. Unsure of the whereabouts of enemy cavalry, Rosecrans on June 28 suggested but did not require that Granger move troops toward Manchester. He told Granger to bring up more troops from Nashville and provide intelligence. Granger was also guarding railroad repair crews and protecting and extending telegraph lines. The railroad supply line was particularly important because of the continued wet weather—which probably allowed Bragg to avoid a major battle. In his report on the campaign, Rosecrans paid tribute to Granger's role in capturing Shelbyville and making the feint successful, and extended thanks "for subsequently dispatching our supplies when they were so pressingly needed."[65]

On June 29 Granger reported to Rosecrans he now had 600 prisoners and the Confederates had suffered several hundred other losses. They appeared to be retreating "in the direction of Chattanooga," in the southeastern corner of the state. This Rebel retreat had allowed Granger the day before to start Stanley through Shelbyville to the Manchester area, where his force arrived June 30. Meanwhile, Rosecrans put Granger in command of the Union rear—all the posts north of Duck River. Granger's actions, including the intelligence he provided, allowed almost all the rest of the Army of the Cumberland to concentrate on what had been its left flank.

On June 30 Granger advised Rosecrans, "I do not consider there is any probability that the rebels will make a stand at Tullahoma," and sure enough Bragg did withdraw that evening. The message also advised Rosecrans that Granger was having supplies sent to him at Manchester, but that the roads over which they would travel were in bad condition, and that he was rebuilding rail and telegraph lines, which would probably extend from the rear up to Shelbyville by the next day. The message also says: "I do not think I have troops sufficient to hold Wartrace. You must do it."[66] Wartrace is northeast of Shelbyville and northwest of Manchester. A commanding officer might have resented being told what he "must" do by a subordinate, but Rosecrans was familiar by now with Granger's rough ways, as well as his military ability which was contributing to a dazzling success for the Army of the Cumberland.

Rosecrans pursued the Confederates over the next few days as Bragg continued to retreat toward Chattanooga, abandoning middle Tennessee. Rosecrans' significant and brilliant victory came with low casualties—he initially reported 85 killed, 462 wounded and 13 missing—and Granger had played a key role.

That was not, however, the way it was seen in Washington or the country at large. Rosecrans' victory did not involve a major battle with the Confederates, unlike the early-July Battle of Gettysburg in Pennsylvania, where Lee's invading army was defeated and thrown back to Virginia. At the same time in the west, the last two Confederate posts on the Mississippi River, Vicksburg and Port Hudson, were captured along with their substantial garrisons. Those eastern and western victories were much greater than the Army of the Cumberland's achievement through maneuver and minor battles, and Stanton kept the pressure on Rosecrans to pursue and engage Bragg's army.

Early July 1863, with its Union victories by Meade, Grant, Nathaniel Banks and Rosecrans on the war's three major fronts (Grant and Banks both operating in the Mississippi Valley), marked the military turning point of the Civil War. It was a war in which, so far, Granger had played a fairly small role. His part was still a significant one, because the war effort was so huge, and his leadership in various areas had been productive. But he had not fought in a large battle since Wilson's Creek, two years in the past. Compared to most major generals, he had precious little experience commanding troops in combat. Through no fault of his, only happenstance, he had missed battles like Pea Ridge, Fort Donelson and Shiloh, and he left Rosecrans' command in Mississippi just before the battles of Iuka and Corinth. While his onetime subordinate Sheridan had made a name for himself at the battles of Perryville and Stones River, Granger missed both. For better or worse, the war's main events seemed to be passing him by.

In August and into September he was back in Nashville taking care of the army's rear. That included repairing telegraph lines, railroads and bridges after Rebel sabotage. Sometimes bringing up reinforcements could be combined with other useful activity, as in the August 24 message: "Tell the commanding officer to clear the country of guerrillas as he goes."[67] Reports were coming in of guerrillas destroying bridges. But Granger told Garfield on August 27 that rail and telegraph lines for 12 miles south of Columbia were "in good condition . . . citizens will do all in their power to prevent its being destroyed."[68] Even in central Tennessee, he now had hopes of winning civilian support.

Granger also had the responsibility of coordinating with Major General Burnside's command, which had advanced into east Tennessee, and extending Rosecrans' lines to Athens, between Chattanooga and Knoxville.

Among his rear area responsibilities were army hospitals, and in June, after he sent an assistant surgeon to investigate facilities in Nashville, he recommended to Rosecrans that steps be taken to hasten the return of hospitalized soldiers to active service. But later that summer he showed humane concern by defending the actions of Colonel Gustavus Smith, who had been gravely wounded the year before at the Battle of Pea Ridge and as a result was serving as commander of the convalescent camp in Murfreesboro. Officers in the field had been complaining that Smith was holding back men fit for active service. Granger, in forwarding a message of Smith's to army headquarters on August 15, added a note of his own concluding, "I know that he does not detain men unnecessarily."[69]

Granger's own health seems again to have been a matter of concern. On August 26 he was told, "Prepare to advance to the Tennessee and cover the rear of the army." In his reply, he reassured James Garfield, Rosecrans' chief of staff: "My health is excellent."

Blackford notes that Granger was chastised on August 21 by Rosecrans' headquarters for failing to adequately communicate, and was told to make daily reports. "I have telegraphed daily when there was anything to communicate,"[70] Granger replied.

Says Blackford: "For all his courage and skill, Granger may well have been something of a trial to headquarters. 'How are you, and what are you up to?' he breezily asked in the conclusion of an August 29 telegram." However, in an August 27 response to a complaint that he was not communicating enough, Granger told Rosecrans, "I have not failed to telegraph you daily,"[71] and provided some supporting evidence.

Rosecrans had embarked in mid-August on another skillful campaign of deceit and maneuver which culminated on September 8 by compelling Bragg to evacuate Chattanooga, just as he had Tullahoma two months before. In this campaign, Granger deployed the Reserve Corps from Nashville as it brought up the rear.

One young officer serving under him in the 10th Illinois, Ephraim A. Wilson, wrote in a postwar memoir: "We used to think that Granger, being the ranking officer as he was, and of course in command, and in the regular service, felt the importance of his position to an unwarranted degree, and he would often make it convenient to 'walk on' the volunteers. However, Granger was a good officer . . . and we freely forgave him his pompous ways for the good work he did."[72]

Rosecrans reorganized the Nashville supply command on September 2, and on September 4 Granger was told by Garfield: "You must leave minimum garrisons in all your posts and come forward with all the force you can possibly spare. We want you with us."[73] Garfield wrote this to Granger, who was in Nashville, from Stevenson in northeastern Alabama, west of the Tennessee River and southwest of Chattanooga. But the Reserve Corps commander remained responsible for forwarding the army's supplies over insecure rail lines and bad roads.

On September 6, when Granger was still organizing in Nashville, Rosecrans ordered him to bring as much of the Reserve Corps as could be spared from guarding the rear to Bridgeport, Alabama, northeast of Stevenson, closer to Chattanooga and the front line. The same day, Granger sent a 5:40 p.m.

message to Garfield saying he would be bringing about 8,500 troops to the front (small for a corps, but he had to leave garrisons behind him). Sent on a Sunday, the message closed: "Shall start on Tuesday. My health worthless."

Perhaps he was willing to be open about his health problems with Rosecrans' chief of staff because Garfield himself had had a prolonged medical leave of absence the prior year. Such leaves were common in the front-line South, where conditions were typically conducive to dysentery and fever, killing many soldiers far from the battlefield. But, as the message itself indicated, Granger's bad health was not going to stop him from reporting for duty. The Reserve Corps came up over the next few days, travelling mostly by rail.

Although Rosecrans, grown overconfident, did not yet quite believe it, the Confederates were preparing for battle. Bragg, like his Union counterpart, had been under increasing pressure from his political superiors to fight. The Confederates were, indeed, to fight hard for almost two more years, even after the war seemed lost. But it did not seem lost yet, despite the Rebel reverses in July. And it was almost won for the Confederacy, many of its partisans believed all their lives, during that September.

In the second half of 1863, both sides reinforced the Tennessee-Georgia front, which had become the focal point of the Civil War. The conflict's two major battles in that period were fought there, the first of which came close to destroying the Army of the Cumberland. Granger would be in the middle of both.

NOTES

1. *OR*, Additions and Corrections, Series 1, Vol. 8, 88.
2. Stephen Z. Starr, *The Union Cavalry in the Civil War, Vol. 3, The War in the West* (Louisiana State University Press, 1985), 57.
3. *OR*, op. cit., 90.
4. *OR*, Vol. 10, Pt. 1, 727.
5. Robert W. Blackford, *The Civil War Service of General Gordon Granger, U.S.A.*, unpublished master's thesis (Southern Illinois University, Edwardsville, 1990).
6. *OR*, op. cit., 729.
7. Frank Burr and Richard Hinton, *'Little Phil' and His Troopers: The Life of Gen. Philip H. Sheridan* (New York, Hurst & Co., 1890), 46–48. This specific, sourced account is credible, although others, including Sheridan himself, wrote in vague terms about how Granger may have been responsible for influencing Blair. Granger's role is also confirmed in Friend Palmer's *Early Days in Detroit*, p. 409.

8. Starr, op. cit., 61.

9. Ibid.

10. Ibid., 62.

11. *Personal Memoirs of P.H. Sheridan* (Vol. 1, London:, Chatto & Windus, 1888), 182.

12. Ibid., 63.

13. Ibid., 67.

14. *OR*, Vol. 17, Pt. 1, 18.

15. *OR*, Vol. 17, Pt. 2, 132.

16. Benjamin Franklin Cooling, *A War Anything but Civil, The Legacies of Forts Henry and Donelson* (Hallowed Ground Magazine, Winter 2011).

17. *OR*, Vol. 17, Pt. 2, 162.

18. Ibid., 163.

19. Starr, op. cit., 77.

20. *OR*, Vol. 17, Pt. 1, 42.

21. Ibid., 40–41.

22. Ibid., 42.

23. *OR*, Vol. 17, Pt. 2, 197.

24. Ibid., 200.

25. Kenneth P. Williams, *Grant Rises in the West: From Iuka to Vicksburg, 1862–1863* (University of Nebraska Press, Bison Books, 1956, 1997), 60.

26. *OR*, Vol.16, Pt. 1, 426.

27. Granger's recorded testimony about his arrival date is self-contradictory. At one point he says it was Sept. 16 or 17, and at another Sept. 21. The latter date, based on the overall evidence, is implausible.

28. Ibid., 428.

29. Ibid., 429.

30. Ibid., 446.

31. Ibid., 446–7.

32. Ibid., 452.

33. Ibid., 448.

34. *Freedom, a Documentary History of Emancipation, 1861–1867*, Vol. 1, (Cambridge University Press, 1985), 544–45.

35. Aug. 22, 1862, letter to Horace Greeley, published Aug. 24 in *The New York Times*.

36. May 29, 1863. The unpublished letters of Preston to his wife are in the private collection of his descendant Patricia Bays, used by permission.

37. Preston was then in Turchin's brigade of Baird's division of Palmer's 14th Corps.

38. *OR*, Vol. 20, Pt. 2, 178.

39. *Freedom*, op. cit., 557.

40. *OR*, Vol. 20, Pt. 2, 162.

41. Ibid., 160.

42. Ibid., 282.

43. Ibid., 287.

44. Robert W. Blackford, *The Civil War Service of General Gordon Granger, U.S.A.*, unpublished master's thesis (Southern Illinois University, Edwardsville, 1990).

45. James A. Ramage, *Rebel Raider: The Life of General John Hunt Morgan* (Lexington, University Press of Kentucky, 1986), 116.
46. Starr, op. cit., 95.
47. New York Times, Jan. 4, 1863.
48. *OR,* Series 1, Additions and Corrections to Vol. 20, 86.
49. T.J. Wood, in *Seventh Annual Reunion of the Association of the Graduates of the United States Military Academy at West Point, New York* (1876), 59.
50. Henry M. Cist, *The Army of The Cumberland* (1882; Castle Books ed. 2002, Edison, NJ), 141.
51. Ibid., 142.
52. Starr, op. cit., 229.
53. Ibid., 230.
54. Jack D. Welsh, *Medical Histories of Union Generals* (Kent, Ohio, Kent State University Press, 1996), 136.
55. *OR,* Vol. 23, Pt. 2, 117.
56. Starr, op. cit., 231.
57. *OR,* Vol. 23, Pt. 2, 183.
58. *OR,* Vol. 30, Pt. 3, 223.
59. Henry J. Aten, *History of the Eighty-Fifth Regiment, Illinois Volunteer Infantry* (Hiawatha, Kansas, 1901), 73.
60. John Fitch, *Annals of the Army of the Cumberland* (Philadelphia: J.B. Lippincott, 1864), 431–32.
61. Ibid.
62. *OR,* Vol. 23, Pt. 1, 322.
63. Ibid., 536.
64. Ibid.
65. Ibid., 409.
66. *OR,* Vol. 23, Pt. 2, 486.
67. *OR,* Vol. 30, Pt. 3, 157.
68. Ibid., 193.
69. Ibid., 22.
70. Ibid., 104.
71. Ibid., 192.
72. Ephraim A. Wilson, *Memoirs of the War* (Cleveland, Ohio: Bayne Printing, 1893), 160–61.
73. *OR,* Vol. 30, Pt. 3, 351.

5
Chickamauga

On joining his troops in the field, Granger found their discipline not up to his or Rosecrans' standards. On September 8 he had the adjutant-general and a regimental colonel investigate a case of breaking and entering and theft, from the house of a British subject. On September 12, even as battle was approaching, an assistant adjutant-general was complaining to a Reserve Corps colonel stationed in Stevenson, slightly to the rear of the army, about soldiers "killing stock and committing other acts of vandalism.... The general commanding [i.e. Rosecrans] directs that you take immediate measures to prevent a repetition of such disgraceful acts."[1] These turned out to be ominous signals.

Granger also found a diminished Reserve Corps, because so many soldiers had had to be left behind guarding the army's communications. Of the corps' three divisions, he had only three brigades at immediate hand, amounting to about 5,400 men. Two of the brigades, under Brig. General Walter Whitaker and Colonel John Mitchell, served in Steedman's First Division. The other brigade was commanded by Colonel Daniel McCook, brother of Major General Alexander McCook who was commanding the right wing of Rosecrans' army.

The Confederate government had decided to reinforce Bragg with a corps commanded by Lt. General James "Pete" Longstreet from Lee's Army of Northern Virginia. Longstreet would not arrive until September 19, and make his presence felt with devastating effect the next day. But Bragg was looking to fight well before that, trying to combine his forces against exposed elements of Rosecrans' army as it advanced east after crossing the Tennessee River southwest of Chattanooga. Bragg could not, however, manage an effective combination, although he did give Rosecrans a scare and set him scurrying to unite his scattered forces.

Granger was still in Bridgeport, Alabama on September 12, west of the Tennessee River, but he sensed with impatience what was going on. He sent a message that day to Garfield asking, "Shall I order the 89th Ohio Volunteer Infantry to join General Reynolds? Shall I order McCook's brigade from Shellmound to Chattanooga? Please keep me posted on all that is taking place. Do not be so slow in answering my dispatches."[2]

Garfield replied: "We are concentrating the army to support General Thomas and fight a general battle." Garfield told him to order an officer not in his command, Brig. General John King, to march to support Thomas through Stevens' Gap. "Come to this place [Chattanooga] immediately with Steedman's division," the chief of staff's message continued. "Move in light marching order by the shortest route, and direct your trains to follow. If all reports are true, we have not a moment to lose. The Shellmound brigade (McCook's) should move at once."[3]

Another message from Garfield the next day told Granger, "The enemy has concentrated the bulk of his army in the neighborhood of LaFayette, and seems determined to give us battle." Granger was ordered to Rossville, located at a pass through the heights just south of Chattanooga, so that he could watch the roads to the south and southwest where the Confederate army was, and also protect Rosecrans' line of retreat should he be defeated. Garfield told him to support Major General Thomas Crittenden, who commanded Rosecrans' left wing, "in case he attacks or is attacked. . . . In case of an engagement in front, close up toward the sound of battle."[4]

Also on September 13, another member of Rosecrans' staff told Granger to go straight to Rossville, on the Georgia-Tennessee line, bypassing Chattanooga. "Crittenden is probably engaged with the enemy in force," this staff officer told Granger. "Pass your troops through by forced march as rapidly as possible. By order of Major-General Rosecrans."[5]

On September 14 Granger told Crittenden that he and his three brigades were at Rossville. They got there, he wrote in his report later that month, "through a suffocating dust and over a very rocky and mountainous road, on which it was exceedingly difficult for troops to travel."[6] The 22nd Michigan Infantry, in Whitaker's brigade of Steedman's division, began marching from Bridgeport at 7 a.m. September 13 and reached Rossville at 11 a.m. the next day after marching more than 35 miles past the base of Lookout Mountain.

The concentration of the Reserve Corps and other Union troops changed and delayed Bragg's plan for attack, and Granger's next big problem was with his own troops, as he lost his temper over extensive violations of the ban against foraging, and apparently regained his composure only just in time.

Granger had previously shown willingness to punish actively disloyal residents of Confederate states. But in this mountainous part of north Georgia, near loyalist east Tennessee, he was, as in Kentucky, concerned not to alienate civilians, and to comply with Rosecrans' orders on the subject. Further, the Union army was getting crucial intelligence at this time about the location of Confederate troops from civilians, whom it was obviously vital not to alienate. One of the main functions of the Reserve Corps over the next few days was providing intelligence to army headquarters.

However, none of these reasons nor any lingering effects of illness and exhaustion can excuse Granger's overreaction and lapse in judgment on this occasion. Accounts differ, but he apparently ordered hungry soldiers to be tied up, and threatened to whip them for the offense of foraging for food. This almost had disastrous consequences, but according to James Holmes, an officer in the 52nd Ohio Volunteer Infantry: "It was not done. If it had been," Holmes wrote in a postwar memoir, "I think Gordon Granger would have been killed then and there, for enlisted men were, from starvation, so far ripe for mutiny if a soldier had been struck by Granger's order."[7]

Another account by Henry Aten of the 85th Illinois says that Granger, "in order to impress the command with a due regard for his authority, caused several men to be tied up by the thumbs near his headquarters. Instantly the camp filled with indignation at the needlessly cruel treatment of the men. Officers demanded the release of the men, and thousands of soldiers gathered near by. General Granger was profane as usual, and made terrible threats, but the murmur of suppressed excitement that ran through the ever-increasing crowd indicated that this was to be a test case. The men had determined that intelligent volunteers should not be thus cruelly treated in an active campaign in the enemy's country and on the eve of battle. But not until a battery was trained upon headquarters, and a given number of minutes allowed for the release of the men, did the general yield. Then he gave the order for their release, and slunk away into his tent, cursing everybody."[8]

Granger tended to bark more than he bit on matters of discipline, as in a case related by Thatcher, which apparently happened earlier in the war, when "an officer who deceived him, disregarding truth and promises, was put under arrest, charges preferred against him, and he would have been dismissed from the service promptly but for his humble apologies and appeals for mercy. Then the officer was released, and placed on duty again—a faithful and truthful subaltern ever after."[9]

But this was a more serious matter, in which Granger appears to have backed down only just in time—although Blackford is likely right in suggesting of Aten's version (which was published in 1901): "One might take this with a grain of salt, since it is difficult to believe such an incident took place."[10] Still, even if Aten's account is very probably exaggerated, something did go awry with Granger's command at Rossville, and it does not reflect well upon him.

Granger was short of cavalry, and Rosecrans' headquarters could not supply him with any, but he was able to send a mounted reconnaissance force five miles down the Ringgold road on the 15th, reporting the possible presence of four Rebel cavalry brigades on that flank. A separate Union cavalry command went back there without finding any Rebels, but trouble was indeed coming from that direction.

The situation was fluid, both armies fairly groping for the other. "You hold our left," Rosecrans told Granger from Crawfish Spring in a message dated 5 p.m. September 16, "with Minty on your front to the southeast, between you and Ringgold."[11] Robert Minty was a cavalry colonel currently in Crittenden's command, who in June had fought well under Granger and Stanley at Shelbyville. "Burnside will move down soon, I hope," Rosecrans continued. "He will allow you to come forward." The commanding general's hopes were disappointed. Despite repeated prompting from Halleck, Burnside declined to move southwest from the Knoxville area.

Garfield followed up with another message, ordering Granger "to send out a brigade to reconnoiter the road toward Ringgold, and direct it to bivouac for the night well out in that direction. Colonel Minty is at Peeler's Mill, and has been attacked by the enemy, who appears to be attempting to get in his rear."[12]

Granger sent Steedman early the next morning, September 17, with six regiments and an artillery battery. They skirmished with Confederate cavalry west of Ringgold, driving them out of town and across Chickamauga Creek. But the Rebel presence was strong enough to induce Steedman to withdraw about six miles before bivouacking for the night, returning to Rossville the next day. Granger reported to Garfield about Steedman's encounter with Rebel cavalry and that his bivouac camp at Battle Springs was shelled during the evening. He also enclosed notes from Minty.

Granger also had to keep in touch with his command in the rear. His responsibilities continued to stretch back to Nashville in middle Tennessee, and he was responsible for securing the army's lengthening supply line with reduced troop strength in hostile territory. On September 18 a colonel in Shelbyville asked permission to "concentrate my forces" and attack 1,000 Confederate cavalry and guerrillas. On the same date, a staff officer in Chattanooga informed him that part of a Union forage train had been captured.

But everyone's focus was now on the coming battle. Although Crittenden had been dismissing Minty's reports of Confederate activity, Steedman's confirmation caused Rosecrans to strengthen his left. He sent a brigade of mounted infantry under Colonel John Wilder from Thomas to support Minty. More important, he marched the rest of Thomas' corps behind Crittenden to form as the army's new left wing, extending it closer to Chattanooga, and had General Alexander McCook close up his corps from the south to support Crittenden's right. These were the correct moves to counter Bragg, whose battle plan, which he would stick to over the next three days, was to turn the left, or northern flank, of the Army of the Cumberland, and cut it off from Chattanooga.

Minty skirmished with Confederates on the morning of September 18, and shortly before 11 o'clock reported from Pea Vine Ridge to Crittenden and Granger that large numbers of Rebels were preparing to attack. Minty, supported by a detachment sent by Wilder, fought a delaying action around Chickamauga Creek, gradually being pushed back in the afternoon. Wilder's main force, to the south of Minty, also came under attack. They had encountered Forrest's cavalry, which was spearheading the Confederate surge.

Rosecrans had concluded his message to Granger on the evening of September 16 by saying, "I would have been glad to see you here," which helps explain why the Reserve Corps commander was at army headquarters on the 18th. Steedman, having returned from his reconnaissance, was left in command at Rossville, but Granger remained in close touch. Rosecrans, no doubt after conferring with Granger, told Steedman to send a brigade in support of Minty, and Dan McCook's was sent. At 3:45 p.m., Garfield ordered Granger to "send another brigade out toward Minty in direction of Reed's Bridge, to assist him in falling back if necessary."[13] Granger sent John Mitchell's brigade to follow McCook's.

He had already dispatched the corps' other brigade, led by Brig. General Walter Whitaker, to seize a bridge over the Chickamauga on the Rossville-Ringgold road, "if it could be done without bringing on a general engagement," as Whitaker put it in his report.[14] Whitaker did not reach the bridge, instead running into a skirmish, and the brigade spent the night near McAfee Church, about three miles from Rossville on West Chickamauga Creek.

Granger spent the night of September 18 at the army headquarters at Crawfish Spring, presumably advising Rosecrans and trying to get as explicit directions as possible from him, while telegraphing orders to the Rossville signal station, and returning there before 7:30 a.m. on the 19th.

McCook, despite not finding Minty, was not inclined to fall back on the morning of September 19. He had captured 22 prisoners in a skirmish on the previous evening, which led him to believe he could advance through the woods and capture a Confederate brigade. He planned to attack with Mitchell that morning, but instead received an order from Rosecrans via Granger to withdraw. Before doing so, McCook rode up to Major General Thomas, who was in the vicinity having travelled through the night with his corps, and urged him to countermand the withdrawal order. Thomas declined, but sent two of his own brigades into the woods, which had the effect of starting the main Battle of Chickamauga, though not how Bragg had planned. McCook and Mitchell obeyed the withdrawal order. Then Steedman took Mitchell's brigade to support Whitaker's.

The Reserve Corps did not play a major role for the rest of that day, September 19. The troops "were engaged in some skirmishing and stood at arms expecting an attack," wrote Major Joseph Fullerton, Granger's chief of staff, in a magazine article 24 years later.[15] At 3:10 p.m., Granger reported to Garfield that Whitaker had come under attack on the Red House road. At 4:50 he reported he had sent Whitaker reinforcements. Steedman reported at 9 p.m. from McAfee Church, and said part of his command had been "engaged this evening with a superior force of the enemy, much to the credit of my troops engaged."[16]

But the Reserve Corps' involvement that day was minor compared to the battle to the south, which was pithily summed up by Thomas in a message to Granger: "We had a severe engagement with the enemy today, driving the rebels on the left and holding our own on the right."[17] Granger remained worried about reports of Confederate cavalry threatening the far left, and asked Thomas to send Minty's cavalry there. A colorful description of Granger's state of mind at this time comes from an 1893 essay by onetime 22nd Michigan Captain William F. Atkinson:

"Gordon Granger had for two days been rambling around the country with the Reserve Corps. On the 19th we were at Ringgold, on the morning of the 20th we were on the Lafayette road, not far from Rossville Gap, and there we would have remained if General Granger had been one of the kind who wait for orders. He had, I can truthfully say, been swearing his way through the woods and over the hills during the 19th, and on the morning of the 20th his temper was not angelic. He knew he was doing no good where he was, and that he could be of use over where Thomas was fighting."[18]

On the19th a terrible, inconclusive battle had been waged along the line to the south, and once again Granger had—so far—missed it, mostly sending and receiving reports while other men fought. No wonder his ever-volatile temper was not angelic.

It likely was not improved by the implicit contradictions in several messages he received that evening from Garfield giving orders for the next day. The one sent at 8:10 p.m., said in part, "You must help us in the fight tomorrow by supporting Thomas." At 10:20 p.m., Garfield said "The general [Rosecrans] places your corps in reserve tomorrow, and directs you to post it on the eastern slope of Missionary Ridge [which extends far south of Chattanooga] to support [Gen. Alexander] McCook or Thomas." If attacked, Granger was "to return slowly, contesting the ground stubbornly."

Garfield's next message, sent at 11:45 p.m., said: "The line of battle for tomorrow is your present line. . . . General Crittenden will be held in reserve on the eastern slope of Missionary Ridge, in rear of your right. You will defend your position with the utmost stubbornness. In case our army should be overwhelmed it will retire on Rossville and Chattanooga. Send your trains back to the latter place."[19]

That chilly night, according to Aten, the men lay in line without removing their clothes, "every one clutching his rifle and thinking of the morrow. No fires could be built; even the solace of a cup of hot coffee was denied them, and the teeth chattered as the weary hours rolled slowly by."[20]

Granger's forces were in front of Missionary Ridge, which extends far south of Chattanooga. They were defending Rossville Gap to the west, through which Rosecrans thought the army might have to retreat on September 20. In fact, the army commander and other key generals would flee that day through McFarland's Gap, which is further south on Missionary Ridge, although everyone was headed north to Chattanooga. But it was through Rossville Gap that Granger and the remaining Union troops would go after nightfall, following the rest of those who stood with Thomas.

Granger's instructions did not become more clear on the morning of September 20, when Rosecrans sent two messages. The first began and ended, "Is

Missionary Ridge available, supposing we should fall back?" and his second said, in toto: "Do the ridges in front and left of Rossville admit of placing artillery in position with any possibility of commanding the valley and road?"[21]

Rosecrans was a brilliant commander, but his flaws included being subject to nervous strain, which caused his orders to become unclear. This was to be demonstrated tragically later on the 20th, when General Thomas Wood disastrously obeyed a muddled order of Rosecrans by pulling his division out of line, opening the way for Longstreet's attack to break apart the Union army.

Despite having spent much of the 18th conferring with Rosecrans, on the morning of September 20 Granger was unclear about what the commanding general wanted and expected. Granger was left to figure out what exactly he was supposed to do on the 20th by interpreting implicitly contradictory orders. Was he to support Thomas or McCook? Even in his new position several miles southeast of Rossville at the Ross house (sometimes called the McFarland house) by the McAfee Church, he was too far away to plausibly support General McCook, whose forces were stationed south of Thomas. Should he expect to be attacked? Was Rosecrans expecting to "fall back" or "be overwhelmed" and "retire on Rossville and Chattanooga," in which case the depleted Reserve Corps must protect the escape route to those places? But Thomas' message on the 19th did not indicate any danger of collapse on the left.

At 8 a.m. on the 20th, Thomas sent Granger another message asking, "Are we in supporting distance of each other? If not, you had better report to General Rosecrans at once."[22] Granger was to Thomas' north or left, which was where the Union-loyal Virginian feared new Confederate attacks.

—————————

The attacks on the morning of September 20 did not come against the Reserve Corps. After the brutal but chaotic fighting of the day before, when both sides fed units into the battle on an ad hoc basis, quelling emergencies as they arose in a seesaw fight, Bragg sought to fulfill his original plan on the 20th. Longstreet had arrived the previous evening, and Bragg had promptly put him in command of the entire left wing of the army; Polk was named commander of the right. This reorganization has often been called "risky" in the face of the enemy, but it is difficult to see how any move assigning more responsibility to the commander of the renowned First Corps of the Army of Northern Virginia could be criticized.

Bragg's plan was for Polk to attack first, starting with his rightmost division, with each successive division in line following it up. The object was to hammer in the Federal left and drive Rosecrans' army southward, away from its supply line at Chattanooga.

Due to confusion in relaying orders, the attack began later than the "day dawn" Bragg intended. The delay was fatal for many Confederates because it meant Federal troops were given several hours of daylight to perfect the breastworks they had already been busy constructing the night before. Nevertheless, when Breckenridge's division on the far right stepped off, supported by a dismounted division of Forrest's cavalry, two of the brigades overlapped Thomas's works, prompting the first crisis of the day. Federal reinforcements piled in and were able to beat back the assaults in bloody, close-quarters fighting. Polk's other divisions ran up against the breastworks themselves and could make no inroads, but everywhere kept up a steady fight.

It became apparent that all the Rebel attacks were coming against the Union left. Thomas called for a succession of reinforcements, which Rosecrans was more than willing to provide. He knew as well as Bragg that if the Rebel army could interpose between the Federals and Chattanooga, the Army of the Cumberland was done for. Brigade after brigade was pulled from Rosecrans' right and dispatched to help support the left. At one point, due to a mistaken perception of the Federal alignment, Thomas J. Wood's division was ordered to pull out of its position on the right and shift toward Joseph Reynolds' division on the left.

This vague but fateful order has been a matter of controversy ever since. Wood was ordered to "close up" on Reynolds and "support him" (two contradictory terms). But there was another Federal division under John Brannan already between Wood and Reynolds—set back some distance and concealed by trees, Rosecrans either wasn't aware of it or had forgotten about it. Wood apparently realized the order made no sense, but obeyed it anyway. Earlier that day he had been harshly berated by Rosecrans in front of others for supposed slowness in executing an order. He has often been accused of spitefulness in obeying this one, but it also would have been difficult for him to override the army commander's judgment with his own in the middle of a battle.

The problem, which Wood and other Union soldiers on the right realized but evidently Rosecrans did not, was that Longstreet's entire wing was sitting out there waiting. Though the Confederate left hadn't moved yet, and the woods provided it cover, the presence of 25,000 men is impossible to completely conceal, and Federal commanders had been sending out scouts and patrols all morning so knew they were there. And as fate would have it, it was precisely at the moment when Wood pulled his men out of the line that the Rebel left wing attacked.

Longstreet had by now had over two months to ruminate on his failure to drive the Federals at Gettysburg, almost invariably because his lead units could not receive sufficient support. Determined not to repeat the experience, at Chickamauga he assembled a veritable battering ram—eight brigades on a two-brigade front, five lines deep. It was this juggernaut that suddenly swept into the hole where Wood's division had been. It tore through the Union right, overrunning everything in its path, including Rosecrans' headquarters. Split down the middle, McCook's and Crittenden's corps disintegrated through casualties or flight, although some units, including Wood's, were able to join Thomas, who was still holding out on the left.

Longstreet and his sub-commanders immediately grasped the new situation. Instead of adhering to Bragg's battle plan to drive the Federals south (there were no more organized Federals in that direction) they instead shifted north where there was a chance to encircle and destroy Thomas' entire command. Now Thomas, who had been facing Polk's wing on his own left and front, had Longstreet's wing attacking his right and rear. And much of the army's ammunition train had been swept from the field. It was a desperate situation.

Ironically, while Granger had been ordered to hold Rossville to hold open an escape route should the army be defeated, most of the army's right wing, including corps commanders McCook and Crittenden and Rosecrans himself, who went all the way back to Chattanooga, retreated headlong through McFarland's Gap, leaving Rosecrans and the others out of touch with the Reserve Corps. So was Thomas, as he desperately defended what was left of the Union line.

(Crittenden testified later at a court of inquiry that he had expected to find Granger at Rossville. He didn't because Granger had gone south to Thomas, although Crittenden didn't know that. In any case, Granger's absence did not stop Crittenden from proceeding north to join Rosecrans in Chattanooga.)

Minty's cavalry brigade, following Rosecrans' order, reported that morning to Granger, who posted it at Missionary Mills on the far left of the army.

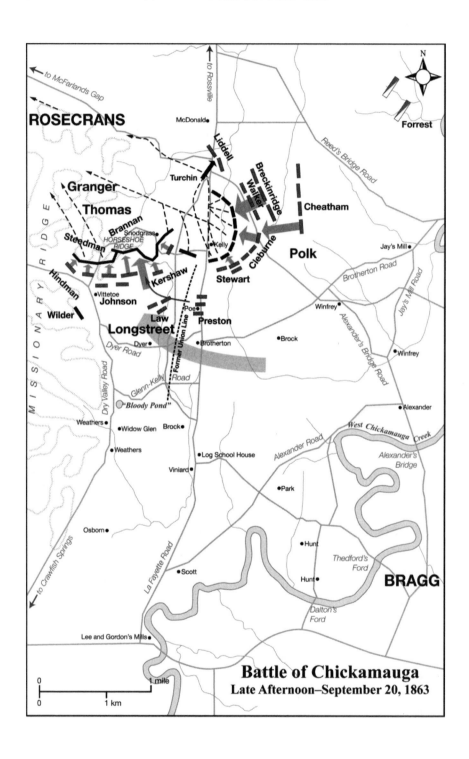

Battle of Chickamauga
Late Afternoon–September 20, 1863

Granger heard Polk's attack start before 10 a.m. Granger sent out three staff officers that morning seeking instructions from Rosecrans, but they came back, one after the other, unable to find the commanding general. That's because, Thatcher says, Rosecrans' "headquarters had been moved and the enemy was there." Granger was left "chafing like a caged lion."[23]

Granger and Steedman went a mile to the front to reconnoiter, without finding much. He pointed out a dust cloud to the south, saying to his chief of staff Fullerton, "That is where we ought to be." He wondered aloud, "Why the [expletive, removed by Fullerton] does Rosecrans keep me here? There is nothing in front of us now. There," pointing to the south, "is the battle."[24]

The noise, dust and smoke from Thomas' direction grew more obvious, but it was not clear who was prevailing in the fight. Granger and Fullerton climbed a haystack, and sat watching and listening for 10 minutes. A local guide and some officers thought the Confederates were retreating, but Granger determined accurately that the opposite was happening.

"Granger jumped to his feet, thrust his glass into its case, and exclaimed with an oath: 'I am going over to Thomas, orders or no orders.'"

When Fullerton suggested acting thus without specific orders "may bring disaster to the army and you to a court-martial," Granger responded: "There's nothing in our front now but ragtag, bobtail cavalry. Don't you see Bragg is piling his whole army on Thomas! I am going to his assistance."[25] (While Granger had some attitudes in common with McClellan, his old army friend who commanded in the east in 1861–62, he did not share McClellan's tendency to fearfully exaggerate Rebel numbers.) According to another aide, J. Gordon Taylor, Granger listened to the noise of battle from Thomas' front for about an hour, and with the three staff officers having returned unable to find Rosecrans, said: "I can't stand this any longer. We are needed over there and if we don't hurry up it will be too late."[26]

In his report, Granger described his reaction to listening to the fight on Thomas' front, "being well convinced, judging from the sound of battle, that the enemy were pushing him hard, and fearing that he would not be able to resist their combined attack, I determined to go to his assistance at once."[27]

Steedman agreed with the move, and Granger sent Rosecrans a message at the stated time of 10:30 a.m. saying he was going to Thomas—although in his report he says the time was 11 a.m., which seems to be more accurate.

There are many discrepancies regarding timing in the various accounts of this day. There was also an odd postwar controversy, properly dismissed by Cozzens,[28] regarding a claim that Steedman had advanced to support

Thomas on his own initiative, without Granger's orders. This inaccurate narrative seems to have started with William Shanks, who said in an 1866 book that "While Granger was looking for orders [from Rosecrans], Steedman marched forward, and it was thus that he happened to reach Thomas's position before Granger did. Steedman has acted without orders in this way on more than one important occasion."[29]

Shanks' account is contradicted by various authorities, including Granger's aides and Steedman's own report[30] on the battle, which says: "At half past 11 o'clock, General Granger becoming satisfied, from the heavy and receding sounds of artillery, that the enemy was pressing the left of our line severely, ordered me to move to the battlefield as rapidly as possible with two brigades of my command, General Whitaker's and Colonel Mitchell's."

However, Steedman was also capable of misleading journalists, as he probably did Shanks. In an 1879 interview, three years after Granger's death, Steedman said: "In battle I always gave the cannonading the benefit of the doubt and marched toward it. That is why I left my place on that bloody afternoon and marched to the relief of Thomas. I disobeyed orders, but I helped save the day by it. Had I not disobeyed orders history might have been different."[31] It is arguable that Granger was disobeying orders, and to the extent he was, no doubt Steedman encouraged him to do so. But Steedman himself was not, yet seems on occasion to have let himself be carried away into a false implication that he marched on his own authority.[32]

Granger set Steedman's two brigades in motion by 11:30, leaving Dan McCook's at the McAfee Church to cover the Ringgold road. Granger, with his staff and cavalry escort, rode south at the head of Steedman's rapidly marching infantry down the Lafayette Road. They brought 95,000 extra cartridges with them—at least one wagon load—which would soon be shared with and prove of crucial importance to the troops holding out under Thomas, about four miles away.

Two miles down the road, they came under fire from artillery and sharpshooters in the woods to the east. Granger, typically, galloped off to a battery and directed return fire. As it turned out, the Confederates were not just "ragtag, bobtail cavalry," but the redoubtable command of Bedford Forrest, who had been charged with guarding the Confederate flank. Granger, in his second crucial decision that day, determined they were not strong enough to justify further delay of his movement. He declined to be intimidated by the Wizard of the Saddle or any Confederate.

Granger called off Steedman's infantry attack and sent word back to bring up McCook to hold off Forrest, and guard the Lafayette road and the country south and west between that position and Thomas. McCook's artillery was engaged in mid-afternoon, and he held the position until ordered back that evening.

Now the whole Reserve Corps was committed to the fight, and no longer guarding Rossville gap. Granger ordered Minty's cavalry to cover the Rossville-Ringgold road, i.e. the position which he had abandoned to march to Thomas' support.

Granger then redirected Steedman's brigades to the southwest, across farmland and off the Lafayette Road. This brought them away from Forrest and the road but more directly toward Snodgrass Hill, which was the epicenter of Thomas' position. Enroute they were able to liberate a Union field hospital, which had been overrun by Forrest's troops.

The movement was not without cost. Whitaker reported that his soldiers marched "at nearly double-quick time, up the valley for near a mile, under a heavy fire of shell from a rebel battery. Several were killed and wounded." And then the men began to come across the gruesome debris of the earlier fighting, including bodies mangled in every manner. Lt. Colonel D.W. Magee, commanding the 86th Illinois, wrote: "We passed through a narrow skirt of woods and across a field which had been fired by the shells in previous conflict on that ground early in the day. A more desolate sight never met the eye. The entire country seemed to be one smoking, burning sea of ruin. Through this blazing field we marched, while the rebel battery played upon us with spherical case, shell, and almost every conceivable missile of death."

Granger had sent a courier in advance, but the man never reached Thomas, just as a message sent by Thomas at 1:00 p.m. did not reach Granger. Thomas was left to gaze with apprehension on the troops approaching from the north, not knowing which side they were on. If they were Confederates, the army was doomed. Then the journalist Shanks told Thomas he could make out the stars and stripes. With a huge sigh of relief, Thomas realized that instead of receiving his force's deathstroke, he was seeing its possible salvation.

Granger rode up and reported to "Pap" Thomas about 1:30 p.m.—or perhaps as late as 2:00. Thomas at first ordered him to deploy the reinforcements on the left of the Snodgrass Hill position, but a new advance of Confederate troops on the far right changed his mind. There, on Horseshoe Ridge, the Union line faced south against Longstreet's breakthrough. The Confederates now threatened to turn and roll up Thomas' flank, launching an attack on his rear that would almost certainly have resulted in decisive defeat of the remaining Union forces on the battlefield.

"Those men must be driven back," said Granger in Fullerton's account. "Can you do it?" asked Thomas.

Granger's reply was laced with his customary accurate cynicism: "Yes. My men are fresh, and they are just the fellows for that work. They are raw troops, and they don't know any better than to charge up there."

He was right. Just as a Rebel division under Thomas Hindman was coming over a rise against Thomas' exposed flank, Steedman's troops charged and met them on the height, sweeping them back down the ridge. The Reserve Corps men then took position and fought off new attacks, with both sides taking severe casualties. Granger spent much of his time with Thomas, whose headquarters was in a field some distance behind the Snodgrass house, helping organize the desperate defense of Snodgrass Hill. The house was being used as a field hospital, the family having fled to take refuge in a ravine. This field headquarters, which became Granger's after Thomas left to coordinate the overall withdrawal, including the troops from Kelly Field to the east, was situated below the corner of the Union position on Snodgrass Hill.

"Fifteen minutes more, General, might have been too late," Thomas said to Granger after seeing Steedman's successful charge and defense of the right flank on Horseshoe Ridge, underlining the significance of Granger's timely decision that morning. In his report on the battle, Thomas said: "This opportune arrival of fresh troops revived the flagging spirits of our men on the right, and inspired them with new ardor for the contest. Every assault of the enemy from that time until nightfall was repulsed in the most gallant style by the whole line.

"By this time," Thomas continued, "the ammunition in the boxes of the men was reduced, on an average, to 2 or 3 rounds per man, and my ammunition trains having been unfortunately ordered to the rear by some unauthorized person, we should have been entirely without ammunition in a very short time had not a small supply come up with General Steedman's command. This, being distributed among the troops, gave them about 10 rounds per man."[33]

Steedman's two brigades on Horseshoe Ridge held the right end of the Snodgrass Hill position, next to portions of Brig. General John Brannan's and Thomas Wood's divisions, and fragments of other divisions, brigades and regiments. Granger helped coordinate all these troops while Thomas remained, and assumed command of them after his departure. Wood's report praised and thanked Granger for sharing his ammunition, as did that of one of his brigade commanders, Colonel Charles Harker. Wood also said: "The gallant bearing of General Granger during the whole of this most critical part of the contest was a strong reinforcement."[34]

Brannan later testified: "If General Granger had not come up at the time he did, I could not have held my position fifteen minutes longer, having been entirely out of ammunition."[35]

Granger worked as usual with artillery batteries, but this was no distraction. One of them had been driven off Horseshoe Ridge in what Cozzens describes as a loss of nerve by its commander, Captain Charles Aleshire—although Whitaker, Aleshire's commanding officer, said he showed "great gallantry and courage through the engagements of Saturday and Sunday, and rendered effective service."[36] (Three months earlier, Aleshire had provided covering fire for Minty's famous cavalry charge at Shelbyville.)

Granger, says Fullerton, then brought up Aleshire's battery at the other end of the line, "to Thomas's left to assist in repelling another assault about to be made on the Kelly farm front."[37] Snodgrass Hill was virtually unconnected to Kelly Field, to its east and northeast, where other troops under Thomas' command were facing east against Forrest and Polk. The Confederates were attacking from the direction of Kelly Field, moving into an area where the Union line was particularly weak to the point of nonexistence, and trying to break the left of Thomas' defenses on Snodgrass Hill. In fact, Thomas had originally ordered Steedman's division to this position on the left flank of Snodgrass Hill before seeing an imminent and greater danger on the right at Horseshoe Ridge, and telling Granger to put Steedman in there instead.

Aleshire and his battery continued to do good service on the left flank of Snodgrass Hill throughout the afternoon until about 7 p.m., supporting elements of Wood's division, including Hazen's brigade which was brought over from Kelly Field at about 3:30 p.m. Brig. General August Willich's brigade was sent to partly plug the gap between Kelly Field and Snodgrass Hill.

There were only three artillery batteries on Snodgrass Hill. Another battery commander, Lt. Frank Smith, reported: "At about 3 p.m. General Granger joined us on the hill. . . . We fought almost constantly from noon until sunset, when we withdrew with but 6 rounds of ammunition to the gun, having suffered a loss of 1 man killed, 9 wounded and 3 horses disabled."[38]

The seesaw fighting on Horseshoe Ridge continued. Granger wept at the death of his friend and staff officer Captain William Russell.[39] He wrote later in his report: "He fell with his face to the enemy, in the thickest of the battle, while discharging an important duty. His loss is severely felt."[40]

When they had ammunition, the defenders fought in two lines, the one in advance firing and the other reloading. When positions were lost, they were typically retaken. At one point, when the 115th Illinois gave way, Steedman personally rallied them, taking the regimental colors and leading a successful counterattack up to the crest, where his horse was shot down and he continued to lead on foot.

Garfield showed up at 3:35, and 10 minutes later telegraphed back to Rosecrans in Chattanooga: "Granger is here, closed up with Thomas, and is fighting terribly on the right. . . . I hope General Thomas will be able to hold on here till night, and will not need to fall back farther than Rossville; perhaps not any. . . . I think we may in the main retrieve our morning disaster. I never saw better fighting than our men are now doing. The rebel ammunition must be nearly exhausted. Ours is fast failing. . . . Granger thinks we can defeat them badly tomorrow if all our forces come in."[41]

The Confederates threw in a fresh division against Horseshoe Ridge. Says Longstreet in his memoirs: [They] "gained a height and intervening dell before Snodgrass Hill, but the enemy's reserve was on the hill, and full of fight, even to the aggressive. We were pushed back through the valley and up the slope."[42]

Thomas left Granger in command in late afternoon. Thomas' report puts the time at 5:30, but from others' accounts it seems to have been half an hour or so earlier. Fullerton says it was "soon after five o'clock."[43] Rosecrans, before receiving Garfield's message, had ordered Thomas to "assume a threatening attitude at Rossville." The "threatening attitude" phrase was hokum, and the significance of the order is all in the word "Rossville," telling Thomas to withdraw to that place. The time on Rosecrans' message, 12:15 p.m., is obviously incorrect. It seems actually to have been sent at 4:15.[44]

Garfield's message to Rosecrans later that evening said the order was not received until after sunset. Sunset came soon after 6:00 that day, but the smoky, dark and tense battlefield may have misled Garfield, Thomas and others, leading them to think the time was later than it was. Contemporary accounts of the battle differ widely on timing. Fullerton, for example, says Granger first reached Thomas at 1 p.m.; Cist says it was at 3. It wasn't just battlefield confusion and distraction; the telling of time was less standardized in the 19th century. All that any modern historian or reader can do is make his or her own judgment based on the preponderance of evidence. Thomas' biographer Christopher Einolf puts Granger's arrival at "at about 1:45 p.m.,"[45] which seems reasonable.

Granger opposed withdrawal, he and Garfield both thinking Rosecrans should send troops and supplies forward from Rossville and Chattanooga. Thomas, however, given the shortage of ammunition and his troops' tenuous hold on their positions, decided to delay but obey Rosecrans' order, holding on until dark. Carrying it out, withdrawing in gathering darkness in the face of a victorious enemy, predictably caused some confusion and additional losses—which does not mean Thomas' decision was wrong. The losses involved in the withdrawal were not nearly as high as they would have been if the Union line had collapsed under attack, and holding their position risked being surrounded and cut off from the rest of the army and Chattanooga.

Thomas chose to begin the withdrawal from Kelly Field, which Polk's Confederates had resumed attacking from the east. As Thomas moved north up the Lafayette Road he encountered Confederates on the west side of the road. He directed Brig. General John Turchin's brigade to drive them off, which it did with artillery support from McCook's brigade of the Reserve Corps. This cleared the road to McFarland's Gap, Rossville and Chattanooga.

More of Longstreet's attacks on Horseshoe Ridge were repulsed, but then the Rebels, supported by effective artillery fire, gained ground, with some of Steedman's troops, out of ammunition, resisting with their bayonets. At 6 p.m. Granger ordered Steedman back to another ridge 300 yards in the rear.

A few minutes earlier, in the middle of the Snodgrass Hill position, Cozzens relates the incredible story of the 18th Ohio (part of Major General Negley's command, another of the senior officers who had fled the battlefield). It charged back up to regain a position lost the previous hour, "bayonets fixed;" then someone began singing *"The Battle Cry of Freedom,"* and "the whole line took up the strain."[46]

The ammunition shortage grew ever more critical, and Granger several times issued orders to hold positions with the bayonet. His report cites three successful bayonet charges.

The battle did not have a storybook ending. Some men in the 21st Ohio, capping a day of heroic service, drove off an attack after 6:30 with their last ammunition, but then in the darkness and confusion were among several hundred of Horseshoe Ridge's defenders who were captured—although some of them escaped in the continuing muddle. Granger, conferring at Snodgrass Field with Generals Steedman, Brannan and Wood, got Thomas' final order to withdraw about 7 p.m., as stated in his report. He passed the order along to the generals, sending two relieving Indiana regiments, the 68th and 101st under Lt. Col. Thomas Doan, to Lt. Col. Henry Boynton, of Brannan's division, who was still on Snodgrass Hill with his 35th Ohio, the 9th Indiana and fragments of other regiments.[47] Boynton says in his report that the 35th had scrounged enough ammunition to repel a Confederate attack just before he got the withdrawal order. According to a battlefield monument (which were constructed under the supervision of Boynton as parks commissioner), he got the order "soon after 7:30 p.m." His troops then pulled back under the cover of Doan's regiments, which in turn marched back down the hill. By 8:00 p.m. the position was evacuated and the battle was over.

Granger seems to have left after 7:00 to catch up with Garfield and Thomas and coordinate the retreat. Colonel McCook was told to cover the rear of the withdrawing troops, and Granger was with him as night fell. According to J.T. Holmes, serving with the 52nd Ohio under McCook, Granger fell into his familiar fascination with artillery, directing a battery's fire "in the gloom of the falling night. . . . There was no response from the enemy. It was growing darker. He said: 'Give them another salvo.' . . . There was no reply; the battle of Chickamauga had become history."[48]

Of the 3,913 men in Steedman's two brigades who went into action that afternoon, 235 were killed, 936 wounded and 561 went missing (most of the latter captured, many of whom would die in the Andersonville prison camp). The other brigades under Thomas' and then Granger's command on Snodgrass Hill also suffered heavy losses. Their battlefield monuments, however, are on the top of the hill, facing those on the slopes below of Longstreet's Confederates, whose 25,000 men in dozens of assaults had not succeeded in carrying the position until dark, when the Union withdrawal was ordered.

Wood's blunder earlier on September 20 had lost the battle, although his superior officers McCook and Rosecrans also were at fault. But Wood fought well with Thomas and Granger for the rest of the day, and at Chattanooga two months later. Wood says Granger's "heroic bearing" at Chickamauga "was worth a thousand men in its inspiring influence. On the field of hotly contested battle, amid the roar of artillery and the sharp rattle of musketry, in the presence of imminent danger, and in the frenzied heat of assaulting columns and charging squadrons, Granger was a true hero."[49]

Steedman's performance at Horseshoe Ridge was to earn him the rank of major general (a promotion recommended by Granger). The next year, he, Wood and Thomas were reunited at the Battle of Nashville, where the West Pointer Wood's attacks were conducted more skillfully than Steedman's. But Steedman's leadership at Chickamauga was exemplary.

At about 10 p.m., McCook's Reserve Corps brigade would be the last Union troops to leave the battlefield that evening, having helped keep the lines of retreat open for the rest of the army. Minty was left on the Ringgold Road, about a mile and a half in advance of Rossville Gap, through which he withdrew the next morning from the advancing Confederates. At 1:30 a.m. on the 21st, Thomas was at Granger's headquarters in Rossville, probably instructing him what to tell Rosecrans in Chattanooga later that day.

At 8:40 p.m. on the 20th, in Rossville, Garfield sent Rosecrans another message, indicating he feared the previous one had gone astray: "General Granger's troops moved up just in time and fought magnificently," Garfield wrote. "Generals Thomas and Granger . . . have successfully repelled the repeated combined attacks, most fiercely made, of the whole rebel army, frequently pressing the front and both flanks at the same time. . . . I believe we can crown the whole battle with victory. Granger regards them as thoroughly whipped tonight, and thinks they would not renew the fight were we to remain on the field."[50] Wisely or not, and to some extent because he was an exhausted man, Rosecrans did not renew the fight, only holding the army at Rossville for a day before withdrawing to Chattanooga.

Granger's performance at Chickamauga was warmly praised by Thomas and Rosecrans, and by others such as Gen. David Stanley, who says in his memoirs: "Gordon Granger's conduct this day was splendid. . . . This timely arrival of Granger undoubtedly saved Chickamauga being a terrible defeat."[51]

Yet Granger has always had his critics, even on this occasion. The most ferocious of them was Archibald Gracie IV, son of a Confederate general who had participated in the assault on Horseshoe Ridge and was killed later in the war. The younger Gracie devotes a chapter and more to denouncing Granger in his 1911 book, "The Truth About Chickamauga."

Gracie raises some valid points about inconsistencies in the various records, and is by no means an untalented writer and researcher. Nor is he dishonest, just blinded by determination to paint a picture of the last glorious victory for his father's Lost Cause. While he also disputes the versions of other Union participants, including Thomas, he is wise enough not to directly attack the iconic "Rock of Chickamauga," and saves his venom for Granger. But his attack on the veracity of Granger's report dismisses or ignores supporting evidence, and eagerly misinterprets an admittedly confused record to Granger's disadvantage.

Thus Granger refers in his report to a period near the end of the day when his troops were out of ammunition and he ordered them to defend their positions in three successive and successful bayonet charges. Gracie calls him a liar: "It seems as if the man behind the gun should know better than the general in the rear, as to whether, after the exhaustion of his ammunition, he had, on three occasions before dark, charged upon the enemy and driven him from the field; yet these men who were actual participants in what they described tell no such tale. In all of the Official Reports mentioned, there is not one of them which claims that they even maintained their position at the point of the bayonet . . . The evidence of Granger's division, brigade and regimental commanders is overwhelmingly against his statements."[52]

While there is evidence, e.g. from Atkinson of the 22nd Michigan,[53] that elements of the Reserve Corps did charge with bayonets fixed, the ammunition shortage was worse elsewhere in the line, and it's from there that most of the bayonet charges seem actually to have been made as evening neared. Gracie assumes that Granger's report is referring just to his Reserve Corps troops, and it's true that Granger, while lauding the other troops at Snodgrass Hill, says "they were not under my command." But that's really a *pro forma* acknowledgement that those soldiers were not in the Reserve Corps. In fact, Granger soon after he arrived was involved in coordinating the defense all over the position, not just with his own Reserve Corps at Horseshoe Ridge. After Thomas' departure and as evening drew on, all the Union troops at Snodgrass Hill, including but not limited to those on Horseshoe Ridge, were under his command. It is likely his report is referring to bayonet charges made not just by Steedman's division at Horseshoe Ridge, but to others in other parts of the Snodgrass Hill position.

Granger's report was submitted September 30 in Chattanooga, a city then under siege, when he had just been promoted to command the Fourth Corps and had more urgent matters on his mind than recapping past events. The report does contribute to the confusion surrounding accounts of the battle, for example going back and forth on the time line, but is nonetheless backed up by other sources.

Gracie himself cites evidence from Fullerton that as the hour neared 6:00, Granger was told by Brannan that his troops were out of ammunition and in response ordered: "Fix bayonets and go for them."[54] Gracie also cites evidence from two colonels in Whitaker's brigade, Caleb Carlton and Heber

Le Favour, that when Granger was told they were out of ammunition, he ordered "that they must use the bayonet, and hold the position at all hazards."[55]

Also in the Reserve Corps, a letter from Col. Darius Warner of the 113th Ohio, serving under Steedman, confirms that his regiment was ordered by the brigade commander Col. Mitchell to defend its position with the bayonet after it ran out of ammunition, and then made a successful charge—although he adds: ". . . but the Rebels seemed not very anxious, and willing to stay back."[56]

Col. Emerson Opdycke, commanding the 125th Ohio in Wood's division, says Thomas began ordering use of the bayonet when ammunition ran low. Granger's arrival brought new ammunition supplies, but soon enough he had to follow his commander's example and order bayonet attacks.

Colonel Ferdinand Van DerVeer, commanding a brigade in Brannan's division immediately to Steedman's left, says in his report that their ammunition ran very low despite being resupplied with "a small quantity furnished by Maj. Gen. Gordon Granger" and taking cartridges from dead, wounded and prisoners. Then, Van DerVeer says his soldiers "fixed bayonets, determined to hold the position. Here again the 9th Ohio made a gallant charge down the hill into the midst of the enemy, scattering them like chaff, and then returning to their position on the hill. . . . At length night ended the struggle," and they received the withdrawal order at 7:00.[57]

Col. Boynton, who was in Van DerVeer's brigade and became the pre-eminent historian of the battle, confirms that the troops "on Snodgrass Hill, when their ammunition was gone, they awaited Longstreet's assaults, and repelled them time and again with their empty barrels and bayonets." He cites how when Longstreet's troops neared the summit, "Wood's men and Brannan's rushed at them with the bayonet and broke their ranks, rolled them down the slopes." Boynton quotes the report of Confederate Major-General Thomas Hindman, whose troops battled Steedman's: "As showing the fierceness of the fight, the fact is mentioned that on our extreme left the bayonet was used and men were also killed and wounded with clubbed muskets. . . . I have never known Federal troops to fight so well. It is just to say, also, that I never saw Confederate soldiers fight better."

As evening came on, Boynton says: "The Union right, though its ammunition ran low, and its officers were constantly searching the boxes of the killed and wounded for cartridges, was becoming practiced in the use of the bayonet against assaulting lines."[58]

Henry M. Cist, a veteran of Chickamauga as a staff officer for Thomas, wrote about the ammunition shortage in his history of the Army of the Cumberland, and said, "The troops were ordered to use their bayonets and give the rebels cold steel, and in the final charges the enemy was met and repulsed in this way."[59]

Nor were such attacks unprecedented. Less than three months earlier, Longstreet's troops at Gettysburg were assaulting Little Round Top, which was defended by the 20th Maine Infantry Regiment. With their ammunition running out, the Union troops led by Col. Joshua L. Chamberlain saved the position (and possibly the battle) with a bayonet charge.

Gracie also makes an extraordinary fuss about matters of no moment, minimizes the achievements of Union soldiers, implausibly suggests Granger sought to avoid danger, twists everything to his disadvantage, and dismisses those witnesses who back up his version of events.

Because the reports of Charles Dana, the War Department representative who was with the army, are favorable to Granger, Gracie speculates that Granger was cultivating him to advance his career, and that the reason Granger went to Chattanooga on September 21 "was for the purpose of seeing this friend . . . leaving his command in the rear with Steedman, in case there should be any real fighting to be done."[60] He also mocks this admittedly florid description of Dana's: "Granger, his hat torn by bullets, raged like a lion wherever the combat was hottest with the electrical courage of a Ney."[61] (The reference is to the courage displayed by French Marshal Michel Ney in Napoleon's 1812 retreat from Moscow.)

Dana had fled the battlefield on September 20 and did not witness Granger's actions. But Fullerton, who did, says "Granger's hat had been torn by a fragment of shell."[62] Dana's source probably was Garfield, and he, too, was there.

It is true that Granger did not plunge with Steedman into the attack, and that it is a good deal easier to order a bayonet charge than participate in one. But Granger's place was not in the charge. He was responsible, at first with Thomas and then for a couple of hours on his own, for the main battlefield, and staving off disaster. Nor is it true, as critics following Gracie have asserted, that Granger, in the words of the National Park Service Web site, "remained only a little longer than Thomas." Thomas, from about 5 p.m., had left Snodgrass Hill to attend to the withdrawal from Kelly Field, leaving Granger in a command which he exercised for about two hours on Snodgrass Hill as the troops continued to fight despite a crippling shortage of ammunition.

Not that his leadership was faultless. It appears three regiments did not get orders to withdraw, which contributed to the loss of prisoners. But Granger was improvising after the army had been defeated and was being forced into a night withdrawal under enemy attack. It was hardly likely everything would run smoothly in such circumstances.

The men who were there, like young Union officer Ambrose Bierce, who later became a famous writer with a reputation for cynicism even exceeding Granger's, appreciated what he did. The enemy, wrote Bierce in a memoir, was in early afternoon about to outflank Thomas on Horseshoe Ridge, "which but for gallant Gordon Granger he would inevitably have done." When on his way to join Thomas that day, Bierce had encountered Major General James Negley, whom he offered to bring with him, but "my good offices were rejected a little uncivilly, which I charitably attributed to the general's obvious absence of mind. His mind, I think, was in Nashville, behind a breastwork." On a day when other major generals scurried to the rear, Granger was "moving soldier-like toward the sound of heavy firing."[63] Bierce moved in the same direction, and was at Snodgrass Hill.

Bierce corresponded later with Gracie, and explicitly rejected the latter's "strange views of Thomas, Granger and Brannan," which "are (to me) so obviously erroneous that I find myself unable to account for them on the hypothesis of an entirely open mind. All defeated people are 'bad losers'."[64]

Granger's military record included hard fighting in the Mexican War, and with Indians on the frontier, and service throughout the Civil War, with seven brevet promotions for gallantry in combat. The journalist William Shanks, by no means an uncritical admirer, said "Granger is a man without any sense of fear—is more thoroughly indifferent to the dangers of battle than any man I ever remember to have met . . . so totally and absolutely fearless that it was not merely apparent, but remarkable, and called forth frequent allusion from his fellow-officers, and the constant admiration of his men."[65] The unanimous reports of his heroism at Wilson's Creek tell the same story, and anyone who honestly considered what he did at Chickamauga would realize Gracie's imputations of cowardice are false and completely out of Granger's character.

Also out of character are the notions that Granger was prone to flattery and was a sophisticated player for political advantage, much less a friend of Dana. In fact, he shared the general hostility of senior officers to the man accurately seen as Secretary of War Stanton's spy, and described him as a "loathsome pimp" in a letter to Rosecrans the next year.[66] The fact that he was writing to Rosecrans, a general equally out of favor as himself with the Army establishment, and describing a powerful person in such pungently negative terms, fits Granger's character. Gracie's charges do not.

One might argue that the crack about Dana does not speak particularly well of Granger, failing as he did to reciprocate the admiring tone Dana used in writing about him to Stanton in the month after Chickamauga. But Granger was aware that on September 20, when Dana fled the battlefield, he also discouraged an attack by Colonel John Wilder's brigade on Longstreet's flank. In fact, Dana's conduct that day was similar to and as damaging as that of the senior officers whom he was essentially describing as cowards to Stanton—although his civilian status may provide some excuse. Granger also was aware that Dana's attitude toward him had become much less favorable—in fact outright hostile—with the arrival of Grant on the scene, and that general's ascent to ever more exalted command.

Gracie's suggestion that Granger went on his own initiative to Chattanooga on the morning of September 21, in part to avoid "real fighting," is complete nonsense. According to Shanks, he was told to there go by Thomas, "to represent the situation to Rosecrans, and obtain his order to retire upon Chattanooga." When Rosecrans began drawing up a detailed and elaborate order, Granger interrupted his commander with typical brusqueness: "Oh, that's all nonsense, general! Send Thomas an order to retire. He knows what he's about as well as you do." Rosecrans followed this advice.[67]

Thomas also must have realized that Granger, as commander of the Reserve Corps and (since June 24) of the District of the Cumberland, was urgently needed in Chattanooga to address the immediate crisis in the rear—how to supply and defend the approaches to the almost besieged city where the Army of the Cumberland took refuge.

The rest of the army retreated to Chattanooga that night, with the movement complete by the morning of September 22. (Fifty-six pickets of the 78th Illinois whom Steedman had neglected to withdraw when he fell back with the army were captured by the Confederates. Twenty-four of them died in prison camps, according to the regimental history.)

Gracie's attack damaged Granger's reputation because it went with the tide of historical interpretation. The soldiers who had fought were dying off by 1911, when Gracie published his book, and in a spirit of national reconciliation, a pro-Confederate "Lost Cause" spin was coloring mainstream accounts of the war. It continues to be influential. Thus the National Park Service Web site on Chickamauga in 2012 inaccurately disparages Granger's performance after Thomas left the Snodgrass field headquarters. It also includes a section, "The Historiography of Chickamauga," which deprecates, without evidence, Boynton's history of the battle. Boynton, who was gravely wounded on Missionary Ridge at the Battle of Chattanooga, played a key role in developing the Chickamauga-Chattanooga Park Commission after the war.

That does not mean Southern sources are necessarily unreliable or unfavorable to Granger. Retired Marine Col. Samuel Taylor wrote an article for "About North Georgia" titled *Granger Saves the Federal Right at Chickamauga*, in which he vividly describes a bayonet charge ordered by Granger due to lack of ammunition just before 6 p.m., which drove back the Confederate attackers and at one point broke through their line.[68] Nor were Northern sources necessarily favorable to Granger, with Grant's hostility being the most obvious and influential example.

Grant, however, did not write about Granger at Chickamauga. Southern historians who did were often aware of how close the Confederates had come to complete victory before Granger arrived to join Thomas. Right after the battle, Forrest, Longstreet and Polk urged Bragg to move immediately against Chattanooga. But in truth Chickamauga was a Pyrrhic victory, and Bragg may have been right that his army was in no condition to take further aggressive action.

Casualties were appalling for both sides: about 18,500 Confederates, including 3,800 killed and missing. Federal casualties were 16,179, including 1,656 killed and 4,774 missing, many of whom would never return. It was one of the most costly battles in the war—a war which killed more Americans, by far, than any other in the history of the United States.

But the Union could and did replace its dead, wounded and captured soldiers, and was to send reinforcements to Chattanooga from east and west. The Confederates had already sent theirs under Longstreet, who won Chickamauga for them. The Confederate army had outnumbered Rosecrans on the field, but could not now replace its casualties.

If Granger's Reserve Corps had not come to Thomas' defense and fought so effectively, helping rally the remaining troops to hold off Longstreet, Bragg would very likely have had a real victory. He and Longstreet might have defeated Thomas as thoroughly as they did the rest of Rosecrans' army, and gone on to capture that army as Grant did the Confederates at Donelson, Vicksburg and Appomattox. That kind of loss would have badly shaken army and civilian morale in the North, and the overall war effort. Granger's actions on September 20 had a significant effect on the history of the Civil War and the United States of America.

NOTES

1. *OR,* Vol. 30, Pt. 3, 587. Capt. T. Wiseman to Col. John Tillson.
2. Ibid., p. 586, Granger to Garfield.
3. Ibid., Garfield to Granger.
4. Ibid., 613.
5. Ibid., 614, Col. C. Goddard to Granger.
6. *OR,* Vol. 30, Pt. 1, 853.
7. J.T. Holmes, *Then and Now* (Columbus, Ohio: Berlin Printing Co., 1898), 6.
8. Henry J. Aten, *History of the Eighty-Fifth Regiment, Illinois Volunteer Infantry* (Hiawatha, Kansas, 1901), 102.
9. Captain Marshall P. Thatcher, *A Hundred Battles in the West: St. Louis to Atlanta, 1861–65. The Second Michigan Cavalry* (Detroit, Mich., 1884), 275.
10. Robert W. Blackford, *The Civil War Service of General Gordon Granger, U.S.A.,* unpublished master's thesis (Southern Illinois University, Edwardsville, 1990).
11. *OR,* Vol. 30, Pt. 1, 687.
12. Ibid.
13. *OR,* Vol. 30, Pt. 1, 66.
14. Ibid., 861.
15. J.S. Fullerton, *The Reserve Corps at Chickamauga, The Century Magazine,* April 1887 (New York: The Century Company, Vol. 23, New Series Vol. 11, Nov. 1886 to April 1887, 1887), 962.
16. *OR,* Vol. 30, Pt. 1, 135.
17. Ibid.
18. William F. Atkinson, *The Rock of Chickamauga, War Papers Read Before The Michigan Commandery of the Military Order of the Loyal Legion of the United States,* Vol. 2 (1898), 8.
19. *OR,* Vol. 30, Pt. 1, 69.
20. Aten, op. cit., 105.
21. *OR,* Vol. 30, Pt. 1, 139–40.
22. Ibid., 139.
23. Thatcher, op. cit., 272.
24. Fullerton, op. cit., 963.
25. Ibid.
26. Taylor is quoted by Peter Cozzens in *This Terrible Sound, The Battle of Chickamauga* (Urbana: University of Illinois Press, 1992), 440.
27. *OR,* Vol. 30, Pt. 1, 854.
28. Cozzens, op. cit., 440 and 605.
29. William F.G. Shanks, *Personal Recollections of Distinguished Generals* (New York:

Harper & Bros., 1866), 287. The reference was called to the author's attention by a 2007 comment by Dave Powell on a post by Joe Meyer on *TOCWOC, A Civil War Blog.*

30. *OR,* Vol. 30, Pt. 1, 860.
31. *Cincinnati Commercial,* reprinted in Nov. 24, 1879, *New York Times.*
32. A pamphlet *Honors at Chickamauga* by Clark Waggoner that took Granger's side in the controversy was published in Steedman's home town of Toledo in the year of his death, 1883.
33. *OR,* Vol. 30, Pt. 1, 253.
34. *The Rebellion Record: A Diary of American Events, with Documents, Narratives, Illustrative Incidents, Poetry, etc. . .,* ed. Frank Moore, Vol. 10, (New York: Van Nostrand, 1869) 331.
35. *OR,* Vol. 30, Pt. 1, 1041.
36. Cozzens, op. cit., 447. Whitaker's report is in *OR,* Vol. 30, Pt. 1, 863.
37. Fullerton, op. cit., 963.
38. *OR,* Vol. 30, Pt. 1, 438.
39. Shanks, op. cit., 275–6.
40. *OR,* Vol. 30, Pt. 1, 856.
41. Ibid., 141.
42. James Longstreet, *From Manassas to Appomattox: Memoirs of the Civil War in America,* Second ed., (Philadelphia: J.B. Lippincott, 1908), 453.
43. Fullerton, op. cit., 964.
44. *OR,* Vol. 30, Pt. 1, 140.
45. Christopher J. Einolf, *George Thomas, Virginian for the Union* (Norman, OK: University of Oklahoma Press, 2007), 177.
46. Cozzens, op. cit., 480–81.
47. Ibid., 508.
48. Holmes, op. cit., 139–40.
49. T. J. Wood, *Seventh Annual Reunion of the Association of the Graduates of the United States Military Academy* (New York: A.S. Barnes & Co., 1876), 62.
50. *OR,* Vol. 30, Pt. 1, 145.
51. *An American General, The Memoirs of David Sloan Stanley,* ed. Samuel Fordyce (The Narrative Press, 2003), 170.
52. Archibald Gracie, *The Truth About Chickamauga* (Boston: Houghton Mifflin, 1911), 136.
53. Atkinson, op. cit., 9.
54. Gracie, op. cit., 140.
55. Ibid., 141.
56. Combat Studies Institute, U.S. Army Command and General Staff College, *Staff Ride Handbook for the Battle of Chickamauga* (1992).
57. Col. Ferdinand Van Derveer report, *Minnesota in the Civil and Indian Wars, 1861–1865* (St. Paul, Minn.: 1891, 2nd ed.), 392.
58. H.V. Boynton, *Chattanooga and Chickamauga,* reprint of letters to the Cincinnati Commercial Gazette, (Washington, D.C.: Gray and Clarkson, 1888), 45–7.

59. Henry M. Cist, *The Army of The Cumberland* (1882; Castle Books ed. 2002, Edison, NJ), 211.

60. Gracie, op. cit., 157.

61. *OR*, Vol. 30, Pt. 1, 195.

62. Fullerton, op. cit., 963.

63. Ambrose Bierce, *A Sole Survivor: Bits of Autobiography*, Ed. Joshi and Schultz (Knoxville: University of Tennessee Press, 1998), 31–33.

64. Ibid., 34.

65. Shanks, op. cit., 268.

66. Quoted in Cozzens, op. cit., 80.

67. Shanks, op. cit., 273.

68. http://ngeorgia.com/history/granger.html

Gordon Granger saw his first major action of the war at the Battle of Wilson's Creek in Missouri. Though a Federal defeat, he was cited for gallantry and afterward promoted to colonel. *The Library of Congress*

The ironclad gunboat *Carondelet*, upon which Granger, serving under John Pope, conducted a reconnaissance in force against Confederate fortresses on the Mississippi. *The Library of Congress*

Phil Sheridan began his rise to prominence as commander of a regiment of cavalry under Granger during the drive against Corinth. He went on to become one of the most renowned Union generals of the war.
The Library of Congress

Ulysses S. Grant, in an early depiction on the cover of *Harper's Weekly*. Though Granger got along with most of his superior officers, he never found favor with Grant, who would later become the most important one of them all. *The Library of Congress*

Granger enjoyed a good relationship with Andrew Johnson while the latter was military governor of Tennessee. Johnson's favor, however, became problematic to his friends once he became president and alienated much of the country, soon to be succeeded by U.S. Grant. *The Library of Congress*

General Thomas "Bull" Nelson, who preceded Granger as commander of the short-lived Army of Kentucky. Nelson was shot to death by a fellow Union officer, Jeff C. Davis, during an argument, though Davis was never prosecuted for the slaying. *The Library of Congress*

The remains of Fort Granger still exist today, just north of the Harpeth River outside Franklin, Tennessee.

Thomas J. Wood, who many blame for Longstreet's breakthrough at Chickamauga. However, the orders he received were vague as well as ill-timed, and Wood himself continued to serve with distinction in the Army of the Cumberland. *The Library of Congress*

Rebel cavalryman Nathan Bedford Forrest vied with Granger in central Tennessee during the spring of 1863, and later tried to prevent his arrival at the Battle of Chickamauga. *The Library of Congress*

Below: General James Steedman (seated at left) with his staff. Leading a division of Granger's Reserve Corps, he personally led the attack that forestalled Longstreet's men from flanking the Union position on Horseshoe Ridge. *The Library of Congress*

General William Rosecrans, whose stellar career came to naught as the Confederates broke his right at Chickamauga, and he opted to organize further resistance at Chattanooga rather than remain with the rest of his men on the battlefield. *The Library of Congress*

Below: A sketch of Steedman's charge at Chickamauga by Alfred R. Waud. *The Library of Congress*

Stedmans charge at Snodrass hill.
Battle of Chickamauga
In two line

George H. Thomas, whose stand on the Federal left won him the name "The Rock of Chickamauga." However, if Granger had not reinforced him in the nick of time, the Union defeat that day might have become a catastrophe. *The Library of Congress*

David Sloan Stanley served with Granger both before the Civil War and during it, and afterward succeeded him as commander of the District of New Mexico. *The Library of Congress*

Rossville Gap in Missionary Ridge, which Granger's Reserve Corps was originally ordered to safe-guard in the event of the army's disaster at Chickamauga. But it was Granger's decision to join the battle instead of staying there that prevented a disaster from occuring. *The Library of Congress*

The home of John Ross, the Cherokee chief after whom the village of Rossville was named. *The Library of Congress*

A view of Missionary Ridge and part of the battlefield of Chattanooga, where the Army of the Cumberland revenged Chickamauga by storming the heights without orders. While his men were in triumph upon the ridge, Granger jokingly rode among them saying he should court-martial every one of them. *The Library of Congress*

General Gordon Granger was never considered the most likeable of Union officers; however his role in helping to win the Civil War in the west exceeded that of many of his contemporaries. *The Library of Congress*

"The Battle of Chattanooga" by Thure de Thulstrup. The three men on the rise at left are Grant, in the lighter coat, with Granger on the left and George Thomas on the right.
The Library of Congress

General Edward Canby, who commanded the Department of the Gulf and welcomed Granger's participation at Mobile, after Sherman declined to assign him a role in his drive on Atlanta and march to the sea.
The Library of Congress

Granger and Admiral David Farragut during the campaign for Mobile. Granger led the land forces attacking the Confederate forts while Farragut led his fleet into Mobile Bay itself, at one point famously declaring, "Damn the torpedoes; full speed ahead!"
The Library of Congress

Two views of Fort Morgan, which along with Fort Gaines guarded the entrance to Mobile Bay. While Farragut's fleet was able to pass the fort, afterward bombarding it from the sea, Granger's men assaulted the formidable bastion on land. *The Library of Congress*

Photo of Gordon Granger taken sometime between his marriage in 1869 and 1875, now hanging in the Virginia home of his great-grandson, Gordon Granger IV. The photo of the photo was taken by Champe Granger, daughter of Gordon Granger IV and great-great-granddaughter of the general. It hangs alongside the photo of Gordon's wife, Maria, at right. *Photo courtesy of Gordon Granger IV and Champe Granger*

Gordon Granger IV in a 2013 photo, at his home in Virginia.
Photo courtesy Champe Granger

Maria Letcher Granger, the daughter of a doctor in Lexington, Kentucky, whom the general married rather late in his life, at the age of 46. *Photo courtesy of Gordon Granger IV and Champe Granger*

The overgrown grave stone of Ellen Gordon Granger, Granger's infant daughter who died in 1875. *Photo courtesy of Steven Dunn*

Two views of the monument
marking Gordon Granger's
grave in Lexington, Kentucky.
Photos courtesy of Steven Dunn

6

Chattanooga

O n September 22, Rosecrans ordered Granger to send Whitaker's brigade "at once across the river to occupy the heights opposite the point of Lookout Mountain."[1] Whitaker was being sent to Moccasin Point, the bulge inside a sharp bend of the Tennessee River, across which to the south stands the dominant feature of Lookout Mountain, about 2,300 feet high. At the same time, Rosecrans decided to abandon the mountain itself. Dana reported that Granger and Garfield objected to that move, which Rosecrans made to shorten his defensive lines around the town of Chattanooga. The army began to seriously fortify those lines.

Also on the 22nd, Dana telegraphed to Stanton that Rosecrans was considering retreating from Chattanooga entirely, judging he could not hold it without reinforcements. But the commanding general had second thoughts, very likely after conferring with Granger and other senior officers. In a second message sent that evening, Dana reported that "Rosecrans has determined to fight it out here at all hazards,"[2] but was short of food and ammunition. Those shortages, especially of food, would soon grow critical as the Confederates closed in.

The obvious disadvantage of vacating Lookout Mountain was that it allowed the Confederates to take it, which Bragg promptly did. Lookout Mountain is to the southwest of Chattanooga, and the Confederate line stretched east from there to Missionary Ridge, which runs north-northeast to above the town near the river. Missionary Ridge also extends several miles south of Chattanooga into Georgia. While much lower than Lookout Mountain, it was still a formidable defensive position, rising almost 500 feet and

113

blocking Union advances to the east. The Rebels looked down from the high ground onto Chattanooga, which was increasingly besieged.

Longstreet had occupied Lookout Mountain, and the first tactic he and Bragg tried was bombardment. Colonel Edward Porter Alexander, Longstreet's capable artillery chief, fired down on the town from the mountain, and traded shots with Whitaker's brigade at Moccasin Point. However, "though we probably made some of them unhappy," according to Alexander, the distance was too far for the Rebels to do much damage.

On September 28, Major Generals McCook and Crittenden were relieved of duty by the War Department. Two other major generals who had fled from the Chickamauga battlefield, Negley and Rosecrans himself, would soon be getting their relief orders. Though Philip Sheridan had vacated the field also, he escaped censure. McCook's and Crittenden's corps were consolidated into a new Fourth Corps, to be commanded by Granger.

Meanwhile, however, Granger was still trying to consolidate the Reserve Corps in the rear and react to Confederate raids, including a major one by Wheeler's cavalry launched into central Tennessee from October 1 to 9. His main concern was to protect the supply base at Murfreesboro, and accordingly he ordered the abandonment of several other posts to concentrate troops there and at a bridge over the Duck River, while sending support to the cavalry forces that engaged with the Confederates. Wheeler began his raid by swooping into the Wauhatchie Valley where he caught and destroyed a huge Yankee supply column of up to 1,000 wagons. The Rebel cavalry then headed north in search of Federal depots.

Wheeler's destructive raid, along with an October 8 advance and attack by Longstreet, brought the army's supply problems in Chattanooga from dangerous to a point of utter crisis. Longstreet's action cut off the last direct route from the Union supply depot and railhead in Bridgeport, Alabama. Now the Army of the Cumberland had to rely on a tortuous wagon train route of almost 60 miles over bad mountain roads. Food was running out, with most regiments going down to quarter rations by late October. More than 10,000 horses and mules starved to death. Ammunition was in even shorter supply, but Whitaker (whose brigade would move with Cruft from the Reserve Corps to the Fourth Corps), got enough to continue his artillery duels with Porter on Lookout Mountain.

Granger took up his new assignment of commanding the Fourth Corps on October 10. It was a significant promotion and a tribute to his performance at Chickamauga, for which he also was breveted lieutenant colonel in the regular army for "gallant and meritorious services." The Fourth Corps consisted of three divisions initially under Generals Sheridan, Wood and John Palmer. After Rosecrans was replaced by George Thomas on October 19, Palmer took over Thomas' Fourteenth Corps and General Charles Cruft replaced Palmer in the Fourth Corps. Granger was now the second most senior officer (after Thomas) in the Army of the Cumberland—although more senior major generals would soon be arriving in Chattanooga with reinforcements.

Replacing as he was two generals who had left under a cloud, Granger was properly sensitive in taking over his new command of hungry and somewhat discouraged soldiers. In his first general order, issued October 10, he said: "Being unexpectedly called to the command of troops so deservedly distinguished for bravery, endurance and discipline, upon the battlefield or wherever duty has called, this is a proper occasion for me to say that I am proud to be with you and identified with such gallant defenders of the cause so dear to American people. Let there be unity of sentiment, concert and harmony of action among us until this accursed rebellion is crushed and the noble Army of the Cumberland rests its flanks, the right upon the Gulf of Mexico, the left upon the Atlantic Ocean."[3] As usual, the soldiers placed under him would live up to the confidence he placed in them, most of them coming to respect their hard-bitten, often tactless, but loyal commander.

The Fourth Corps became immediately engaged in protecting supply trains and skirmishing with Rebel sharpshooters. Whitaker was ordered by Granger to drive off Rebels from their rifle pits in the area of Brown's Ferry on the Tennessee River, which would soon become the focus of Federal efforts to effectively break the siege and secure adequate supplies for Chattanooga.

Brigadier General William F. "Baldy" Smith, Granger's West Point classmate, had recently arrived in Chattanooga and been appointed by Rosecrans as the Army of the Cumberland's chief engineering officer. Smith quickly came up with a plan to seize Brown's Ferry and cross the Tennessee there west of Chattanooga so as to reopen a much shorter supply line from Bridgeport. Rosecrans having been relieved, Smith sold the plan to Thomas and then to Grant, who arrived in Chattanooga on October 23 as the newly appointed commander of most of the western armies.

Granger sent various elements of Fourth Corps to assist Smith's operation in late October to open the "cracker line." A key role was played by Gen. William Hazen's brigade in Wood's division. Most of the brigade floated at night down the Tennessee, launching a successful surprise attack on the Confederate pickets at Brown's Ferry. Smith, coming from Chattanooga, linked up with reinforcements that had been sent from Virginia under Major General Joseph Hooker. Hooker's two corps were coming northeast from Bridgeport in Lookout Valley, on the west side of Lookout Mountain.

Hooker's soldiers fought off Longstreet's night attack October 27–28 at the Battle of Wauhatchie, although neither general had good command of his troops. Then Hooker remained camped in Lookout Valley, with two of Cruft's brigades from the Fourth Corps, to guard the cracker line.

The result of this successful if limited offensive under Smith and Hooker was a gradual improvement and increase of supplies for the army in Chattanooga, whose condition had become desperate. But the still underfed Army of the Cumberland had by no means recovered sufficient strength to take the offensive by capturing Missionary Ridge to the east of Chattanooga, as Grant ordered it to do on November 7. (Grant's rash order was partly motivated by pressure from Washington, where the administration was concerned about the safety of Burnside's army in Knoxville, nearly 100 miles to the northeast.)

Thomas, with Smith's support, persuaded Grant to rescind the order and await the arrival of Sherman, who was marching east to Chattanooga with reinforcements from the Army of the Tennessee. Granger almost certainly supported Thomas' position, which was fully justified by the military circumstances. The soldiers—and even more so their surviving horses and mules—had only begun to receive somewhat adequate food supplies after lengthy deprivation. Most were still on short rations. Nevertheless, the reluctance of Thomas and Granger to attack served to confirm Grant's low opinion of them.

Whatever the differences among the Union generals, they were dwarfed by the dissent on the Confederate side. Bragg was, as usual, at odds with most of his senior officers, and the opening of the cracker line had removed much of the advantage of his position, effectively lifting the siege of the Union army.

Bragg's army still remained ensconced on the high ground around Chattanooga from the northeast to southwest of the city. Bragg was so confident he could defend those positions that, at the suggestion of President Jefferson Davis, he sent Longstreet, with whom he was feuding, away from Chattanooga toward Knoxville, to crush Burnside or drive him out of East Tennessee.

Grant, meanwhile, came under increasing pressure from Washington to take the offensive in order to protect Burnside. By November 17, Burnside's army was besieged by Longstreet's in Knoxville. Its plight would continue to be a key consideration for Grant, Stanton and Lincoln up to and following the Battle of Chattanooga.

While Bragg thus weakened his own army, the Union side continued to get reinforcements. Sherman's strong contingent of the Army of the Tennessee arrived in mid-November in time to take part in Grant's coming offensive. As Grant prepared for battle, he moved Sherman's troops up behind a ridge north of Chattanooga, keeping the Confederates guessing whether they were headed there or to Knoxville. Grant's plan was to have Sherman cross the Tennessee, form the new left wing of the eastward-facing Union line, and attack the north end of Missionary Ridge. Granger was at first ordered to move north to link up with Sherman, but the latter's slow progress caused the orders to be rescinded.

Bragg, bizarrely, was ordering further depletions of his own ranks to reinforce the campaign against Burnside, although he was to rescind those orders when he became aware of Sherman's move and Thomas' strength. Meanwhile, Granger's troops were getting indications of Confederate withdrawals from Missionary Ridge, prompting Grant to order Thomas to conduct a reconnaissance in force on November 23. On the 22nd, Granger ordered Sheridan and Wood to issue rations and ammunition to the troops, who "will be held in readiness to move at a moment's warning."

"What [Thomas] was supposed to do was pure routine," wrote historian Bruce Catton. "Advance just enough men to make the opponent show his hand. What he actually did was move up everybody he had, in a massive advance of unlimited potentialities. Not for Thomas was the business of tapping the enemy's lines lightly. If he hit at all, he hit with a sledge hammer; and on November 23 he put the better part of two army corps in line and sent them rolling forward in a movement that had a strange, unintentionally spectacular aspect.

"Thomas' lines, in front of Chattanooga, were perhaps two miles away from the foot of Missionary Ridge. Between the ridge and the town lay open country, mostly a rolling plain, and halfway across there was a chain of low hills, of which the highest was called Orchard Knob. On Orchard Knob and the modest elevations that tailed away from it, Bragg had a skirmish line, and it was this skirmish line that Thomas proposed to dislodge. To do it he put three divisions in line of battle, with a fourth massed where it could go in and help if needed. The Federals spent half an hour ostentatiously dressing their ranks, and from the top of Missionary Ridge the Confederates looked down, saw it all, and concluded that the Yankees were going to hold a review. Then Thomas sent his men forward."[4]

Whoever had the idea of this parade-ground surprise in plain sight, it was the Fourth Corps that did most of the advancing in double-quick march at the center of the Union line. Granger decided, as he told Thomas, to put Wood's division in the lead with Sheridan's in support. Cruft's two brigades were not there, having been detached to support Hooker at Lookout Mountain, while Major General O.O. Howard's Eleventh Corps, which had been under Hooker, was now held by Thomas in reserve behind Granger, to the left of Wood's division. Brigadier General Absalom Baird's division of the Fourteenth Corps was to the right of Sheridan.

"The troops moved into line and position with such regularity and precision," Granger said in his report, "as to present the appearance of a formation for review or parade, and the enemy's pickets, but a few hundred feet off, were apparently awaiting a display or military pageant when our skirmish line advanced and opened fire."[5]

Fullerton paints the scene of the almost 25,000-man deployment, making up the bulk of the Army of the Cumberland, although most would not actually attack the Confederate line this day: "Flags were flying; the quick, earnest steps of thousands beat equal time. The sharp commands of hundreds of company officers, the sound of drums, the ringing notes of the bugles, companies wheeling and counter-marching and regiments getting into line, the bright sun lighting up ten thousand polished bayonets till they glistened and flashed like a flying shower of electric sparks—all looked like preparations for a peaceful pageant, rather than for the bloody work of death."[6]

This confident array was no longer composed of the defeated, besieged soldiers who had been led by McCook and Crittenden. Wood's reports says: "My division seemed to drink in the inspiration of the scene, and when the 'advance' was sounded moved forward in the perfect order of a holiday parade. ...not one straggler lagged behind to sully the magnificence and perfectness of the grand battle array."[7] Says Thomas in his report: "The formation being completed about 2 p.m. the troops were advanced steadily and with rapidity directly to the front,"[8] surprising the enemy and capturing more than 200 of them.

Howard's memoir says: "Granger was in his element. He deployed Wood's division in plain view, Sheridan's a little farther to the right. . . . The enemy were attracted by this bold maneuvering, and stood up in groups on their works to look at the Yankee parade. Immediately after the rapid formation the forward movement began. Away the skirmishers went over the rough broken ground, appearing and disappearing among rocks and trees, or emerging from small ravines and hollows; and the main lines followed on at equal pace. The Confederates this time were really taken by surprise. They, however, did not run away; they hurried into position, and commenced their fire."[9]

Unlike many Civil War battles fought in obscure woods, much of the Battle of Chattanooga was in plain view of both armies, and "the spectacle was one of singular magnificence," according to Dana's report. "At last, everything being ready, Granger gave the order to advance, and Hazen and Willich pushed out simultaneously."[10] (Brig. General August Willich was another of Wood's brigade commanders.) The troops advanced under a barrage of Union artillery.

The fiercest resistance that afternoon was encountered by Hazen's brigade, which carried a strong position in what Granger called a "quick and gallant" bayonet charge, and suffered 125 killed and wounded. The badly outnumbered Confederates could not hold and were not reinforced, so Granger's troops quickly captured Orchard Knob and the ridge to its right. Granger joined Wood there immediately afterward, and according to the latter, "Personal observation assured him of the extensiveness and completeness of our success. The result being reported to General Thomas, commanding the department, he ordered that the position should be held and intrenched."[11] (The communication with Thomas was apparently by wig-wag flag signals.) Grant was persuaded to hold the ground, rather than withdrawing as after an ordinary reconnaissance, and Bragg decided not to bring on a general engagement by trying to retake it. The Confederates did commence a fierce but ineffective artillery barrage from Missionary Ridge. Granger obeyed Thomas' order to "hold and strengthen your position" by having trenches dug with breastworks built of logs and stones, and putting out pickets.

The Fourth Corps soldiers had performed very well—much better, according to Cozzens, than their comrades just to the north: "On Wood's left, Howard's Eleventh Corps embarrassed itself,"[12] with at least one regiment refusing to advance. Howard said in a postwar account he was "unaware of the muddle into which [his troops] had fallen," and was waved down by Granger, who "good-naturedly chided" him saying, "Your troops on the left haven't squared up."[13]

Howard, indeed "finding my troops too much retired, went from brigade to brigade and dressed up the lines to Granger's satisfaction." Soon, says Howard, his Eleventh Corps was "ahead of our neighbors and proud of it," having "swept the front beyond the [Citico] creek of all Confederate sharp-shooters who were inclined to loiter in that region. Granger was pleased."

Granger's and Wood's versions are a bit different. Granger wrote in his report that he observed Howard's advance was stalled, so ordered Brig. General Samuel Beatty, commanding a brigade on the left of Wood's division, to send two regiments quietly through the woods to make a surprise flank attack on the Confederates facing Howard. This worked, but during the night Howard still failed to advance and the Confederates reoccupied their position, so Beatty's two regiments had to drive them out again next morning.

Howard describes Granger, as usual, "expending a little of his extra enthusiasm by showing a battery commander how to point and serve his guns." And after the fighting, an expansive Granger was all too ready to tell this one-armed veteran of the Army of the Potomac and other combat-hardened officers "how the battle had been fought and to show us the way to fight all battles."[14] His propensity to be a blowhard did not necessarily endear Granger to other soldiers, or to modern historians. This time, his exuberant bluster probably came partly out of relief that his corps did not experience the "heavy loss" he had told Thomas he was expecting that afternoon.

Orchard Knob became Union headquarters for the coming battle, and the jumping-off point for the attack on Missionary Ridge on the 25th. The demonstrated threat to his center limited Bragg's options in reinforcing his flanks, which were threatened by Sherman and Hooker, respectively, and caused him to recall troops, including Major General Patrick Cleburne's division, which had been en route to Knoxville. The latter decision would make the Union task harder at Chattanooga—and easier at Knoxville. But the small yet significant victory of Orchard Knob also raised Union and lowered Confederate morale, a crucial factor in the much larger engagement two days later.

After the battle Thomas chose a portion of this area for a national military cemetery, which continues to exist today. Granger's troops went over that ground on their way to take Orchard Knob, which is now a "military reservation" with imposing old memorials. The modern neighborhood is working-class African-American, looking over a commercial and industrial area up to the fancier houses on top of Missionary Ridge. At the time, of course, all of this was well outside the built-up area of Chattanooga.

The next day, November 24, belonged to Hooker's corps. Thomas had finally persuaded Grant to let Hooker attack Lookout Mountain on the Union right. Part of Granger's corps was involved in this fight, and one of its brigade commanders, Whitaker, asked him for ammunition and reinforcements in the afternoon, which Thomas sent from the Fourteenth Corps. The Army of the Cumberland also provided artillery support. This was another clash fought in sight of both armies, with low-lying mists giving it the look of a "battle above the clouds." Hooker essentially captured the mountain that day, with the Confederates withdrawing overnight.

Granger's artillery also dueled with the Confederate batteries on Missionary Ridge. According to Sheridan's report, his division was "at several times subjected to a very heavy artillery fire from rebel batteries on Mission Ridge,"[15] although it seems the long range made the fire largely ineffective.

Grant told Thomas that he and Sherman were both to advance at dawn the next day, November 25: "Your command will either carry the rifle-pits and ridge directly in front of them, or move to the left [i.e. in the direction of Sherman], as the presence of the enemy may require."[16] Granger, told to prepare "for an offensive movement the next morning," issued the appropriate orders: "You will make every preparation for such movement," Fullerton told Sheridan and Wood on Granger's behalf.

But the next morning did not bring on a major engagement on Granger's front. Skirmishers were sent out from Wood's division to reconnoiter, driving back their Rebel counterparts to their rifle pits and finding as expected that the Confederates were amply prepared to defend their entrenchments. Sheridan drove off Confederate pickets without resistance, "so as to prolong my line of battle on that of Wood, the necessity of continuing to refuse my right having been obviated by the capture of Lookout Mountain and the advance of Palmer."[17] (Brig. General Richard Johnson's division of Palmer's Fourteenth Corps was on Sheridan's right.)

Grant was waiting for Sherman, who was slow to come up on the left. When he did, Sherman's attacks at the north end of Missionary Ridge were poorly coordinated and unsuccessful, failing to make use of his superior numbers. He was opposed by the Confederates' most effective division commander, Cleburne, known by some as the "Stonewall of the West." Hooker, meanwhile, whom Grant and Thomas also were waiting for, pressed on from Lookout Mountain on the army's right, but was held up at Chattanooga Creek, where retreating Confederates had burned the bridge. After much indecision, Grant decided to support Sherman by having Thomas advance to capture the rifle pits in front of Missionary Ridge, the steep, seemingly impregnable position east of Chattanooga that extended northeast to southwest for about 15 miles.

There is a persistent myth that Granger failed to pass on the attack order because he was playing with artillery again. It seems to have originated with Grant and particularly with Dana, now acting as Grant's spokesman rather than Granger's. Dana said in a message to Stanton that evening: "Grant gave orders at 2 p.m. for an assault upon their lines in front of Thomas, but owing to the fault of Granger, who devoted himself to firing a battery instead of commanding his troops, Grant's order to the division commanders was not transmitted until he repeated it an hour later."[18] Grant at the end of his life said that he had "directed Thomas to order the charge at once," but that an hour later this order had still not been transmitted to Wood."[19] A particularly damaging version of these events came from the journalist Sylvanus Cadwallader, who had Granger explicitly contradicting Thomas in front of Grant. However, Cadwallader acknowledged that he did not witness all this, but got some of it "from information."[20]

It is certainly the case that Granger liked to involve himself with artillery fire. While this was usually in combat, that day he also used a cannon-fire signal to start the attack on Missionary Ridge.

Granger's fondness for artillery has become something of a standing joke among some historians, but his active involvement in fighting seems to have helped rather than hurt his standing with the troops under his command. It did irritate Grant that afternoon. But the notion that Granger disobeyed an order to attack and then "lied"[21] in public to Grant, in front of Thomas and other generals and staff officers, telling him untruthfully that he had not received the order, is inherently implausible. The real tension at Orchard Knob was between Granger's superior officers, Grant and Thomas. Grant was frustrated at Sherman's lack of progress and unsure how hard to push against Missionary Ridge, and Thomas was reluctant to order an attack in the center until he saw better results on the right and left flanks, especially from Hooker on the right. If anything delayed Grant's order, it was the coolness and differences in opinion between him and Thomas, and their failure to effectively communicate with each other. The Union's best generals were at Chattanooga, but the most senior of them were to have precious little direct influence on the coming assault, which would be a soldiers' victory.

The mood of the three top generals on Orchard Knob was likely not improved by Rebel gunfire, which was at last becoming more accurate. According to Dana's postwar memoir, "The enemy kept firing shells at us, as I remember, from the ridge opposite. They had got the range so well that the shells burst pretty near the top of the elevation where we were, and when we saw them coming we would duck, that is, everybody did except Grant and Thomas and Gordon Granger. It was not according to their dignity to go down on their marrow bones."[22]

The delayed attack is partly explained in Thomas' report. With Sherman running into trouble, Grant and Thomas decided to move Baird's division from Palmer's corps to his support. But it turned out Sherman did not need more troops; they were simply piling up before a position he couldn't carry, so Baird was put in place to the left of Granger's divisions. "Owing to the difficulties of the ground,"[23] says Thomas, "his troops did not get in line with Granger's until about 2.30 p.m." Another of Palmer's divisions, commanded by Johnson, was on Granger's right. The two Fourth Corps divisions, commanded by Wood and Sheridan, were in the center, and would lead the coming attack. But Baird's and Johnson's divisions would also participate in the assault, made by more than 23,000 men.

Another, more significant, reason for Granger's and Thomas' inaction was that Grant had not ordered them to act. The most junior general on Orchard Knob that day, Grant's staff officer James H. Wilson, was with the commanding general's chief of staff, the volunteer officer John Rawlins. A hot-tempered lawyer in civilian life, Brig. General Rawlins had an easily aroused suspicion of West Pointers who failed to be sufficiently deferential to his boss.

As Wilson wrote after the war: "Grant himself seemed anxious but undecided and gave no positive orders, but as time continued to drag with nothing done Rawlins finally, at my suggestion, urged Grant to silence Granger and give Thomas positive orders for a general advance."[24] The silencing of Granger meant having him desist from assisting the artillery, but the point is that Grant's staff officers were aware no order had been given to Thomas or Granger to advance. Grant had probably deferred somewhat to Thomas, giving him a suggestion which the Virginian did not interpret as an order.

When Grant did act, he told Thomas to order an advance to take the enemy's line of rifle pits of Missionary Ridge. The order was immediately obeyed—Thomas, as Wilson says, "recognizing at once the difference between a suggestion and a positive order."[25] Even Cadwallader acknowledges that Granger "obeyed promptly and rushed into the fight like a wild Irishman,"[26] which sounds like the man.

One of the many points of confusion is the role of Baird's division, on Wood's left. Cadwallader cites Baird's non-receipt of an order to attack as something to do with Granger, although Baird was in Palmer's Fourteenth Corps.

The confusion is compounded in Stanley's memorial, citing an anonymous staff officer who says Granger said to Thomas: "'Give me Baird's division of the Fourteenth Corps, and we will break their center.' Baird's division was given him, and the center was broken."[27] This version seems too neat. It is a rare case of the battle's history being written to favor Granger, as opposed to versions by the partisans of Thomas or Grant. But the truth about the sudden, surprising and complete victory of Missionary Ridge is that it cannot be ascribed to any of these generals, but rather belongs to the lower-ranking soldiers under their command.

Grant's *Memoirs* do not speculate about why his order was purportedly delayed, but say he finally got action by giving the attack order directly to Wood. Wood's version is somewhat different. In an account written after the war, he says Grant approached him and engaged him in conversation about Sherman's unsuccessful attacks. "I think if you and Sheridan were to advance your divisions and carry the rifle pits at the base of the Ridge, it would so threaten Bragg's center that he would draw enough troops from the right, to secure his center, to insure the success of General Sherman's attack," said Grant, according to Wood, who replied: "Perhaps it might work in that way; and if you order it, we will try it, and I think we can carry the intrenchments at the base of the Ridge."

Says Wood: "General Grant walked immediately from me to General Thomas, distant about ten paces. I did not accompany him, though there would have been no impropriety in my doing so. Generals Grant and Thomas were in conversation a very short time, perhaps two or three minutes, when General Thomas called General Granger, who stood near to him. After perhaps two minutes conversation between Generals Thomas and Granger, the latter came to me and said: 'You and Sheridan are to advance your divisions, carry the intrenchments at the base of the Ridge, if you can, and, if you succeed, to halt there.'

"He further said, 'The movement is to be made at once, so give your orders to your brigade commanders immediately.'"[28]

Granger quickly issued final instructions for the attack. He had Wood and Sheridan bring all their brigades out of the trenches and into close columns, each with a double line of skirmishers in advance. It was the skirmishers' job to put down covering fire, while the columns were ordered to keep going at the double-quick, not stopping to fire, the skirmishers at last melding into the assault. Setting off at about 3:40 p.m., the troops had to cover several hundred open yards. These shock tactics worked well, as the mass of four rapidly advancing divisions intimidated the Confederate defenders in their rifle pits, who tended to overestimate their number. Confederate cannon targeted the advancing troops, and were in turn shot at by Union guns. Fortunately for the Army of the Cumberland, the Confederate artillery was poorly placed and inaccurate. Many of the defenders in the pits fired a volley and fled; those who stayed put were quickly overwhelmed or routed by flank fire from the Union troops who had broken through.

The attack so far had been a brilliant success, on a larger scale than what had happened two days before at Orchard Knob. But this day's Union plan was fatally flawed. The rifle pits provided no defense from Confederate fire from higher up the ridge, and their artillery was becoming more accurate, no longer out of effective range. The troops were vulnerable and taking casualties, yet they had no further orders either to advance or retreat. So they began advancing without orders, or under orders from commanders who were exceeding their own authority. They began an upward climb.

"As soon as this movement was seen from Orchard Knob," wrote Fullerton, "Grant quickly turned to Thomas, who stood by his side, and I heard him say angrily: 'Thomas, who ordered those men up the ridge?' Thomas replied, in his usual slow, quiet manner: 'I don't know; I did not.' Then, addressing General Gordon Granger, he said, 'Did you order them up, Granger?'

"'No,' said Granger, 'they started up without orders. When those fellows get started all hell can't stop them.' General Grant said something to the effect that somebody would suffer if it did not turn out well, and then, turning, stoically watched the ridge. He gave no further orders.

"As soon as Granger had replied to Thomas, he turned to me, his chief-of-staff, and said: 'Ride at once to Wood, and then to Sheridan, and ask them if they ordered their men up the ridge, and tell them, if they can take it, to push ahead.' As I was mounting, Granger added: 'It is hot over there, and you may not get through. I shall send Captain Avery to Sheridan and other officers after both of you.'"[29]

Henry Cist also writes that Grant had ordered Thomas to conduct a "demonstration . . . to take the first line of rifle-pits and hold his command there," and aggressively questioned Thomas when they saw the troops going up the ridge. When Thomas told him they were probably going up on their own authority, Grant responded it was "all right if it turned out all right. If not, someone would suffer."[30] Major General Howard described in *The Century* magazine the same sequence of events, with Granger first crying out, "They are going up the ridge without orders," Grant then questioning Thomas and stating, "Somebody will suffer for it if they don't stay there."[31]

Grant in his report praised the soldiers for "following closely the retreating enemy without further orders."[32] But there is an odd footnote in his memoirs saying that in his prior order to Thomas, "authority was given for the troops to reform after taking the first line of rifle-pits preparatory to carrying the ridge."[33] Cozzens is justly skeptical that the order said anything about carrying the ridge, which clearly came as a shock to Grant when it actually happened. Grant seems to have been unable to permanently accept the fact that the aggression and courage displayed by the Army of the Cumberland is what won the battle, not his own leadership or that of his friend Sherman, who he had intended to strike the decisive blow.

Sheridan had sent back a staff officer, Captain Ransom, to clarify the attack orders and determine whether he was authorized to move up the ridge. Ransom talked to Granger and unfortunately only understood the order to stop at the rifle pits. According to Granger, Ransom said Sheridan "wished to know whether the order that had been given to take the rifle pits 'meant those at the base of the ridge or those on top.' My reply was that the order had been to take those at the base. Conceiving this to be an order to fall back to these rifle-pits," Ransom, on his way back to Sheridan, so reported it to one of Sheridan's brigade commanders, Brig. General George Wagner. Wagner accordingly withdrew many of his troops, thus increasing their casualties when they had to advance again. These costly errors are honestly acknowledged in Granger's report.[34]

Wood had already ordered his troops up on his own authority by the time Fullerton reached him, which removed any ambiguity about what should be done. He says in his report he was acting to keep up with "the enthusiasm and impetuosity" of his men, who were going up on their own accord. To a certain extent, this also had been done by Sheridan and Wagner, although Sheridan's initial report said Avery did play a role by relaying Granger's new order that Sheridan should take the ridge if in his judgment he thought he could. "My judgment was that it could be carried," Sheridan said, "and orders were given accordingly, obeyed with a cheer, and the ridge was carried."[35]

Granger "in the meantime sent all the rest of my staff officers," some to
Wood and Sheridan to make sure the new orders got through, "and others
to order up the reserves and every man that remained behind to the support
of the troops starting up the ridge."[36] (Lt. Obadiah German of the 8th Wisconsin Battery reported getting a 4:30 p.m. order from Granger "to move forward and take position on Mission Ridge, on the right of General Willich's
brigade."[37]) Baird's and Johnson's divisions also were ordered up the ridge.

Brig. General Samuel Beatty, commanding a brigade in Wood's division,
like other commanders saw two of his regiments going up the ridge without
orders. "Being unable to obtain communication with General Wood," as he
says in his report, he ordered up two other regiments to support them. He
then sent forward the two remaining regiments in his brigade, "and soon after
received the order from General Granger to send up all my troops."[38] Granger
arrived on the ridge in time to move the 17th Kentucky, supported by the
19th Ohio, to a position where, "by his personal command, [they] fired a full
volley after the fleeing rebels."[39]

Thomas in his report attributed the advance to the troops being "apparently inspired by the impulse of victory," acknowledging that "the original
plan of operations was somewhat modified."[40] As the Cincinnati *Gazette*
reported at the time: "Here [at the rifle pits], according to original orders,
our lines should have halted; but the men were no longer controllable."[41]
Granger's report says: "They started without orders along the whole line of
both divisions.... Officers caught the enthusiasm of the men."[42]

Grant is his memoirs says: "Without awaiting further orders or stopping
to reform, on our troops went to the second line of works; over that and on
for the crest—thus effectually carrying out my orders of the 18th for the battle and of the 24th for this charge."[43] That last part is a stretch, although it
can be argued it was Grant's bulldog insistence on the offensive which eventually paid off. And while Sherman fought ineffectively against Cleburne,
Grant's putting him in place to attack on the left, and approving Hooker's
advance on the right, did contribute to the successful outcome. When Hooker
broke through Rossville Gap, after surmounting his delay at the creek, then
turned his troops to north to roll up the Rebel left, he perhaps had a greater
influence on the crushing outcome of the battle than commonly acknowledged. At the same time as Granger's men were charging them in front, the
Confederates in the center were already hearing Yankee fire on the ridge to
their left.

Granger may have blundered in instructing Ransom, but he was the first general on Orchard Knob to act to remedy the defective orders in light of the new situation. The coming victory did not belong to any of the generals. It belonged to the ordinary soldiers, defeated at Chickamauga and besieged in Chattanooga, still on short rations, who now clambered up Missionary Ridge under fire, huddled beneath overhangs near the summit fixing their bayonets, and then charged up to capture cannons and turn them upon the enemy, spreading north and south on the ridge-top to destroy remaining Confederate resistance—except at the north end where Cleburne, facing Sherman and now Thomas (Baird's division), held out until after dark before withdrawing in good order. From Orchard Knob to the top of the ridge was about three miles, and the Union soldiers got there in not much more than an hour.

They were fortunate that the Confederate artillery was poorly placed high on the ridge, unable to aim down far enough at the advancing enemy (which also was the case the day before on Lookout Mountain). The Confederate rout built on itself, as the defenders held fire to avoid hitting their own retreating comrades. Historians have been harsh on Bragg's report after the battle in which he blamed the conduct of his own troops who fled from the ridge, but there is a kernel of truth beneath his uncharitable verdict. The Confederates had spent two months seeing their enemy reinforced and their own ranks reduced, and two days observing steady Union advances on this battlefield. Union morale was higher, and Federal troops fought better. But Bragg's blundering mean-spiritedness, and superior Union leadership including Granger's, contributed to the difference in morale.

Dana's verdict that "the storming of the ridge by our troops was one of the greatest miracles in military history"[44] cannot be gainsaid. ("Neither Grant nor Thomas intended it," he accurately added.) The action has rightly gone down as one of the most significant and effective displays of military valor in American history, winning as it did the Battle of Chattanooga. While the victory won by those troops, with the Fourth Corps in the lead, was not the result of their senior generals' acumen, it cannot help but reflect favorably on those commanding officers, Granger included. Ending his report, Granger paid tribute to the commanders of his divisions and brigades, to their officers and his staff, also noting that "to the private soldiers in the ranks, not merely my own acknowledgments, but those of the whole country, are due."[45]

Wood's division encountered the fiercest resistance and was first to the top, although Thomas reported to Halleck, "Missionary Ridge was carried simultaneously at six different points."[46]

"Shortly after the battle was over," said Colonel John Martin of the 8th Kansas Volunteers (in Brig. Gen. Willich's brigade of Wood's division), he encountered his irrepressible corps commander: "General Granger rode along our lines, and said, in a joking way, to the troops, 'I am going to have you all court-martialed! You were ordered to take the works at the foot of the hill, and you have taken those on top! You have disobeyed orders, all of you, and you know that you ought to be court-martialed!'"[47]

Grant and Thomas visited the ridge before withdrawing to Chattanooga. Granger stayed on top, and was to spend the night at Bragg's former headquarters there.

Before that, there were rations to be brought up for the army spending the night atop Missionary Ridge, and wounded men from both sides to be brought down, most of them spending the night in the huts at the bottom or near bonfires built to keep off the late-November cold. This had been no easy victory. Granger later reported his casualties in Wood's and Sheridan's divisions at Missionary Ridge as 2,544, including at least 291 killed. These two divisions took much higher casualties than any other in the Union Army during the battles for Chattanooga, and played a correspondingly larger role in winning the victory.

There was also the question of pursuit. Sheridan with Granger's authorization had pressed on into the valley on the far side of the ridge, capturing nine guns and then outflanking and driving off Confederates under General William Bate from a delaying position, taking more guns and wagons. But with night fallen, he realized he needed reinforcements if he was to press on to Chickamauga Station and get in the rear of the troops who had faced Sherman, so he went back to Missionary Ridge to try to get them. Granger approved another limited advance by Sheridan, but declined to go further until he had gotten a reply to a message he had already sent to Thomas—who, like Grant, was no longer on the ridge.

Grant says that while on Missionary Ridge, "I ordered Granger to follow the enemy with Wood's division, but he was so much excited, and kept up such a roar of musketry in the direction the enemy had taken, that by the time I could stop the firing the enemy had got well out of the way."[48] Cozzens says reasonably that "doesn't ring true, particularly in light of his intended use of Granger's corps as expressed later that night. Also, Grant already had come to loathe Granger for his sharp tongue and preoccupation with shooting cannon, so his memory of events may have been clouded by lingering acrimony."[49] Grant's account was written more than 21 years later, but one detail of it, that Granger was directing fire from Missionary Ridge, is confirmed in Beatty's report. Granger was surely easy to dislike, and Grant undoubtedly did so, at least since 1862 (as Sheridan reported) and probably well before that. Unfortunately, the coming Knoxville campaign would solidify and partly justify Grant's prejudice against him.

Granger says in his report that he was resting Wood's division that evening to get it "ready for the anticipated pursuit of the enemy." Wood says that instead of pursuing the fleeing troops in front of them, his troops were mostly "deployed to the right and left to clear the ridge and relieve the pressure on our troops that had not gained the summit,"[50] and that afterward they needed to reorganize and rest for the night. Sheridan was prepared to drive his troops harder.

Grant and Thomas had gone back to Chattanooga before 7:15 p.m. That's when Granger sent a message to Thomas from Missionary Ridge urging "a bold dash upon the Chickamauga" against the enemy forces which "evidently are badly demoralized. Our men are in great courage and spirits. I am ready for any orders or dispositions you may be pleased to make."[51]

Says Cist: "At midnight, on Granger's suggestion, Sheridan in the advance was again ordered with his division to press the enemy."[52] But until he was assured of Thomas' support, Granger told Sheridan to continue advancing only as far as Chickamauga Creek, which Sheridan reached at about 2 a.m. and followed the order to stop. Granger wisely declined to risk a night engagement with Cleburne's rearguard, on territory known to the Confederates but not to the Union (Granger had difficulty procuring guides that night), without higher authority. Cleburne was retreating along with the rest of Bragg's army but in much better order than most of it. When Hooker caught up with Cleburne on the morning of the 27th at Ringgold Gap in Georgia, his attacks were repulsed with severe losses.

Granger's message on the evening of the 25th said, "We have captured about 40 pieces of artillery and about 2,000 prisoners." The next day, he upped the prisoner catch by Fourth Corps to more than 3,000; on the 27th, Thomas was reporting to Halleck the taking of more than 5,000 prisoners, and Grant ultimately reported more than 6,000. Says Howard: "General Grant, summing up our losses in the several combats of Hooker, Sherman and Thomas, gave them as 757 killed, 4,529 wounded, and 330 missing. Bragg's losses, as nearly as I can get the figures, were 3,000 killed and wounded, and about 6,000 prisoners left in our hands. Forty cannon fell to us, and at least 7,000 small arms. Many of the prisoners were wounded, and of them an unusually large number of commissioned officers."[53] Sheridan's divisions alone captured 1,762 prisoners, many of them in the pursuit on the night of November 25–26.

That pursuit also produced its share of tendentious mythologizing to further damage Granger's reputation. In Sheridan's memoirs, he describes a November 26 conversation with Grant, in which the commanding general "realized what might have been accomplished had the successful assault on Missionary Ridge been supplemented by vigorous efforts on the part of some high officers, who were more interested in gleaning that portion of the battlefield over which my command had passed than in destroying a panic-stricken enemy."[54] In part, this refers to a tiresome dispute which would go on for decades that Sheridan conducted with Hazen and Wood over which units should get credit for capturing particular battle flags, guns and positions at the top of Missionary Ridge. But, coming right after an account in Sheridan's memoirs in which Granger, in the middle of the night, authorized only a limited pursuit, it is also an implicit criticism of him and Thomas—criticism with which Grant, given his prejudice against those officers, was likely happy to join.

In reality, though, as Cozzens implies, Granger and Thomas were following Grant's orders. This is actually proven by the Official Records of the Army, documenting Thomas' midnight reply to Granger's message. Thomas said nothing about a pursuit of Bragg's fleeing army, but instead pointed Granger and his troops in a different direction:

"Your dispatch of 7.15 p.m. was duly received. Please accept my hearty congratulations on the splendid success of your troops, and convey to them my cordial thanks for the brilliant style in which they carried the enemy's works. Their conduct cannot be too highly appreciated. I have just seen General Grant, who desires that you make preparations to move up the river as soon as possible."[55] That meant northeast up the Tennessee River, away from Bragg and into the eastern part of the state. Granger accordingly withdrew Sheridan before daylight, as he began preparing to bring the Fourth Corps to the rescue of Burnside's army, which was still besieged by Longstreet in Knoxville.

NOTES

1. *OR,* Vol. 30, Pt. 1, 163
2. Ibid., 197.

3. *OR,* Vol. 30, Pt. 4, 254.

4. Bruce Catton, *Grant Takes Command* (Boston: Little, Brown and Company, 1968), 71–72.

5. *OR,* Vol. 31, Pt. 2, 129.

6. J.S. Fullerton, in *Battles and Leaders of the Civil War,* ed. Johnson and Buel, Vol. 3, *The Army of the Cumberland at Chattanooga* (New York: The Century Co., 1884, 1888), 721.

7. *OR,* Vol. 31, Pt. 2, 255.

8. Ibid., 94.

9. *Autobiography of Oliver Otis Howard* (New York: Baker & Taylor, 1907) 478.

10. *OR,* Vol. 31, Pt. 2, 65.

11. Ibid., 256.

12. Peter Cozzens, *The Shipwreck of Their Hopes: The Battles for Chattanooga* (Urbana: University of Illinois Press, 1994), 133.

13. O.O. Howard, *Chattanooga,* in *The Atlantic Monthly,* Vol. 38 (Boston: H.O. Houghton and Co., 1876), 212.

14. *Autobiography of Oliver Otis Howard,* op. cit., 479.

15. *OR,* Vol. 31, Pt. 2, 189.

16. Ibid., 44.

17. *Personal Memoirs of P.H. Sheridan,* Vol. 1 (New York: Charles Webster & Co., 1888), 308.

18. *OR,* Vol. 31, Pt. 2, 68.

19. *Personal Memoirs of U.S. Grant,* Vol. 2, (New York: Charles L. Webster & Co., 1886), 78–79.

20. Sylvanus Cadwallader, *Three Years With Grant* (New York: Knopf, 1956;. University of Nebraska Press, 1996), 153–54.

21. Cozzens, op. cit., 248. Thomas' biographer Einolf, op. cit., follows Cozzens' lead.

22. Charles Anderson Dana, *Recollections of the Civil War* (New York: D. Appleton & Co., 1909), 149.

23. *OR,* Vol. 31, Pt. 2, 96.

24. James H. Wilson, *Under the Old Flag,* Vol. 1 (New York: D. Appleton and Co., 1912), 297.

25. Wilson, op. cit., 298.

26. Cadwallader, op. cit., 154.

27. (David Stanley), *Society of the Army of the Cumberland Fifteenth Reunion* (Cincinnati: Robert Clarke & Co., 1884), 221.

28. Thomas J. Wood, *The Battle of Missionary Ridge,* in *Sketches of War History, 1861–65,* Ed. Chamberlain (Cincinnati: Robert Clarke Company, 1896), 34–35.

29. J.S. Fullerton, op. cit., 725.

30. Henry M. Cist, *The Army of The Cumberland* (1882; Castle Books ed. 2002, Edison, NJ), 261–62.

31. O.O. Howard , *Ulysses S. Grant* in *The Century Magazine,* Vol. 74, May–October 1907 (New York: The Century Co., 1907), 958.

32. *OR,* Vol. 31, Pt. 2, 35.

33. *Personal Memoirs of U.S. Grant*, Vol. 2, op. cit., 78.
34. *OR,* Vol. 31, Pt. 2, 133.
35. Ibid., 191.
36. Ibid., 133.
37. Ibid., 560.
38. Ibid., 301.
39. Ibid., 302.
40. Ibid., 96.
41. *The Rebellion Record,* Vol. 8, Ed. Frank Moore (New York: Van Nostrand, 1865), 233.
42. *OR,* Vol. 31, Pt. 2, 132.
43. *Personal Memoirs of U.S. Grant*, Vol. 2, op. cit., 80.
44. *OR,* Vol. 31, Pt. 2, 69.
45. Ibid., 135.
46. *The Rebellion Record*, Vol. 8, op. cit., 191.
47. John Martin, quoted in *Battles and Leaders of the Civil War*, ed. Johnson and Buel, Vol. 3, *The Army of the Cumberland at Chattanooga* (New York: The Century Co., 1884, 1888), 726.
48. *Personal Memoirs of U.S. Grant*, Vol. 2, op. cit., 82.
49. Cozzens, op. cit., 349.
50. *OR,* Vol. 31, Pt. 2, 259.
51. Ibid., 117.
52. Cist, op. cit., 256.
53. *Autobiography of Oliver Otis Howard*, op. cit., 488–89.
54. *Personal Memoirs of P.H. Sheridan*, Vol. 1, op. cit., 318.
55. *OR,* Vol. 31, Pt. 2, 117.

7

East Tennessee

S ome historians, following Grant's lead, have disparaged Granger's purported slowness in marching to relieve Knoxville, where Burnside's Union army was besieged by Longstreet. But an examination of what actually happened that late November, and over the next few months, provides substantial justification for Granger.

On November 26, the day after the capture of Missionary Ridge, an order from Grant to Granger was apparently delayed for six hours en route to Thomas. Still, Granger (through Avery) ordered Sheridan that day: "Make every preparation for moving upon Knoxville tomorrow with four days' rations and 50 rounds of ammunition per man; no wagons will be taken; everything in light marching order. A steamboat will pass up the river abreast of the command, loaded with supplies, from which your troops will be furnished at points to be designated hereafter. You will report at these headquarters in person the moment your command is in readiness to march."[1]

But later on the 26th, Granger's staff officer Fullerton told the divisional commanders, Sheridan and Wood, they would not be moving the next day. On November 27, Granger told Sheridan and Wood to start the next morning, the 28th, with a few wagons as well as the steamboat.

There is conflicting evidence about exactly when Granger started for Knoxville—although the contemporary documents in the Official Records should remove any doubt—but whenever it was, it wasn't soon enough for Grant. It actually seems to have been on the afternoon of November 28. That is the date reported by Granger, and also the date Grant sent a message from Chattanooga to Major General John Foster in Cumberland Gap saying

Granger and his Fourth Corps "left here today" for Knoxville. The next day, Grant sent a message indicating he was aware that Granger had started. Grant had returned to Chattanooga on the 28th after spending the days after the battle with Hooker at Ringgold and with Sherman.

Grant errs in his memoirs, putting the date of his return to Chattanooga and confrontation with Granger as the night of the 29th,[2] by which time Granger had actually been en route for more than a day. Sheridan's memoirs, written after Grant's in the 1880s, also put the departure date as November 29, probably as a result of picking up Grant's error.

Grant says "Granger had not only not started but was very reluctant to go, he having decided for himself that it was a very bad move to make"[3] — which prompted Grant to send Sherman and much of his army to Knoxville too, putting his friend in charge of the expedition.

While he exaggerates Granger's tardiness, there is every reason to suppose Grant did find his subordinate in an argumentative mood. Granger had spent the two days since Missionary Ridge trying to ensure adequate provisions for his troops in their new endeavor—having first been ordered to have his corps collect and bury the Union dead on the battlefield, and count the dead Confederates and collect enemy battle flags.

Granger's soldiers, as Wood related after the war, "had had no clothing issued to them since leaving Middle Tennessee in the preceding summer. . . . The troops were in very poor condition indeed for a forced march of a hundred and twelve miles. The clothes on their backs were much worn, and their shoes about worn out; in fact, not a few of the men were as good as barefooted. As soon, however, as a very slight, absolutely necessary preparation could be made, Granger was ready to proceed with his command."[4] That preparation now included bringing along one wagon per regiment, minimal provisioning for his short-rationed soldiers but an improvement over the zero wagons specified in the November 26 order, and one that likely saved many of their lives in the very hard winter months to come.

Stanley's Army of the Cumberland memorial says: "The whole thing amounts to this: General Granger wanted to tarry two days, to get shoes for his men; General Grant wanted him to march without shoes."[5] Granger also had the temerity to suggest that other forces under Grant's command might be better prepared to relieve Knoxville.

On the other hand, Grant did have legitimate concerns about Burnside, which he expressed in a November 29 letter to Granger. On the 23rd, Grant said, Burnside had telegraphed that he had ten to twelve days' worth of rations left; and since then, communications with Knoxville had been cut off by the Rebels. This meant, Grant told Granger, there was "a necessity for forced marches. I want to urge upon you in the strongest possible manner the necessity of reaching Burnside in the shortest time."[6]

On the same day, November 29—in fact in the next message listed in the Official Records—Grant wrote to Sherman: "Granger is on the way to Burnside's relief, but I have lost all faith in his energy and capacity to manage an expedition of the importance of this one. I am inclined to think, therefore, that I shall have to send you."[7] He did send troops under both generals to Knoxville, with Sherman in command.

Sherman adopted Grant's low opinion of Granger, at least in communicating with his superior. In an 1864 message to Grant, Sherman deprecated another general (Romeyn B. Ayres) by calling him "as bad a growler as Granger."[8]

Granger, however, was now on board with Grant's sense of urgency. He sent a message on the 29th from Ooltewah Creek—indicating he was under way to Knoxville—ordering Brig. General James Spears to link up with him, saying "My column will move rapidly" and adding: "P.S. Burnside can hold out but a few days longer, and unless we reach him soon, he will be obliged to surrender. I say never!"[9]

November 29 also was the date Longstreet attacked Burnside's lines at Knoxville and was repulsed with heavy losses, and received confirmation of the Confederate defeat at Chattanooga. He lingered in the area in order to compel the Union relief columns to keep coming—drawing off their strength from the beleaguered Army of Tennessee—and then on December 4 he retreated toward northeastern Tennessee, lifting the siege. It turned out that Burnside's plight for provisions had never been that bad, and his troops were eating better than those rushing to their aid—although Grant, Granger and the other Union generals did not know that.

On November 30 Granger reported to Grant he was making good progress, but that "there is little or nothing to be gleaned from the country," which was largely depopulated.

The plight of the Fourth Corps soldiers was made worse when Sherman told Granger he must share his supplies with Sherman's troops, and also ordered him to take a more direct route to Knoxville, away from the Tennessee River and its supply boat. Wood's December 29 report describes the soldiers' plight, and their indomitable response: "Thinly clad, some of the men being absolutely barefooted and all deficient in clothing, and after having been more than two months on short rations, the march was cheerfully and rapidly made at a most inclement season of the year. The line of march having been changed after leaving Chattanooga, it was impossible to draw subsistence from the commissariat department, and during the remainder of the march it was necessary for the troops to subsist on the country."[10] They sometimes marched 21 miles in a day over frozen ground, with their bare feet tied up in rags.

The army was back in generally friendly territory. East Tennessee was a mostly loyal area where much of the population was happy to see them, and had helped sustain Burnside in Knoxville. But this also was a poor area, war-ravaged, weary, and unable to adequately supply its liberators.

Wood's report also noted: "When we marched from Chattanooga, the troops were allowed but one wagon per regiment for the transportation of baggage, shelter and cooking utensils."[11] The orders on November 26 had called for no wagons at all to be taken. That Granger managed to get them changed by the next day, allowing for one wagon per regiment, speaks well for his concern for the troops under his command, no matter what trouble it might get him into with his superiors. Had those wagons not been taken, the condition of his soldiers would have been that much worse, likely resulting in more deaths from malnutrition and exposure.

Sherman found more local supplies on his route. On December 1, Granger told Sheridan to order citizens to bring in "beef, bacon, flour, corn-meal, forage, &c., upon promise of immediate payment." But on December 3, Granger told Sherman he would go to Loudon on the river the next day to meet the steamboat and "obtain rations, as the command is entirely out. . . . In case our troops are caught in a cold rain in these mountains at this inclement season of the year, many of them must perish and many more become disabled, without the means of sheltering, feeding, or otherwise providing for their comfort."[12] This got the attention of Sherman, who permitted Granger to "halt your column where you please" and make arrangements to gather food and grind flour. However, the steamboats stopped far short of Loudon, finding the river not navigable. Some supplies were unloaded down river, but Granger lacked wagons and draft animals to bring them up, and his troops remained imperiled by lack of food and shelter.

Sherman's and Granger's forces linked up, and on December 6 the two major generals rode ahead into Knoxville. They found Burnside's army receiving some supplies from sympathetic local residents in addition to provisions hauled down the supply line from Cumberland Gap. The three generals discussed what to do about Longstreet.

Sherman says in his memoirs: "I offered to join in the pursuit, though in fact my men were worn out, and suffering in that cold season and climate. . . . Burnside explained to me that, reinforced by Granger's two divisions of ten thousand men, he would be able to push Longstreet out of East Tennessee, and he hoped to capture much of his artillery and trains. Granger was present at our conversation, and most unreasonably, I thought, remonstrated against being left; complaining bitterly of what he thought was hard treatment to his men and himself. I know that his language and manner at that time produced on my mind a bad impression, and it was one of the causes which led me to relieve him as a corps commander in the campaign of the next spring."[13]

No doubt Granger was intemperate, but he hardly lacked excuse. His soldiers were every bit as "worn out, and suffering in that cold season and climate" as were Sherman's, and his superior officers were and would remain seemingly indifferent to that fact. Sherman, however, was in charge of the relief expedition, so it was he and his troops that marched south toward Georgia, leaving Granger at Knoxville with Sheridan's and Wood's divisions.

Sheridan's division was placed east of Knoxville, with headquarters at Sevierville, about 20 miles away. "We soon had all the mills in operation," he says in his memoirs, "grinding out plenty of flour and meal. The whole region was rich in provender of all kinds, and as the people with rare exceptions were enthusiastically loyal, we in a little while got more than enough food for ourselves, and by means of flatboats began sending the surplus down the river to the troops at Knoxville."[14] However, like Wood, Sheridan also reported the lack of shoes, clothing and tents as grave hardships for his soldiers.

Because Burnside's garrison was in better shape than the relievers, it assumed the offensive against Longstreet, conducting a leisurely pursuit while leaving Granger's troops at and near Knoxville. On December 8, 9 and 12, Granger requested permission from Burnside and Thomas for the Fourth Corps to go back to Chattanooga, fearful of what would happen to his soldiers if they remained in Knoxville with inadequate supplies through the winter. But Grant told Burnside on December 10: "Keep Granger with you until your forces return [from pursuing Longstreet]. . . . When the river rises and we get the banks more securely, I will try to send you a boat-load of supplies weekly."[15] On December 12, Granger again asked Grant for permission to withdraw the Fourth Corps to Chattanooga, citing the continued severe supply shortages. He said he was confident Longstreet was retreating to Virginia—which turned out not to be the case—and that even if he wasn't, "it is impossible to pursue him and subsist the troops upon his track."[16]

This persistence on behalf of his ill-clad, hungry and suffering soldiers did nothing to endear Granger to his superiors. On December 11 Dana reported to Stanton: "Grant is very angry with Granger for misconduct in the Chattanooga battle, and now for unwillingness to march after Longstreet. ... Granger is certainly unfit to command."[17] This was quite a change in tone from a man who two months before had said Granger "raged like a lion wherever the combat was hottest with the electrical courage of a Ney"[18] (a phrase which the War Department had had to ask him to clarify). Thomas did not share Grant's opinion about their subordinate, which explains Granger's brevet promotion to colonel in the regular Army for "gallant and meritorious conduct" in the Battle of Chattanooga.

Burnside, about to leave Knoxville and be replaced by Foster as commander of the Army of the Ohio, also was appreciative. On December 11 he thanked Granger and the Fourth Corps for their "rapid and vigorous advance" in difficult circumstances which "assisted in compelling the enemy to raise the siege."[19]

On December 12 Granger asked Foster for permission to evict disloyal civilians and use their houses to shelter his troops. The next day, Foster sent Granger two messages, the first rejecting his request and the second partly acceding to it, making available buildings to accommodate 3,000 soldiers of Granger's 11,000-strong command. On December 14, Granger endorsed and sent to Grant's headquarters a report from Wood about the poor condition of the troops, the inadequate food and shelter, and especially the lack of clothing for winter weather, and the resultant threats of sickness and death.

Instead of being relieved or adequately supplied and sheltered, the Fourth Corps was sent into the field once more. They remained there on December 29, when Wood reported: "After remaining at Knoxville a week, a report was received that Longstreet had turned on his pursuers and was driving them back. To support them, we were ordered to make a forced march to this point, and here we have remained ever since, suffering all the privations and hardships that insufficient clothing, insufficient shelter, and insufficient food at the most inclement season of the year can produce."[20] It was a particularly harsh winter that year in mountainous East Tennessee, and a miserable campaign for the ill-supplied army.

Longstreet had indeed turned on his pursuers (commanded by Major General John Parke), fighting the inconclusive Battle of Bean's Station on

December 14–15. The rapid advance of Granger's reinforcements did help induce Longstreet to resume his retreat. The worsening winter weather also contributed to Longstreet's decision not to fight and to withdraw to Morristown. Fourth Corps' soldiers were continuing to do what was asked of them despite the deplorable conditions and inferior equipment with which they were provided.

Now bivouacked at cold and muddy Blain's Cross-Roads, 22 miles east of Knoxville, Granger repeated to Thomas on December 19 his refrain about inadequate supplies, adding, "Many of the command are falling sick with pneumonia, diarrhea, &c. . . . A small supply of clothing and shoes has arrived, about one-third of what is needed. . . . If it is determined that we remain here this winter, I respectfully request that the First Division of the corps be sent up to join us, and with them can be sent our transportation, baggage, camp and garrison equipage, to which they can act as escort."[21]

On December 20 Granger suggested to Foster, back in Knoxville, that cavalry be switched from pressing Longstreet's left flank to his right. The next day, he reported to Parke, who commanded Foster's troops in the field against Longstreet, that he was not able to forage adequate supplies for his troops, and suggested moving south of the river. Wood's division, which had taken the lead in this advance, stayed put for a few days before withdrawing. Sheridan's division was spread between Knoxville and Strawberry Plains, south of Blain's Cross-Roads.

On the 24th, Fullerton, back in Chattanooga, dispatched a supply train to Knoxville for Granger's corps. Steamers also began delivering supplies on December 28.

Granger was back in Knoxville on Christmas Day, when an incident happened which does not reflect well on him and provided some justification for Grant's bad opinion—at least if General Wilson's account can be believed. Wilson, as he relates in his memoirs, was in charge of Grant's Chattanooga headquarters that day, where he was surprised to receive the following message to Grant from Granger: "We are in Knoxville and will hold it till hell freezes over. Tight."[22] Senior officers at Knoxville had apparently been letting off steam by uninhibitedly celebrating the holiday together, when Granger composed the first sentence as a parody of Thomas' message to Grant in October from a besieged Chattanooga ("I will hold the town until we starve"). Foster, the commanding officer, had added the last word "Tight" as an indication to the telegraph operator that Granger was inebriated and the message should not be sent—the latter indication unfortunately not being followed.

When Grant returned from Nashville and saw the message, it confirmed his low opinion of Granger, which he likely did not conceal when visiting East Tennessee for several days from December 31. In his memoir, however, Wilson paints a more balanced portrait:

"Granger was a cavalry officer of the old school. . . . He had an ideal figure with a fine head, a fierce moustache, and a withering glance. While his port and bearing were those of the traditional swashbuckler, he had natural parts and professional acquirements far above the ordinary. Imprudent and reckless in behavior, he would do himself more harm by a day of senseless braggadocio than he could repair by a month of irreproachable conduct. A compound of opposites, inconsiderate, overbearing, and profane to a degree rarely surpassed, he knew how to be a gentleman of the most courtly manners. Brave, brilliant, and aggressive, a bolt of steel in action, he occasionally fell into fits of indolence. . . . With fully as much courage, more brains, and a far more impressive figure and appearance than Sheridan, he fell far below that general in the cheerful alacrity and readiness with which he watched for opportunity and performed the duty that always comes to those who earnestly hunt for it."[23]

Sheridan's "cheerful alacrity and readiness" were always at Grant's service, whereas Granger was prepared to strenuously argue with him or anyone to spare his troops useless suffering and death. He would do so although it might blight his promotion prospects and historical reputation, making himself a convenient scapegoat. While it cannot be denied that Grant had cause for indignation when reading that Christmas message, Wilson also says Grant was angry because he expected Granger to be engaged in pursuing Longstreet. That expectation was completely unrealistic given the troops' lack of basic supplies to contend with the harsh winter weather. Granger's consequent bitterness expressed itself in drunken foolishness which could not be justified; still, there was a case for his passive resistance to unreasonable demands. Yet Grant was his superior officer, and he too had reasonable grounds for his orders to keep the pressure on the Confederate armies, and to try to follow Lincoln's longstanding instructions to liberate the Union-friendly population of East Tennessee. Grant had reason to conclude that Granger was not a reliable instrument to carry out those orders.

A clash of personalities may have been at the bottom of this dysfunctional relationship between the two generals. Grant, like many modern historians and readers, was allergic to the type of swaggering military martinet he perceived Granger to be, especially one who until Chickamauga had had comparatively little experience of hard Civil War fighting compared to many other soldiers. Grant, as he says in his memoirs, was as a young soldier not particularly interested in a military career. Overall he spent less than 20 years in the Army, and worked at various other trades. Granger spent his whole adult life in the U.S. Army, becoming a particular type of officer that did not much appeal to Grant. Both men were courageous in battle, yet reacted to it in very different ways. Grant was calm in the face of danger, Granger aroused and excitable.

At least with Grant now on the scene, from December 31, he discovered for himself some of the severe difficulties with which Granger's corps had been contending. Grant's memoirs note "the thermometer being down as low as zero every morning for more than a week while I was at Knoxville and on my way from there on horseback"[24] to Kentucky. On January 3, 1864, from Strawberry Plains, Grant told Thomas: "Send forward clothing for this command as fast as it arrives at Chattanooga. If you have clothing on hand that can possibly be spared, send it forward. . . . Troops here are in bad condition for clothing, and before making much advance must be supplied."[25] This message implicitly concedes the point Granger had been making all winter—which had provoked rage and scorn in Grant and his influential acolyte, Dana—that the Fourth Corps was in no condition to engage in a winter campaign with Longstreet in the mountains.

Granger and Grant seem to have avoided each other at Knoxville but met at Strawberry Plains on January 3, and on January 5 at Blain's Cross-Roads. Telegraphing Sheridan about the latter meeting, Granger said: "From all that I could learn, we are to move camp to somewhere on the railroad between Strawberry Plains and Knoxville."[26] No move was soon made, though, and on January 11 Sheridan was sounding just as frustrated as Granger and Wood: "My division has been on less than half rations for some days, and are suffering from hunger. . . . Is there no 'God in Israel?'"[27]

On January 13, Grant and Foster had the Fourth Corps move east toward Dandridge, further away from Knoxville and Chattanooga, for what Sheridan called "the twofold purpose of threatening the enemy's left and of getting into a locality where we could again gather subsistence." Sheridan's division had to ford the Holston River, "the water very deep and bitter cold, being filled with slushy ice."[28]

On January 15, Grant had told Foster to send the Fourth Corps back to Chattanooga "as soon as you deem your position secure." But Confederate activity removed any prospect of security. On January 16, Grant told Thomas,

"Longstreet is said to be marching toward Knoxville" with reinforcements, and "It is impossible to spare Granger . . . from East Tennessee until Longstreet is driven out," and urged him to "send Foster all the provisions you can. The question of provisions alone may decide the fate of East Tennessee."[29] Granger had been trying to tell Grant the truth about the lack of provisions for almost two months, to the detriment of his own career, but Grant didn't believe it until he had seen for himself the grim conditions under which Union soldiers were suffering. Actually moving supplies was difficult. A steamer went aground on the Tennessee River in mid-January, and railroad bridges needed repair by Thomas.

On a side issue further illustrating Grant's antipathy, the commanding general on January 17 declined to endorse Granger's well-justified recommendation that Hazen be promoted to major general. The stated objection in Grant's message to Thomas was that Granger's endorsement of Hazen "is calculated to forestall other Officers who will also be recommended for promotion. After the recommendations for promotion have been sent in I will have no objection to then endorsing favorably Genl Hazen's separate recommendation."[30] Thomas may have had a hard time making sense of that.

Foster planned to have his cavalry under Brig. General Samuel Sturgis (once Granger's superior at Wilson's Creek) threaten Longstreet's rear, according to a January 17 message he sent to Grant. Pursuing Grant's orders, the army advanced toward Longstreet. Foster, however, was unwell and stayed in Knoxville, sending Parke in his place, and Parke stayed back at Strawberry Plains. Granger, too, in poor health and still trying to secure supplies, was at first behind the advance to Dandridge, which was led by Sheridan. Sheridan had to support a hard-pressed Sturgis in a skirmish near Dandridge, after which Granger came up.

Sturgis' cavalry "was drawn back," according to Hazen, "when the impression got abroad that Longstreet with a superior army would assail us. At this time, the evening of the second day, Granger arrived on the scene and at once called a council of war."[31] Failing to get all the information he wanted, Granger's temper flared, with the result that he quarreled with Hazen and briefly put him under arrest in the middle of the night. He also decided, consulting with Parke in the rear, to retreat back to Strawberry Plains. A forgiven Hazen was put in charge of the rearguard, which got under way the next night.

"Whatever may have been his faults as a commander," wrote Hazen about Granger two decades later, "he was genial, brave, and generous."[32] Says

Longstreet: "The enemy passed the Holston and broke his bridges behind him. Our army returned to their huts and winter homes."[33]

Grant, ever displeased with Granger and anxious to see Longstreet driven out of the state, sought an investigation. The next month, Major General John Schofield, who had succeeded Foster, sent a message to Grant's assistant inspector-general Lt. Colonel Cyrus Comstock, saying "So far as I have been able to learn the unfavorable report of the conduct of Maj. Gen. G. Granger, in reference to the recent falling back from Dandridge, was without good foundation. . . . I do not at this time deem it necessary to relieve General Granger from his command, but am glad to have the authority to do so if it becomes necessary."[34] (Schofield and Granger had both fought as junior officers at Wilson's Creek.)

Granger's caution regarding Longstreet was only partly attributable to the very difficult conditions under which his soldiers were laboring that winter. He also had a healthy respect for those veteran Confederate troops and their commander, who proved one of the war's most effective generals.

Longstreet tells of meeting a woman in Dandridge, following Granger's withdrawal, who "told us something of General Granger during the night before. She had never heard a person swear about another as General Granger did about me [Longstreet]. Some of the officers proposed to stop and make a battle, but General Granger swore and said it 'was no use to stop and fight Longstreet. You can't whip him. It don't make any difference whether he has one man or a hundred thousand.' Presently she brought out a flask that General Granger had forgotten, and thought that I should have it. It had about two horizontal fingers left in it. Though not left with compliments, it was accepted." Longstreet and his staff drank to the toast: "General Granger—may his shadow never grow less."[35]

Longstreet may have shared something of Grant's low opinion of Granger, since he and Grant were close friends before and after the Civil War, but he does not seem to have shared his friend's hostility. The Confederate-sympathizing woman probably embroidered and exaggerated the story. While Granger did not drive Longstreet out of Tennessee, he was not defeated by him, either, and prevented his Confederate army from doing damage to the Union cause. Granger could and did hold his own with the best Confederate generals, such as Forrest and Longstreet, who often defeated inferior Union commanders.

The Fourth Corps did not go back to Chattanooga, but did move in that direction. Sheridan's division was sent south to Loudon, about 25 miles southwest of Knoxville, where it could be supplied by rail from Chattanooga. Arriving on January 27, they found "supplies were more plentiful, and as our tents and extra clothing reached us there in a few days, every one grew contented and happy. Here a number of my regiments, whose terms of service were about to expire, went through the process of 'veteranizing,' and, notwithstanding the trials and hardships of the preceding nine months, they reenlisted almost to a man."[36] Wood's division also was moved south and southwest of Knoxville, closer to the rail supply line. Not all of his veterans reenlisted, however. Granger had his headquarters from January 25 at Loudon. He was authorized to send draft animals and officers' horses to the rear, if insufficient forage for them was found in the corps' new positions.

On January 26, before the supply situation had significantly improved, Foster's chief of staff asked Granger to address complaints "by Union citizens . . . of depredations by soldiers." Granger replied the same day: "I have issued the most stringent orders and done everything in my power to prevent marauding, but hungry men are difficult to control after fasting for five months on half and quarter rations. Nothing has pained me so much as being compelled to strip the country; friend and foe must fare alike, or the army must starve. The country does not afford the food and forage we require. I think any man caught plundering or foraging on his own hook should be summarily shot."[37] The last sentence shows Granger's righteous indignation of behalf of hard-pressed loyal civilians, but it is highly doubtful that when it came down to it, he would ever have ordered a soldier to be shot for foraging. The familiar pattern is one of Granger using hot words that he would, under consideration, decide not to turn into rash and cruel actions.

As his troops became better supplied, Granger took steps to protect local civilians from being plundered. But his health was not good. When Foster told him on January 29 to check into "the destitute condition of the loyal people in the vicinity of Maryville," he immediately replied from Loudon: "I am too unwell to visit Maryville in person, but will send my inspector-general to . . . give all necessary orders to prevent starvation and prevent their being robbed."[38]

Grant, who had planned a major push against Longstreet in early February, decided against it after conferring with Foster and Schofield—for some of the same reasons that Granger had been articulating for months now.

Longstreet advanced to occupy Strawberry Plains in mid-February, and Colonel Edward McCook's Cavalry Division was placed under Granger's command by Schofield. (Schofield's major-generalship was of more recent

date than that of Granger, who served under him anyway.) Granger told Mc-
Cook to watch for the reported advance of a Rebel cavalry force, "and attack
it if possible." On February 19 Granger reported a skirmish the day before
by the cavalry attached to his command.

The Union commanders were hearing inaccurate rumors that Longstreet
was on his way to Georgia, while remaining concerned that he would threaten
Knoxville and railroad supply lines in Tennessee. On February 20, Schofield
told Granger it looked like his own headquarters town of Loudon would be
Longstreet's target. But Longstreet soon pulled back to Bull's Gap, about 20
miles northeast of Morristown, and became generally quiescent in winter
quarters. Thomas was lobbying Grant to have the Fourth Corps sent back
from Schofield, and told Granger that when it happened he would be moving
to the Army of the Cumberland's left flank in Cleveland, Georgia.

The ever blunt Granger reported to Schofield on February 25 that the
cavalry horses were starving and needed forage brought in by boat or wagon,
not being able to live off the country since "nearly every nook and corner is
exhausted of forage and subsistence." He sent on a similar message from
McCook on March 5. Thomas, meanwhile, was lobbying to have at least
McCook's cavalry sent to him at Cleveland, which Schofield agreed to, telling
Granger on March 6: "I will send you a small force of very poor cavalry to
take its place."[39] Schofield also conceded Granger's point about feeding the
horses, telling him on March 8, "the cavalry sent to Loudon to relieve Colonel
McCook will have to be foraged by rail."[40]

The second and third divisions were left with little fighting to do, which
enabled both Sheridan and Wood to take leaves. Sheridan's Second Division
helped build a railroad bridge over the Tennessee River in March, while
Wood's Third Division was moved north of Strawberry Plains to Rutledge,
and conducted several reconnaissance missions that month. Granger reported
intelligence to his superiors, such as the movement of some of Longstreet's
cavalry to reinforce General Joseph Johnston, who had succeeded Bragg in
Georgia.

Sherman seems to give conflicting accounts of how Granger came to
leave the command of the Fourth Corps. At one point he says he relieved
him, but he also claims that Granger lobbied for and took a leave of absence.
Oliver O. Howard, who succeeded Granger as corps commander, says it was
a leave of absence, but may be following Sherman's version. A March 28 message from Sherman to Grant says "General Reynolds has notified me that
he has a sixty days' leave from the War Department, of which he proposes to

avail himself now, and that he is willing to give up his corps. I would therefore ask that a new corps commander be appointed for the Fourth Corps."[41] It appears Sherman said Reynolds when he meant Granger, but Stanley says: "Granger had made no application for leave of absence, had received no such leave, nor did he desire any."[42]

Granger had not had any leave since the start of the war, and his health had suffered during that harsh winter in Tennessee, so it would not be remarkable if he accepted a leave. But there may have been a mutual understanding that he was out of favor with Grant, and by extension with Grant's close friend and colleague Sherman, who rose to succeed Grant when the latter moved east in March to become commander of the entire U.S. Army. Thomas would have been happy to have him back for the campaign against Atlanta, but Grant and Sherman, who were calling the shots, wanted him gone.

In an April 11 message to Major General Stephen Hurlbut, Sherman referred to Grant as having relieved Granger because he was dissatisfied with his performance. That dissatisfaction seems in part based upon a clash of personalities, and in part is consistent with Grant's views of the alleged slowness and other purported failings of the succeeding commanders of the Army of the Cumberland, Rosecrans and Thomas, with whom he also had poor personal relationship. Grant judged all three men too harshly.

On April 10—which happened to be three days after Longstreet's army was ordered out of Tennessee back to Virginia—Granger, in Loudon, issued a farewell order to the Fourth Corps:

"By this order all official connection between you and myself has been broken; but not so those ties of affection born out of the glorious services of the past. As a corps you have been organized but six months, in which time you have done deeds of arms that will shine on the brightest pages of the history of the war. You have won an undying fame. Lookout Mountain and the heights of Mission Ridge are imperishable monuments to your great achievements!

"Your soldierly fortitude displayed under the most trying circumstances with limited food and clothing, during a laborious Winter campaign—passed in march and open bivouac—has been praiseworthy as your conduct on fields of battle. . . . Soldiers, farewell! The memory of our common service in the past will ever remain fresh and green, cherished by me through all the vicissitudes of life. Again, farewell!"[43]

Howard's order the same day referred to "the past noble record, under

the able and respected Commander whom I succeed."[44] He recognized that
the soldiers who served under him, if not all those above, respected Major
General Granger.

NOTES

1. *OR,* Vol. 31, Pt. 2, 138.
2. *Personal Memoirs of U.S. Grant,* Vol. 2, (New York: Charles L. Webster & Co., 1886), 92.
3. Ibid.
4. T.J. Wood, *Seventh Annual Reunion of the Association of the Graduates of the United States Military Academy* (New York: A.S. Barnes & Co., 1876), 63.
5. (David Stanley), *Reunion of the Society of the Army of the Cumberland,* Vol. 15 (Cincinnati, Robert Clarke & Co., 1884), 217.
6. *OR,* Vol. 31, Pt. 2, 49.
7. Ibid.
8. *OR,* Vol. 39, Pt.2, 442.
9. *OR,* Vol. 31, Pt. 3, 271.
10. *OR,* Vol. 31, Pt. 2, 262.
11. Ibid.
12. *OR,* Vol. 31, Pt. 3, 317.
13. *Memoirs of General William T. Sherman.* Vol. 1, (New York: D. Appleton, 1875), 368.
14. *Personal Memoirs of P.H. Sheridan,* Vol. 1 (New York: Charles Webster & Co., 1888), 327.
15. *OR,* Vol. 31, Pt. 3, 369.
16. Ibid., 393.
17. *OR,* Vol. 31, Pt. 1, 265.
18. *OR,* Vol. 30, Pt. 1, 195.
19. *OR,* Vol. 31, Pt. 1, 281.
20. *OR,* Vol. 31, pt. 2, 262.
21. *OR,* Vol. 31, Pt. 3, 448.
22. James H. Wilson, *Under the Old Flag,* Vol. 1 (New York: D. Appleton and Co., 1912), 305.
23. Ibid., 306–7.
24. *Personal Memoirs of U.S. Grant,* Vol. 2, op. cit., (New York: Charles L. Webster & Co., 1886), 101.
25. *OR,* Vol. 32, Pt. 2, 19.
26. Ibid., 29.
27. Ibid., 64.
28. *Personal Memoirs of P.H. Sheridan,* Vol. 1, op. cit., 330.
29. *OR,* Vol. 32, Pt. 2, 110.
30. *The Papers of Ulysses S. Grant,* Vol.10, Ed. John Y. Simon (Southern Illinois University Press, 1982), 33.

31. Hazen, William. *A Narrative of Military Service.* (Boston: Ticknor, 1885), 240.
32. Ibid.
33. James Longstreet, *From Manassas to Appomattox*, 2nd Ed., (Philadelphia, J.B. Lippincott, 1908), 530.
34. *OR,* Vol. 32, Pt. 2, 424.
35. Longstreet, op. cit., 529–30.
36. *Personal Memoirs of P.H. Sheridan*, Vol. 1, op. cit., 338.
37. *OR,* Vol. 32, Pt. 2, 218.
38. Ibid., 255.
39. *OR,* Vol. 32, Pt. 3, 27.
40. Ibid., 15.
41. Ibid., 171.
42. (David Stanley), *Society of the Army of the Cumberland, Fifteenth Reunion* (Cincinnati: Robert Clarke & Co., 1884), 218.
43. *The New York Times,* April 21, 1864.
44. *OR,* Vol. 52, Pt. 1, 545.

8

Mobile

G ranger did not steep himself in bitterness like some rejected generals, although he had ample reason to think himself hard done by. He focused instead on getting back into the war. That he managed to do so came as an unwelcome surprise to Grant, who wrote in his memoirs: "General Granger had got down to New Orleans, in some way or other, and I wrote [Major General Edward] Canby that he must not put him in command of troops. In spite of this he asked the War Department to assign Granger to the command of a corps."[1] This is actually a reference to the next year, when Granger did command a corps under Canby in the last battles for Mobile. But long before that, in the summer of 1864, he did go to Canby's headquarters in New Orleans, as Grant says, and that general did send him to Mobile Bay.

Granger apparently managed to use political influence to go around Grant to get the appointment. A key supporter was Andrew Johnson, the military governor of Tennessee, with whom he had had a productive relationship. Johnson, a rising star who would soon be running for vice president on Lincoln's ticket, sent a June 25 message to the president saying:

"In justice I desire to say a few words in behalf of Maj. Gen. Gordon Granger, who was relieved from his command in this State. . . . I had some opportunity while he was commanding in this district of observing his conduct as an officer and soldier, and it affords me pleasure to state that in my opinion he had few, if any, superiors at the time he was removed from the command. I look upon it as a public loss and so stated in my former telegram urging his retention. I regard him as bold and energetic. I sincerely hope that the services of such a man will not be dispensed with for want of a command by the 1st of July, the time fixed by act of Congress, as I understand, for mustering out generals not on active duty."[2]

While Johnson's influence was no doubt the crucial factor, Stanley's SAC memorial says that James Garfield, who had the unique status during the year of being both a major general and a Congressman (and who later became president of the United States), also intervened with the War Department on Granger's behalf. Stanley quotes an anonymous onetime staff officer of Granger as saying the department also acted "to quiet the importunity with which he [Granger] had been seeking active service" by sending him to Canby's command in New Orleans at the beginning of July. There, Canby "frankly told him that he was embarrassed by his presence, since he had no command to offer him commensurate with his rank. He gave him, however, his choice of going to St. Louis, to report there to his old commander, General Rosecrans, or of taking command of the small force which was designed to cooperate with Admiral Farragut in the attempt to take the forts at the entrance of Mobile Bay, and thus close that port. . . . Though about but two thousand five hundred men comprised the command, General Granger immediately accepted it."[3]

Granger had had a good relationship with Rosecrans, but serving under Canby in a relatively junior capacity offered the opportunity for immediate action, and he took it. While there were few troops to spare for the coming campaign, Granger would be in independent command of the Army operation.

But he would be junior partner to the Navy, and specifically to Rear Admiral David Farragut. That 63-year-old, Union-loyal southerner was already a legendary sailor, starting from his days as a preteen combatant in the War of 1812. In a devastating blow to the Confederacy, Farragut had captured New Orleans in April 1862. He spent the next year and more helping open up the Mississippi, culminating in Major General Nathaniel Banks' capture of Port Hudson after Grant took Vicksburg in July 1863.

Canby, by contrast, like Granger before Chickamauga, had not seen as much Civil War combat as many other generals, and his rank as major general was more recent than Granger's. A West Pointer, he had served with Granger in the Mexican War. He had commanded in New Mexico as a colonel in 1862, where his cautious strategy helped defeat the Confederate campaign, and then became a senior military bureaucrat in Washington. Canby helped restore order in New York City after the draft riots of 1863, and was sent the next year to replace Banks in New Orleans following the failure of the Red River campaign.

Mobile was, with Wilmington, NC, one of the two remaining major Confederate ports which could not be comprehensively blockaded by the U.S. Navy. (Wilmington was protected by Fort Fisher, which an Army-Navy force failed to take for the Union in December 1864; a second joint operation did capture the fort in January 1865.) Back in 1861, General-in-Chief Winfield Scott's much derided "Anaconda" strategy had called for a naval blockade, which had been put into effect and as predicted by him was damaging the Rebel war effort. Tightening the blockade meant increasing the Confederacy's severe economic difficulties, leaving its government increasingly incapable of supplying troops in the field even with food. That helped spur desertions and military collapse.

Farragut was waiting for the arrival of ironclad gunboats to join his fleet in launching an attack in Mobile Bay. The role of Granger's division would be to cooperate with Farragut in capturing the three forts—Gaines, Morgan and Powell—commanding the entrance to the bay, which in Union hands could blockade the port city of Mobile, 30 miles north. While the Navy's role was crucial, it was Granger's troops who would have to capture the forts, the control of which was the objective of the campaign.

1863 had been the war's turning-point year, in which Granger had played a significant role advancing the Union cause. The Confederates had everywhere been forced on the defensive. By the summer of 1864, however, the war was not going particularly well for the Union Army, which to many northerners seemed bogged down in endless bloodshed. In the west, the Red River and Camden (Arkansas) expeditions had failed. A heavily outnumbered Nathan Bedford Forrest had crushed a combined force of cavalry and infantry under Samuel Sturgis at Brice's Crossroads, Mississippi. Sherman's troops had fought their way slowly to the vicinity of Atlanta, but it still held out against them. On the war's main front, Virginia, the Army of the Potomac under Grant's direction had advanced to besiege Petersburg after a campaign of almost inconceivably high casualties, especially on the Union side.

The Confederates had succeeded in aggravating war-weariness in the North, and their goal of causing Lincoln's political defeat in the fall election, leading to a negotiated peace treaty with the new Democratic president, seemed achievable. The Mobile Bay campaign was to be the Union's first decisive step in breaking the impasse, thus restoring the morale needed for Lincoln's re-election victory.

As at New Orleans two years before, at Mobile Bay it was Farragut's fleet that did most of the fighting. But the army, despite the few troops sent, had more to do with the latter victory than the former. After a personal reconnaissance in January 1864, Farragut had recommended an army supporting force of 5,000 men. But by summer, Canby and General-in-Chief Grant were short of soldiers, and Granger started off with well under half the number recommended. Farragut also determined that he needed at least one ironclad, but the Navy did not send him any until just before the battle.

While both Canby and Granger would wind up being accused by Grant of slowness in later operations, no such criticism can stick to them in this campaign. On July 8, they came together to visit Farragut on his flagship *Hartford* off Mobile Bay.[4] They scrambled quickly and effectively to adapt to lower troop numbers, and wound up launching the campaign ahead of the Navy.

"The force under your command," Canby told Granger on July 31, "is not in number or appointment as large or as complete as I designed to send. ...The present object is simply that of cooperation with the Navy in the operations about to be undertaken by Admiral Farragut against the rebel works in Mobile Bay.... I do not give you any special instructions, as I know that you will make the best possible application of the means under your control."[5] Granger's conduct of the campaign would reward Canby's confidence in him.

Mobile Bay is south-southeast of the city, and the two key forts defending it, Morgan and Gaines, were across from each other at the bay's entrance. Fort Gaines is on the west side, at the easternmost point of Dauphin Island. A third fort, Powell, was behind Gaines to the north. Granger and his little division of 1,700 landed on Dauphin Island on the late afternoon of August 3. Farragut had intended to send in his fleet the same day. Instead he waited for the arrival of a fourth ironclad warship, the ill-fated *Tecumseh*. It would be sunk by a mine (called then a torpedo) with 92 or 93 crewmen killed, when Farragut did attack on August 5. The naval delay allowed the Confederates to reinforce Fort Gaines, Granger's first target, but that did nothing to retard his progress.

The troops landed in the evening on the west end of the island, about 15 miles from the fort, and marched unobserved toward it through deep, heavy sand and drenching rain until midnight, then spent a mostly sleepless night being bitten by innumerable insects. They arrived west of Fort Gaines late the next day, constructing trenches less than half a mile from it. The fort's Confederate defenders fired ineffectively at their besiegers the next morning, August 5, when Farragut's fleet entered the bay on the other side, near Fort Morgan.

Farragut's conduct burnished his legend—he was strapped to the mast shrouds as his flagship *Hartford* made its way through massive enemy fire, ordering "Damn the torpedoes" and full speed ahead.

While this was primarily a naval affair, the army contributed to Farragut's victory using one of Granger's favorite weapons. His light artillery was brought up on the night of the 4th, and Union troops also took possession of two abandoned Confederate guns. They opened up the next morning on the Confederate water batteries, silencing them, according to Canby's report, as the U.S. Navy burst into the bay. Granger also commenced shelling Fort Gaines, silencing two guns which were firing at the fleet.

"A few minutes after the battle between Farragut's fleet and Fort Morgan began," says a biographer of Farragut, "General Granger's forces began an artillery barrage of Fort Gaines. With devastating accuracy, they soon disabled or dismounted every gun in the fort."[6]

The Navy bombarded Forts Morgan and Powell, the latter of which was evacuated by its defenders that night. Granger landed his heavy guns on August 5 on the south side of Dauphin Island, and next day they joined a ship from Farragut's fleet in continuing the bombardment of Gaines.

That evening, August 6, Farragut sent a flag-of-truce to Fort Gaines, to which the Confederates responded the next morning, asking for surrender terms. Farragut and Granger sent the Confederate commander, Colonel C.D. Anderson, a message demanding "unconditional surrender," while pledging "the treatment which is in conformity with the custom of the most civilized nations toward prisoners of war,"[7] and that "private property, with the exception of arms, will be respected." Anderson and an aide met with Granger and Farragut on the latter's flagship, the *Hartford*, that evening, and signed the surrender. The next morning, August 8, Union officers including Granger arrived by boat to accept the surrender of Fort Gaines along with 818 prisoners and 26 guns. The garrison was shipped to New Orleans.

Anderson's superior officers tried to stop him from surrendering, and Confederate Major General Dabney Maury later denounced his conduct, reporting: "It is painfully humiliating to announce the shameful surrender of Fort Gaines."[8] Anderson's superiors, however, had not had to endure Granger's bombardment.

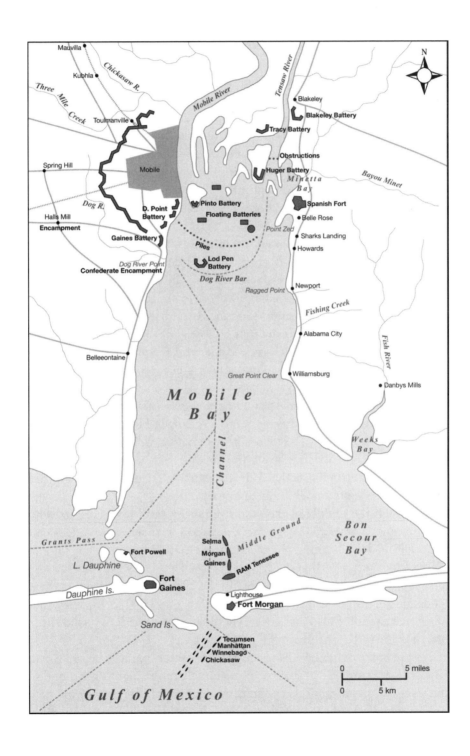

Fort Morgan declined to surrender, and still presented a potential threat to Farragut's fleet if and when the U.S. ships sought to leave Mobile Bay. Granger requested and received more troops, most of whom had just arrived via New Orleans from Texas. Reinforcing success, Canby shipped about 2,000 men in four regiments toward Dauphin Island the same day, enabling Granger to leave small garrisons in the captured Forts Gaines and Powell. Most of the troops who captured Gaines were put back on transports briefly on August 9, disembarking with the reinforcements about three miles east of Fort Morgan on the east side of the bay. A week later, Canby told Granger that more than a thousand additional reinforcements would be sent as soon as possible.

There is a famous photograph taken at this time of Granger and Farragut—at least a famous one of Farragut, often seen in books or articles about him—when they are at Fort Gaines, planning the attack on Fort Morgan. Farragut is relaxed, wearing an admiral's cap, with a slight smile on his clean-shaven face, a few days after his historic and heroic battle. The younger, bare-headed, balding, fiercely bearded but still elegant Granger sits up much straighter, tense and alert. Each commander had fought a long way to this point, where the prospect of Union victory is becoming clearer. They are winning the war.

Granger advanced carefully toward Fort Morgan, making use of an abandoned Rebel trench while digging more of his own. He also kept his men under cover of hills and gullies to minimize casualties, while bringing forward artillery and laying down covering fire, mostly from sharpshooters. From August 13, naval gunners targeted the fort, and on August 15 Granger and Farragut made a joint naval reconnaissance.

Through the middle of the month Granger's guns and mortars were brought up and protected by sandbags, delayed somewhat by persistent rain and what he described in a report as "a terrible storm or hurricane" on the night of the 19th. On August 22, Granger's artillery—22 guns and 16 mortars—opened up along with the Navy. In the 12 hours before the fort's surrender on August 23, Canby said it was hit by about 3,000 shells, destroying much of it. Most of the rebel guns were disabled and the heavy solid shells breached the fort's walls in several places.

A fire broke out in Fort Morgan at 9 p.m. According to an account by a Union lieutenant, Rufus Kinsley, "In the middle of the night signals of distress were displayed from the parapet, whereupon our fire ceased, and they were summoned to surrender, but [Confederate] Gen. [Richard L.] Page replied: 'Never! We will burn first, with our fort!' Gen. Granger told him he could have his choice; but one or the other must be done immediately. He signaled to resume the fire, with all possible energy, and our guns, which had been silent about ten minutes, reopened with such vigor as to keep from six to a dozen shells constantly in the air. Our mortars were so near, and so skillfully planted, that not one of them missed a shot during the day or night."[9]

Page, a cousin of Robert E. Lee, raised the white flag in the morning. "This may safely be regarded as the most remarkable bombardment on record," says Kinsley, with a touch of hyperbole. "An impregnable fortress, mounting two hundred of the best guns in use, besieged by a party who dug through the sand a distance of four miles," and captured after a 24-hour artillery assault.

The Confederates agreed to surrender "with the single condition, which was allowed, of remaining within the fort until two o'clock in the afternoon, to enable the officers and men to pack up their luggage—for they had made no preparation to leave,"[10] according to the diary of Union Brigadier-General George H. Gordon. Page broke his sword over his knee; he was later accused of destroying supplies after the surrender. Granger's casualties were only one killed and seven wounded. Another 600 prisoners and 60 guns were captured. These extraordinarily low casualties for the victorious Union army help explain why Granger's veteran troops tended to admire and like him, and to look more kindly on his devotion to artillery and logistics than other critics have done.

After the surrender, Granger went back temporarily to New Orleans to confer with Canby, leaving Gordon in command. He urged Canby to send reinforcements and to let him attack northward and capture the city of Mobile. But that offensive would be delayed until 1865, when Canby would command an army of more than 30,000 troops. The Confederates by then had responded to the looming threat, reinforcing Mobile and building new forts to defend it, which they would vigorously defend in the spring of 1865.

Still, if the immediate victory was incomplete it was nonetheless significant. Granger had used his small force with promptness and efficiency in support of Farragut's campaign to take the bay forts and close down the major Confederate port on the Gulf Coast. His name was included, with Farragut and Canby, in Lincoln's September 3 proclamation of "national thanks" for the "brilliant success" at Mobile Bay, accomplished by "skill and harmony . . . energy and courage." Even Grant, when he described the campaign in his report on the war's last year (published as an appendix to his

Memoirs), was gracious enough to mention Granger's role without criticizing him.

On September 12, the army forces were reorganized. Granger was appointed commander of the newly formed District of West Florida and Southern Alabama, still under Canby, and headquartered at Fort Gaines on Dauphin Island.

Granger's troops cooperated with the Navy in launching a raid in the Mobile vicinity in September. He also dispatched a raid into the Florida panhandle by 700 mostly cavalry troops under Brig. General Asboth. They won an engagement at Marianna on September 27 and returned with 96 prisoners and some 600 freed slaves, many of whom would enlist in the Union army and fight for it near Mobile in the spring of 1865. (Asboth, who had served with Granger in Mississippi in 1862, suffered a wound in the skirmish which ended his active service.)

Granger reported back to Canby on the Confederate progress on fortifying the Mobile area, which would make the Union army's task harder in the 1865 campaign.

Canby sent Brig. General John Davidson on a cavalry raid in November from Baton Rouge east to Pascagoula, Mississippi. In December, Granger made an expedition west from Mobile Bay to Pascagoula, landing near there on the 15th. His force of about 3,000 mostly infantry troops moved toward Mobile from the west in what amounted to a large raid, with a little minor skirmishing and the capture of a good deal of lumber and other goods including naval stores. A detachment of Granger's cavalry advance ran into stiff resistance on December 22 and had to be supported by infantry. Encountering supply problems, on December 26 Granger began retreating back to Pascagoula. He had had tried to persuade Canby to combine his force with Davidson's, but could get only very limited support before the cavalry was sent back to New Orleans.

According to a December 29 message from Canby to Halleck, these expeditions "have induced the Governors of Alabama and Mississippi to call out the militia of their States under the belief that Selma and Mobile were both threatened."[11] A message sent the week before by Confederate Lt. General Richard Taylor, Maury's superior, mentions Granger being "near East Pascagoula" and confirms the effect. "My arrangements," said Taylor, "have placed every disposable man within my department in position to cooperate in the defense of Mobile and its communications."[12] Those rebel troops defending Mobile were unavailable for other fronts, including Savannah, which Sherman captured on December 21. That diversion was Granger's main contribution to the war effort during the winter of 1864–65.

Granger stayed in Pascagoula until late January, though taking a break for a naval reconnaissance of Mobile Bay. This was a more pleasant winter than the bitter one he had spent the previous year with ill-provided troops in East Tennessee. Lincoln had been re-elected in November, and a Confederate invasion of Tennessee led by John Bell Hood had been crushed by forces under George Thomas in the middle of December. In the New Year, Sherman moved north from Savannah into South Carolina. The tightened blockade—in part due to the Mobile Bay victory—and the loss of territory, property and communications were creating insurmountable economic problems for the Confederacy, with severe shortages of food and other supplies. There would be serious fighting ahead, including on Granger's front. But aside from some self-deluded exceptions such as the Confederate president, most people were increasingly aware that Union victory was coming soon.

An undated letter from Granger to "My Dear Nick" seems to be from this time. "Captain Avery is the only one of my old staff left," Granger writes, "a fine fellow officer and a good friend. If they give me a few more troops I can see hope of smashing this thing generally in this quarter, although you know I am not one of the Elect with the Great Mogul."[13] The Great Mogul was probably Grant, and this relaxed reference indicates Granger was not one for holding a serious grudge. "They hated each other,"[14] according to Granger's great-grandson, but actually his ancestor's hot-tempered character does not seem to have included a tendency toward lasting bitterness.

Hood's complete defeat by Thomas at Nashville in December enabled Canby to focus his attention on Mobile, and in January to start building up his troop numbers for that campaign. He also was promised reinforcements from Thomas' army—the Sixteenth Corps, formerly part of the Army of the Tennessee, under Maj. General Andrew J. Smith.

Granger, back in East Pascagoula on January 24 after a reconnaissance trip to Mobile Bay, told his commander, "I do not like to make suggestions, but I am fearful that we are losing valuable time."[15] Canby's response to this suggestion, if any, is not recorded. Perhaps he contemplated the irony that both his subordinate Granger and his superior Grant were pressing him for speedy and aggressive action.

In the same message, Granger told Canby it looked like the Confederates were abandoning Mobile—an incorrect judgment, like his assessment in December 1863 of the prospects for Longstreet leaving Tennessee. But he soon changed his mind and his reports. He told Canby of new Confederate defenses and reinforcements, which led him to conclude, this time accurately, in a message sent from Fort Gaines on February 17: "Abundant evidence seems to be accumulating to prove that every effort will be made to defend Mobile. . . . However, I apprehend no difficulty in outgeneraling them, capturing everything, or forcing a hasty evacuation"[16] as soon as the Sixteenth Corps arrived. In early February Granger visited Pensacola in west Florida, which was then part of his command.

But in the second half of February he got a new assignment, taking over a reorganized Thirteenth Corps. Some of its troops were at Fort Barrancas near Pensacola, where one of Granger's three division commanders, Brig. General Christopher C. Andrews, said in his campaign memoir that the soldiers "made a beautiful and attractive camp."

Granger's other divisions were under brigadier generals James Veatch and William Benton, and were stationed at the two captured forts, Gaines and Morgan, in Mobile Bay. Smith's Sixteenth Corps began arriving at Dauphin Island on March 7, temporarily reporting to Granger for orders. Also participating in the campaign would be 13,000 men—primarily U.S. Colored Troops—under Major General Frederick Steele, operating from Pensacola. Canby now had over 45,000 men aimed at Mobile, including 18,500 in Granger's Thirteenth Corps.

Although Grant had been suggesting to Canby that Granger was not fit for high command, Canby had a much higher opinion of his subordinate. On February 28 Halleck sent Canby a private letter that touched on this delicate issue. "I also think highly of both Steele and Granger," Halleck wrote, "but General Grant found much fault with the latter in the West, and does not deem him competent for a large command. I know nothing of the cause of his want of confidence in Granger, but he said to me very emphatically, 'Tell Canby not to give Granger any large command, for if he does he is certain to fail'."[17]

Canby nonetheless gave command of the Thirteenth Corps to Granger, a decision entirely justified by its results. Canby was pleased with Granger's work at Mobile in both 1864 and 1865. Granger was to receive two brevet promotions (to brigadier general and major general in the regular Army) for "gallant and meritorious service" and "distinguished gallantry and good conduct" for his actions in the long Mobile campaign.

Grant, however, did not take the news of Granger's employment well. On March 1 he inquired of Halleck: "Was not the order sent for Canby to organize two corps, naming Steele and A.J. Smith as commanders? I so understood. I am in receipt of a letter saying that Granger and Smith are the commanders. If so, I despair of any good service being done."[18] Halleck replied the next day that Canby had not been ordered not to employ Granger, but that Grant's opinions had been passed on to him. Grant replied that he thought Canby should be ordered to put Steele in command of the Thirteenth Corps. Fortunately for Granger, Grant was soon distracted by more immediate concerns closer at hand.

Back at Fort Gaines on March 2, Granger told Steele to have C.C. Andrews' division occupy Pensacola and repair the wharves, so that cavalry reinforcements and railroad equipment could be landed there. However, a plan to lay down rail track was nixed by Grant as a low priority.

As the war's likely end approached, Granger was engaged in negotiations with Confederate commander Dabney Maury on various issues relating to prisoners held by both sides. One involved the authorized shipment and sale of Confederate-held cotton to benefit Confederate prisoners in Union camps. In December, Maury reported that "a recent notification from the Federal naval commander . . . has suspended further action in the business for the present." (That naval commander was no longer Farragut, who in September went north and was to serve the remainder of the war in Washington and Virginia.) Granger cited Confederate delays, but cotton was delivered through Union lines and shipped to New York and New Orleans in the first months of 1865. This was a result of an agreement between senior Union and Confederate authorities that allowances be made for each side to provide for their men held in captivity by the other.

Under the same agreement, Granger sought to send clothing to Union prisoners held in Confederate camps, but Maury responded on February 27 that it probably would not be necessary as "I have been informed that an agreement has been made for the immediate exchange of all prisoners of war of the United States in this department."

These initiatives to exchange or at least ease the plight of prisoners were the result of a change in policy by Grant. In 1864, he had stopped prisoner exchanges, seeking to exploit and increase the Union's numerical advantage in combat-ready troops. But now Grant, like almost everyone else, could see that the Confederacy was too weak to long continue. Another factor was a change of policy in Richmond. According to a modern biographer of Grant, "Confederate authorities abandoned their refusal to include black soldiers in exchanges,"[19] as Lee had refused in 1864. But if there was a new Confederate policy, Maury and his superior, Lt. General Richard Taylor, seemed unaware of it, and the racial issue would complicate Granger's negotiations.

On February 26, Granger complained to Maury that black prisoners of war captured by the Confederates were being used as forced labor in the Mobile defenses, and threatened to retaliate by compelling Confederate prisoners to do similar work. (Granger's message did not make it into the Official Records, but is referred to in Maury's reply.)

Maury was not moved, replying on March 4 that "200 negro slaves, who were captured by Major General Forrest and sent to this district, are engaged in labor upon the fortifications just as other slaves are." Maury said "they were taken away from their homes and their lawful owners by invading parties of U.S. forces, and during the temporary occupancy of portions of C.S. [Confederate States] territory placed in the army or employed for other military purposes, and this against their will. These negroes . . . are earnest in their desire to return to their lawful owners, from whom they were unwillingly taken away."[20] Granger probably doubted the sincerity of this expressed "desire," given the position of the former slaves at the mercy of their captors.

The recapture by the Confederate army of slave "property," Maury continued, "operates to restore it to its original position and it reverts to its lawful owners," who would receive "just compensation" by Confederate authorities for the use of their slaves.

The dispute was kicked upstairs, and Taylor informed Maury on March 6 that Confederate law did provide that "negroes captured from the enemy are . . . considered the property of their respective owners." While "preparations are now in progress for the early delivery [i.e. through exchange] of all prisoners of war held in this department," by "all prisoners" Taylor did not mean former slaves. The "general exchange has been agreed upon under the cartel of 1862" (which was before the extensive employment of black soldiers in the Union army). "I have never been informed," Taylor wrote, "of any agreement on the part of the Government of the Confederate States to exchange negroes as prisoners of war."[21]

Accordingly, Maury informed Granger on the same day that Taylor "instructs me to state that he must adhere to the settled policy which has hitherto prevailed on the subject of negro slaves recaptured by our forces." Three days later, he sent Granger Taylor's letter. But on March 12 an aide to Taylor was asking Maury, "Do you know whether Confederate government has agreed to exchange negro prisoners or not?"[22]

On March 14 Grant, through a staffer, told Canby to exchange or parole any prisoners not facing serious charges. On the same day, Grant sent a message to Robert E. Lee protesting the murder after capture of some black troops and their white officers.

Also on March 14, Granger sent a message to Maury saying he welcomed "information that a general exchange has been agreed upon under the cartel of 1862," which he noted recognized "no distinction of color or former condition." Another major change of policy in Richmond—that the Confederates, too, would start enlisting black troops—appeared to equalize the issue. Granger noted the recent action of the Confederate government "in calling men of African descent into your armies," which, he said, "promises of a quick and proper solution to the question of treatment of colored men captured while in our service." His army expected to receive, Granger said, for exchange purposes "all officers and men of our Army, whether white or black, whom you have captured and now hold."[23]

It does not appear that Maury and Taylor actually permitted the exchange of any black prisoners before the rapidly approaching end of the war. Granger's determination to uphold the rights of his black troops, however, indicates how far he and the Lincoln administration had come since the long first part of the war when their focus was on holding the border states by distancing themselves from abolitionist politics. Granger was on the road that would culminate in his famous June 19—"Juneteenth"—orders in Texas.

But at Mobile, there still was fighting to be done. Canby, very likely with Granger's input, devised a plan to take the city, with his main force, including the Thirteenth Corps, moving to flank it on the east to cut it off from the Confederate heartland. Details of the Union planning are unknown because Canby was killed on duty after the war by Modoc Indians, and, like Granger, never got to write his memoirs. But given his demonstrated confidence in Granger, despite Grant's objections, it is highly likely he consulted with him in formulating the plan to take Mobile. Recognizing this potential plan of attack, the Confederates had built two forts to block any Union advance on the east side of the bay across from the city of Mobile: Spanish Fort, and, five miles to the north, Fort Blakely.

Lengthy field orders for engineering officers, with detailed instructions about what they should report on—including roads, water-courses, "differences of level," woods and towns—were issued by Granger on March 15, showing his consistent interest in obtaining good intelligence: "Officers intrusted [sic] with collecting and transmitting this information should re-member that they are performing one of the highest functions of the service, that they lead and guide every step of the army, and that its success and safety depends on their faithfulness, intelligence and candor."[24]

Grant, meanwhile, was still finding time to try to get rid of Granger, complaining on March 14 to Stanton: "I am very much dissatisfied with General Canby. He has been slow beyond excuse. I wrote to him long since that he could not trust Granger in command. After that he nominated him for the command of a corps. . . . I would like now to have Steele, as I recom-mended long since in a dispatch addressed to General Halleck, put in com-mand of the Thirteenth Corps."[25]

Grant often complained about the slowness of subordinates such as Granger, Canby, Rosecrans and Thomas. In December, he had actually dis-patched a replacement, Major General John ("Blackjack") Logan, to relieve Thomas, who only saved his job by beginning the Battle of Nashville before Logan arrived at his headquarters. It is worth noting in defense of these of-ficers that the Army of the Potomac, under Grant's command, had by March spent the past nine months besieging Petersburg, Virginia. Grant's slow progress there may in part explain his unwillingness to tolerate "slowness" of generals elsewhere, as a sort of psychological defense mechanism.

Staff officer Captain Stephen Cobb, writing after the war, paints a vivid defense of his commander at this time: "Major-General Gordon Granger deserves more honorable mention than he has received since the war. At the time of which I write, he was unfortunate in having a difference with the General-in-Chief. Since then he has been unfortunate in his political opin-ions and actions, and in his friendship for the late President Johnson. Writers knowing all this—for it is his misfortune not to be able to control his likes and dislikes—have tabooed him. His heroism at Chickamauga, where, as the right arm of Thomas, he performed prodigies of valor; his gallantry at Mis-sionary Ridge, and in every battle in which he participated, history must record. Granger was a brave soldier, a true patriot, fit to command."[26]

Granger's Thirteenth Corps commenced the new Mobile campaign on March 17, moving out from Fort Morgan east and then north. As he had experienced in the Island No. 10 campaign three years earlier, the Union troops had to wade through swamps and wet weather and corduroy the road—to avoid quicksand this time. Soldiers had to haul animals, wagons and guns out of the mire, with Granger himself, Andrews says in his memoir, "lending a hand at the ropes." They built a pontoon bridge over Fish River and had two minor skirmishes over the next few days. The Sixteenth Corps had an easier time moving up the bay by boat.

The Thirteenth Corps bridged two more streams, and on the evening of the 26th Granger ordered his skirmishers forward and they ran into resistance. The Rebels were driven off, but, says Andrews: "Granger, being in the advance, narrowly escaped; for it was dark, and he was a few moments between the fire of his own reserves and that of the Confederates."[27] Granger ordered the 21st Iowa to hold the advanced position, relieving it at midnight with another regiment.

The next morning, Veatch's division of Thirteenth Corps was attacked by a vigorous sortie as the Confederates strove to gain time to improve their defenses. But they were soon pushed back toward Spanish Fort, which encompassed batteries and other defensive works including one known as Fort McDermott. Spanish Fort was now besieged and assaulted by A.J. Smith's and about half of Granger's corps, with Canby in overall command. Benton's division took the lead for the Thirteenth Corps, pushing the defenders back to Spanish Fort. Union artillery was brought up and commenced firing.

Granger was in the advance, and kept the troops pressing on. "During the day," Andrews relates, "Granger with a staff officer rode along the line of skirmishers, attracting a fire which struck down the orderly bearing the corps colors."[28] Thirteenth Corps was on the left, its left flank at the bay and its right connecting to the Sixteenth Corps. For several days Granger was put in command of a neighboring brigade next to the Thirteenth Corps' position. When it was returned to Smith on April 3, Granger had to spread out his line accordingly. Canby's command arrangements were fluid, with some of Granger's troops going to serve under Steele, and another brigade of Smith's coming under Granger's command until April 13.

Canby did not yet press the assault home, and Spanish Fort remained for the moment in Rebel hands. Granger had mortars shipped up the bay from Fort Morgan. The besiegers dug trenches and roads, fortifications and gun platforms, advancing in darkness and fighting off occasional Confederate sorties.

Granger was by now very familiar with this form of warfare, and had plenty of scope for his favored practice of directing artillery. A battery of four mortars was brought up, says Andrews, and on April 3 "opened in the afternoon in a satisfactory manner in presence of Gen. Granger and several other officers, the first two shells being dropped directly on the top of the parapet of [Fort] McDermott."[29] The next day, this same battery "exploded a caisson in McDermott, which produced a loud cheer among the besiegers."[30]

The corps' guns were directed both at the large fort and at rebel gunboats and batteries in the bay which were shelling the besiegers. One shell from a gunboat killed six men of the Thirteenth Corps and wounded seven, according to *The New York Times*. The U.S. Navy could give only limited support, since its ships could not move close enough up the bay.

Granger's report on the campaign gives detailed accounts of artillery placement, including how and why different types of guns were placed and sometimes replaced. On April 4, he sent the following written order to the captain commanding the 18th New York Battery: "I send you a detail to extend your right so as to complete six embrasures. You will add temporary platforms to correspond with the embrasures, so as to enable your guns to be used to the front and flank as circumstances may require."[31] Says Blackford: "The siege of Mobile was in one respect an operation after Granger's own heart in that it enabled him to indulge his passion for big guns."[32]

Nor was the infantry idle, being busy digging trenches ever closer to the fort, and constructing gun platforms and fortifications topped by logs. Despite the protections, casualties, though low by Civil War standards, were already much higher than they had been at Forts Gaines and Morgan the year before. Up to and including April 4, the Thirteenth Corps had lost 26 killed and 177 wounded.

Veatch's division was sent with a supply train to meet Steele's force, which was heading west from Pensacola. On April 3 it joined Steele's mostly African-American soldiers in investing Fort Blakely. According to Canby, "by the afternoon of the 5th Spanish Fort and Blakely were both included in the same general line of investment. In the meantime the works against Spanish Fort had been diligently pushed forward, although sharply contested by the enemy at all points." Granger now had a division and a brigade of his corps engaged in the siege.

On April 6, says Andrews, "Granger ordered the two thirty-pounders of Capt. Armstrong's battery (First Indiana) to be brought to bear in an enfilading fire upon the garrison's rifle-pits in front of Red fort. The embrasures not admitting of this, Armstrong proposed to move one of his guns out on open ground some yards to the left, whence there would be good range. After some hesitation, permission was given him to do this." This forced the retreat of Confederate sharpshooters from their trenches. When their fellow sharpshooters opened up on Armstrong's gun from in front of McDermott, they were 800 yards away and did no damage. "Meantime, a rope was attached to the trail of the gun, and men placed in readiness to haul it into the works in case the garrison guns opened upon it."[33]

Says Stanley: "Granger was everywhere—in the trenches, superintending the construction of batteries, placing guns in position, directing their fire; and all the time, pushing up with his left until he had got within a hundred yards of the parapet. His activity was untiring, and his indifference to exposure almost reckless."[34]

On April 8, Colonel Henry Bertram's brigade of the Thirteenth Corps moved up within 100 yards of the fort, and three more guns were brought to bear on Granger's front. The final Union bombardment lasted two hours from 5:30 p.m. Canby had planned an infantry assault for next morning, but the corps commanders had discretion to press any prior advantage. On the evening of the eighth, Carr's division of Sixteenth Corps broke through the Rebel line, followed by other troops including Granger's. Bertram's brigade claimed to capture Fort Alexis, part of the Spanish Fort complex, and raised the U.S. flag there at 12:30 a.m. on April 9—although Smith claimed it was captured by his Sixteenth Corps.

Brig. General Eugene Carr, who commanded a Sixteenth Corps division, sent a message to Granger later that day: "Your men are contending with mine for possession of the captured guns and works. Let us wait until the rebels are whipped before we quarrel amongst ourselves." While Carr seemed good-humored, Granger, perhaps remembering Sheridan's dispute with Hazen after Missionary Ridge, sent a reply at once serious and designed to defuse any controversy: "I am sorry our men are contending for so small a matter as the possession of guns which the enemy has abandoned. General Canby ordered one of my brigades to take possession of all property in Fort Alexis and Spanish Fort. Perhaps your men are not aware of the order."[35]

Canby's forces captured more than 500 prisoners and close to 50 guns in Spanish Fort, but most of the garrison escaped to Fort Blakely and Mobile.

Blakely itself came under increasing pressure from April 2, with similar advancement of trenches and artillery, digging up mines ("torpedoes," which caused significant Union casualties, especially during and after the assault), and fending off sorties from the garrison. At both Spanish Fort and Blakely, much of the fighting and digging was done at night.

The besieging troops showed some of the characteristics of later generations of GIs. At the approach to one trench, Andrews says, "the soldiers with characteristic humor had put up in it a sort of guide-board," which consisted of a drawn hand pointing to the words, "To Blakely".[36]

On the ninth, immediately following the fall of Spanish Fort, Granger was ordered to move his Third Division to the siege of Blakely, where it formed with a brigade of the First Division the right flank of the investing army, with its right on the bay. Blakely was subjected to an all-out assault that day. Steele's African-American troops took the lead and suffered heavy losses. Troops from the Thirteenth Corps made up about half of the 16,000 attackers, where they were under Steele's command. Reported Granger: "Of the splendid behavior of the troops I was a witness."

Thirteenth Corps troops played a major role in storming the fort. Andrews said resistance was heavier than expected; however, the Confederates were swiftly overrun all along the line after intense and costly fighting. Reported Canby: "With a gallantry to which there were no exceptions the troops pressed forward under a heavy fire of artillery and musketry, passing over exploding torpedoes, net-works, and abatis, and assaulted and carried the enemy's works in about twenty minutes, each division carrying the works in its front."[37] Confederate prisoners numbered about 3,500.

With Mobile now indefensible, Maury evacuated his army, marching northwest on April 10. Granger marched two of his divisions at night 10 miles south to take ship across the bay. On the morning of April 12th, they were transported to a point about five miles below Mobile.

Granger and Rear-Admiral Henry K. Thatcher (Farragut's successor) had sent a brief message to Mayor Robert H. Slough: "Your city is menaced by a large land and naval force. We deem it proper to demand its immediate and unconditional surrender"[38]—which the mayor granted. While the troops marched north, one of Granger's staff officers and a naval lieutenant-commander went in advance to accept the city's surrender.

Granger himself entered Mobile on his headquarters boat that afternoon, April 12, avoiding torpedoes and unmolested by the abandoned Rebel batteries. He ordered his troops "not to disturb people or property in or near Mobile. Many of the people are strongly Union, and troops will not be permitted to discriminate in treatment of citizens."[39] With the war almost over, there was no military purpose in treating civilians harshly. While some of that perceived pro-Union sentiment may have been inspired by the Confederate collapse, Granger's order was nevertheless in the magnanimous spirit of Lincoln, who would be assassinated two days later. Nor was he wrong about the existence of pro-Union sentiment, as Cobb, who was travelling with the corps commander, relates:

"The scene that met our view, as we moored the boat at the foot of Government Street, was as novel as it was exciting. This street is the widest and the best street in Mobile. Some two hundred yards up the street, at the crossing of Royal Street, was assembled a motley crowd of five thousand people of both sexes and all ages and colors. In doubt as to our mission or intention, they maintained a breathless silence until the white flag was run up beside the emblem of our nationality, when, with one tremendous cheer, that awoke the echoes in their deserted forts, they rushed down to the 'Yankee vessel'— to it, on board it, over it, through it, everywhere.

"The majority of our visitors were loud in their demonstrations of gladness at our coming. Some were silent—a part with malice and hate, others too overjoyed to give utterance to their feelings.... Taking a dilapidated carriage, the general and his staff rode to the Battle House, established headquarters, posted pickets throughout the city, and breakfasted on corn bread, rye coffee and spoiled bacon. Thus the last city of importance in the kingdom of Jeff Davis had ceased to be of the Southern Confederacy."[40]

Granger ordered Mobile's stores to reopen and instituted a curfew of 10 p.m., extending it to midnight on April 17. The Army was now responsible for law and order, there being no longer a functioning court system.

On April 13 Granger's Third Division of the Thirteenth Corps clashed with Maury's rear-guard at Whistler Station, preventing the Confederates from burning a bridge over Eight Mile Creek. Eight days later it captured the Mount Vernon Arsenal, and, continuing north on April 26–27, occupied McIntosh Bluff on the Tombigbee River. Granger, based in Mobile, also was responsible for territory to the north and west of the Tombigbee. On April 24 he told Benton, in command of the Third Division, that he was sending him 250 cavalry to help attack Confederate outposts guarding railroad supplies, and Benton moved to do so two days later. Recognizing the imminent end of the war, Granger told him, "I do not wish the railroad destroyed unless it should be absolutely necessary." He was appointed commander of the Mobile District.

Richard Taylor and Canby agreed to a truce on April 30, and Taylor formally surrendered on May 4. On May 5, Canby had Granger send troops back to Pascagoula, to protect the area and the New Orleans telegraph line from guerrillas. The same day, Granger sent orders to subordinates confirming that Taylor had surrendered to Canby and telling them to cease hostile operations, "waging war only against marauders."[41] He also moved troops around, sending some to Citronelle, about 40 miles northwest of Mobile, and withdrawing Benton's division back from the Tombigbee to Mobile. Following the end of hostilities, Granger dealt with Taylor on issues relating to the surrender. He followed instructions from Canby on superseding former Confederate civil authorities and preserving their records—tasks he would soon be doing on a grander scale in Texas.

Canby reported total casualties in the campaign of 1,678, including 232 killed. The Thirteenth Corps' share was 643, including 86 killed. About half the corps' casualties came under Steele at Fort Blakely (and a small portion of the Sixteenth Corps' casualties came from units serving under Granger). Confederate prisoners numbered over 5,000, not counting those surrendered at the end of the war.

Grant in his memoirs complained about delays in the 1865 campaigns under the command of Canby and Thomas (Wilson's massive cavalry raid through Alabama to Georgia came under Thomas' remote command). Grant said their successes came too late to do any good.

It's true that the Battle of Fort Blakely happened the same day as Lee's surrender of the Army of Northern Virginia, when Grant nobly ordered his troops not to celebrate, saying, "The war is over; the rebels are our countrymen again." And the war was over at Appomattox—but not in the rest of the country.

None of the participants at Blakely knew about Lee's surrender. The Union troops were informed about that time of the fall of Richmond. News traveled still more slowly in the collapsing Confederacy, where there were still plenty of Rebel soldiers able and willing to fight. They became less willing as the hopelessness of further resistance sunk in, a realization materially helped by Union successes in Alabama. Although President Davis was insisting that the conflict be continued, if necessary by guerrillas, he did not carry his people with him. When Forrest, for example, on May 9 urged his troops to surrender and obey Federal authority, he said: "That we are beaten is a self-evident fact."[42] The Mobile campaign helped make it so, and thus to end the war.

Stanton recognized this in a May 16 congratulatory message to Canby, saying, "the brilliant success of your achievements has exercised an influence that cannot be overestimated in breaking the rebel power, destroying all hopes, and bringing their cause to ruin. The extensive preparations and vigorous defense of Mobile show that the rebel chiefs regarded it as their last refuge."[43]

In his report on the campaign, Granger as usual paid tribute to the unnamed officers and soldiers who bore its brunt: "Continually on the march, in the trenches or upon fatigue ... they have deserved by their services every honor and reward that is to be attached to duty well and faithfully done."[44] Granger, in turn, along with other senior commanders, was praised in Canby's report.

The good performance of the Thirteenth Corps followed a pattern of all Granger's commands. The corps' medical director, Charles White, reported how the "immense labor" of the initial march "was performed with energy, alacrity, and in high spirits.... The morale of the corps was admirable. ... The troops were of robust, full habit, showing high health."[45] They were well supplied and well led.

Mobile had not been much damaged by the war, but on May 25 it experienced a disaster when the Army's main ammunition dump exploded, killing several hundred people and starting fires that destroyed much of the city. The warehouse also contained many explosives recently surrendered by Taylor. It was and remains unclear whether the explosion was sabotage or accident, although the latter supposition is now generally accepted.

Granger, according to a *Mobile News* report, "went to the scene of destruction almost before the flying shells had ceased to explode, and immediately took steps for the relief of the sufferers and the safety of the city." Granger, said the paper, "has employed all available labor to rescue those still alive" underneath the rubble. Many were rescued by men initially still in danger from shells and bullets that continued to go off. "Thousands of men worked hour after hour among the debris, bringing forth one after another of the writhing and dead victims."[46]

Granger also issued orders for the evacuation of nonresident paroled prisoners, for the conscription of able-bodied unemployed men to assist in "cleaning the streets of the city," and said an officer would be designated to take charge of destitute women and children and provide for them. When Canby next day authorized distribution of military rations to the needy, and use of medical officers to treat the injured, Granger told him he had already taken those steps.

While trying to alleviate the grim aftermath of the warehouse disaster, Granger also complied with orders to send Veatch's division to New Orleans. The Thirteenth Corps and Granger would soon be on the move to their next assignment, in Texas. His sometime friend and subordinate, now a superior and confidant of Grant, wrote to him about this from New Orleans on June 3. "My dear Granger: I will be over to see you if possible in a day or two. P.H. Sheridan, Major-General."[47]

NOTES

1. *Personal Memoirs of U.S. Grant*, Vol. 2, (New York: Charles L. Webster & Co., 1886), 410.
2. *OR*, Vol. 39, Pt. 2, 144.
3. (David Stanley), *Society of the Army of the Cumberland, Fifteenth Reunion* (Cincinnati: Robert Clarke & Co., 1884), 219.
4. James P. Duffy, *Lincoln's Admiral: The Civil War Campaigns of David Farragut* (New York: John Wiley & Sons, 1997), 232.
5. *OR*, Vol. 39, Pt. 2, 216.
6. Duffy, op. cit., 241.
7. *OR*, Vol. 39, Pt. 1, 418.
8. Ibid., 426.
9. Rufus Kinsley, ed. David C. Rankin, *Diary of a Christian Soldier* (Cambridge University Press, 2004), 162.
10. George H. Gordon, *A War Diary of Events in the War of the Great Rebellion* (Boston: James R. Osgood, 1882), 337.
11. *OR*, Vol. 45, Pt. 2, 418.
12. Ibid., 723.
13. A copy of the letter is in the files of the National Park Service at the Chickamauga battlefield museum, where I came across it in 2012. The ranger thought the "Great Mogul" was Lincoln, but I told him Granger must have meant Grant.
14. 2012 interview by author with Gordon Granger IV.
15. *OR*, Vol. 49, 580.
16. Ibid., 739.
17. *OR*, Vol. 48, Pt. 1, 1001.
18. Ibid., 1045.
19. Brooks Simpson, *Ulysses S. Grant, Triumph over Adversity, 1822–1865* (New York: Houghton Mifflin, 2000) 403.
20. *OR*, Series 2, Vol. 8, Pt. 1, 355.
21. Ibid., 362.
22. Ibid., 382.
23. Ibid., 396.
24. *OR*, Vol. 49, Pt. 1, 927.
25. *OR*, Vol. 48, Pt. 1, 1164.
26. Stephen A. Cobb, *The Siege of Mobile* (Beloit, WI: Beloit College Archives)
27. Christopher C. Andrews, *History of the Campaign of Mobile* (New York: Van Nostrand, 1889), 43.
28. Ibid., 58.
29. Ibid., 133.
30. Ibid., 140.
31. *OR*, Vol. 49, Pt. 2, 230.
32. Robert W. Blackford, *The Civil War Service of General Gordon Granger, U.S.A.*, unpublished master's thesis (Southern Illinois University, Edwardsville: 1990).

33. Andrews, op. cit., 144.
34. (David Stanley), *Society of the Army of the Cumberland, Fifteenth Reunion* (Cincinnati: Robert Clarke & Co., 1884), 223.
35. *OR,* Vol. 49, Pt.2, 303–4.
36. Andrews, op. cit., 191.
37. *OR,* Vol. 49, Pt. 1, 98.
38. Ibid., 144
39. *OR,* Vol. 49, Pt. 2, 340.
40. Cobb, op. cit.
41. *OR,* Vol. 49, Pt. 2, 625.
42. Nathan Bedford Forrest, quoted in J. Harvey Mathes, *General Forrest* (New York: D. Appleton, 1902), 352.
43. *OR,* Vol. 49, Pt. 1, 104.
44. Ibid., 144.
45. *OR,* Vol. 49, Additions and Corrections, 154.
46. Reprinted in June 4, 1865, *New York Times.*
47. *OR,* Vol. 49 , Pt.2 , 952.

9

"Juneteenth"

Granger had been told in May he was going to Texas. On May 26, General Buckner agreed to surrender Confederate troops west of the Mississippi River to General Canby, an act that was formalized by Kirby Smith, Confederate commander of the Trans-Mississippi, on June 2. By that date, Granger had 6,000 men waiting for transport ships to take them from Mobile to Galveston. The next day, he was ordered by Canby to report to Sheridan, who was now in New Orleans heading the Military Division of the Southwest.

Despite—or because of—the Confederate surrender, Texas was in a chaotic state of affairs. According to a June 4 report from Sheridan to Rawlins (Grant's chief of staff), almost all the Confederate troops had disbanded before the surrender. Some of their leaders, including Kirby Smith, were going into or at least contemplating exile in Mexico. That was a particular concern to Grant, and thus to Sheridan, because France had invaded Mexico during the Civil War, in violation of the Monroe Doctrine. The French-installed emperor, Maximilian, was currently engaged in a civil war, and Grant and Lincoln had sent the opposition some support. Now, with the Civil War over, Grant was inclined to do more, although the State Department was cautious. The ex-Confederates, on the other hand, were supporting Maximilian's forces, bringing them 14 artillery guns from Brownsville. Grant and others feared this alliance might spur new rebellion and fighting in America's biggest state.

On June 10 Sheridan telegraphed Granger: "There is not a very wholesome state of affairs in Texas. The Governor, all the [ex-Confederate] soldiers, and the people generally are disposed to be ugly."[1] Most of the Confederacy east of the Mississippi had been conquered by Federal troops, as the people there could plainly see. Union troops had also conquered some areas west of the big river, like Missouri and Arkansas. But that did not apply to Texas, whose future prospects remained clouded.

Granger, still in the Mobile area at Fort Morgan, was nonetheless engaged with his new command, dispatching troops on June 8 to south Texas ports including Brazos Santiago near the Mexican border, Corpus Christi and Indianola. These were mostly volunteer troops who would have much preferred to go home rather than to Texas now that the war was over. But they followed orders.

On June 13 Sheridan directed Granger: "On your arrival at Galveston assume command of all troops in the State of Texas; carry out the conditions of the surrender of General Kirby Smith to Major-General Canby; notify the people of Texas that in accordance with the existing proclamation from the Executive of the United States 'all slaves are free'; advise all such freedmen that they must remain at home; that they will not be allowed to collect at military posts, and will not be supported in idleness. Notify the people of Texas that all acts of the Governor and Legislature of Texas since the ordinance of secession are illegitimate. Take such steps as in your judgment are most conducive to the restoration of law and order and the return of the State to her true allegiance to the United States Government."[2]

A constitutional amendment abolishing slavery had passed Congress in January but was not ratified until the end of the year, so Sheridan's order regarding slavery was based on Lincoln's Emancipation Proclamation, which had taken effect at the beginning of 1863. That proclamation declared slaves free in states that were part of and controlled by the Confederacy, including Texas. It could only be enforced with the advance of Federal armies, which had made few inroads into Texas before the surrender. As a result, African-Americans there remained enslaved until after the end of the war, when economic conditions were poor, lawlessness was widespread and sources of reliable information scarce. Using the Emancipation Proclamation in this manner was a logical move, and not original with Sheridan. Another Union general, Edward McCook, had read the proclamation aloud on May 20 in Tallahassee, the capital of Florida, to announce the demise of slavery in that state.

Yet there was still widespread white resistance to the idea that slavery must end. The *Marshall Republican*, the most important weekly in east Texas, opined on June 16 about "the ruinous effects" of freeing slaves. The newspaper said the time would come when the people of the North "would be glad to witness a return to a system attended with more philanthropy and happiness to the black race than the one they seem determined at present to establish; for they will find that compulsory labor affords larger crops and a richer market for Yankee manufacturers. . . . the amendment to the Federal Constitution abolishing slavery has not been ratified by three-quarters of the States, nor is it likely to be in the ensuing ten years. When the State governments, therefore, are reorganized it is more than probable that slavery will be perpetuated."[3]

The *Houston Telegraph* took a somewhat different line, saying emancipation was inevitable but that a system of forced labor for blacks (paid, but presumably at a very low rate) was necessary and likely. Granger's new job would include disabusing the many holders of such notions, and communicating the new reality of slavery's complete end to whites and blacks alike.

Sheridan, however, was primarily concerned about pressuring Mexico and disrupting any potential alliance between Maximilian's forces and former Confederates. On June 16 he told Granger—now in New Orleans en route to Galveston—that as soon as possible after his arrival he should instruct Major General Steele in south Texas "to demand of the commander of the French forces in Matamoras the return of all arms and munitions of war taken to Matamoras by the rebels, or obtained from them since the date of the surrender of General E. Kirby Smith. He need not proceed to hostilities to obtain them, but report the reply received to these headquarters for further instructions."[4]

Granger arrived on June 17th with 1,800 troops in Galveston, which is toward the northern end of the Texas coast. He issued general orders saying "the undersigned assumes command of all troops within the State of Texas." (Those troops included another U.S. Army contingent which on the same date, June 17, occupied Marshall, across from northern Louisiana.[5]) Granger was now commander of the District of Texas, with headquarters at Galveston. It was not strange territory to him, for as a junior Army officer in his thirties he had spent much of the 1850s in Texas. As in his other post-Civil War assignments in the South and New Mexico, his effectiveness was increased by his familiarity with the areas from prior active service.

In October 1862, Farragut had sent an expedition to capture Galveston, the biggest port in the state and not far from the city of Houston (then inland). Galveston was retaken by the Confederates on January 1, 1863. Farragut, who was focused on the Mississippi River campaign, wisely decided to leave it in Rebel hands. Union forces made various other forays into Texas, but all were ultimately unsuccessful, and the state remained under Confederate control until the end of the war. The war's last skirmish was in Texas on May 12–13 at Palmito Ranch, and was a Confederate victory. Most Confederate troops avoided surrendering in person to Federal authorities. But as spring advanced it became ever more apparent that their cause was doomed, which prompted widespread desertion and mutiny, and associated riots and looting. Following Kirby Smith's surrender on June 2, the U.S. Navy had raised the stars and stripes over the Galveston courthouse on June 5.[6] It now fell to Granger to institute a Federal occupation of the country's largest state, one that had never been conquered by the Union Army, and that not long before the war had been an independent nation. Many white Texans did not feel defeated, and were not inclined to comply with Federal orders and laws, especially regarding racial matters.

Two days later, on June 19th, Granger issued through his staff officer, Major F.W. Emery, three new general orders. The first of these, General Order No. 3, is the basis for the "Juneteenth" celebrations of slavery's end which continue to this day. It read:

"The people of Texas are informed that, in accordance with a proclamation from the Executive of the United States, all slaves are free. This involves an absolute equality of personal rights and rights of property between former masters and slaves, and the connection heretofore existing between them becomes that between employer and hired labor. The freedmen are advised to remain quietly at their present homes and work for wages. They are informed that they will not be allowed to collect at military posts and that they will not be supported in idleness either there or elsewhere."[7]

Granger apparently read this order aloud, possibly from the balcony of Ashton Villa where he and staffers were living. It follows Sheridan's instructions but goes further than them, in meaningful and constructive ways. It is also better written—and words mattered, as Lincoln had consistently shown. While Sheridan had told him to tell the slaves they were free but "must remain at home," Granger clarified and expanded the matter.

Sheridan's order had contained a contradiction: He proposed telling the slaves they were free but at the same time, for economic reasons and to preserve order, commanding them to stay at their places of enslavement. In much of the South, many slaves had run away to greet incoming Union troops, travelling with them, sometimes congregating at their posts and hoping to be economically supported by them. This was obviously not feasible in Texas, where the Army would have enough trouble supplying its own soldiers. There was also the danger of newly freed blacks who took to the roads falling victim to violence by armed former Confederates angry about emancipation and the outcome of the war.

Granger converted Sheridan's proposed command to the former slaves into a suggestion, meaning they were now unambiguously free. He told them that if they stayed at their former master's place they would now be in the position of "hired labor," and "advised" these newly free citizens to stay "at their present homes and work for wages." Most accepted this advice, according to Texas historian Randolph B. Campbell, but by no means all. The order spurred immediate ecstatic celebration in Galveston's African-American community, which spread across the state, along with considerable movement of the black population, often in search of relatives or employment or to escape oppressive conditions.

The number of blacks in Texas had grown substantially during the war, as slaves were brought there to avoid the Union armies. Granger's announcement told them and all Texans, former slaves and masters alike, that freedom had arrived. The word "Juneteenth" comes from June 19 in contemporary African-American parlance, and was a new word signifying a new world. Its continued recognition as a holiday celebrating the end of slavery in the United States has always been driven by black people.

"A careful reading of Granger's words," says Campbell, "suggested that freedmen could expect only limited assistance from the government."[8] While it's true enough that Granger retained, while modifying, the cautionary admonition to blacks in Sheridan's original order, he also went much farther than his commanding officer in declaring their civil rights.

Significantly, Granger's order crisply asserted the new existence of "an absolute equality of personal rights and rights of property between former masters and slaves." That meant no forced labor, whatever the opinion of the *Houston Telegraph*, and much more. It expressed what was then an extremely controversial position in Texas and throughout the white South, as the history of the next 100 years would demonstrate. Granger's words and actions prefigured the reforms soon to be passed in the 14th and 15th amendments to the U.S. Constitution. But the principles behind them did not win widespread acceptance for a great many years among whites in Texas (which would not soon ratify even the 13th Amendment abolishing slavery), nor in much of the rest of the South. Yet Granger also recognized and communicated the need for the freed slaves to work and keep the peace, and help rebuild the Texas economy.

"Given the size of Texas," says Campbell, "the relatively poor communication system, and the bitter hatred of many owners for the idea of emancipation, it is not surprising that some slaves remained in bondage for months after Juneteenth. . . . Most slaves greeted freedom with the joy that would be expected of people receiving the answer to a lifelong prayer. . . . In some cases, however, whites did not permit such celebrations. One slave reported that in Crockett the slave patrol whipped one hundred celebrants. Another described how he, when told of his freedom, leaped into the air to express his delight, whereupon his master pulled a pistol and fired several shots between his feet. Jump again, he said, and I will shoot you between the eyes."[9]

On the wharves of Galveston, where the news did not have to travel far and Army protection was nigh, there was no impediment to celebration: "Black men pitched their hats high in the muggy June air, scattering the sea gulls which hovered nearby. Men and women screamed, 'We's free! We's free!'"[10]

The reasons Granger's order created such a shock in Texas and beyond, reverberating in celebrations that continue into the 21st century, is both because it was the first official news of slavery's end, and it communicated a view of race relations that in a Southern context was nothing short of revolutionary. It also reflected the huge shift in Northern opinion during the war, including within the U.S. Army.

No longer was there substantial pro-slavery sentiment in the army, as there had been when Granger was dealing with the tense racial politics of front-line Kentucky. The shift was accelerated by the introduction of black troops in 1863. When Thomas was establishing the national cemetery at Chattanooga at the end of that year, a subordinate asked him if the dead soldiers should be buried in areas according to the state they were from. The Virginian famously replied: "No, no; mix 'em up, mix 'em up. I'm tired of states' rights."[11] Still, the gravestones of white soldiers buried there do identify the state regiment they served in. Those of the black soldiers do not, because they did not serve in state regiments. Their grave markers read USCT for United States Colored Troops. (Some blacks did serve in state regiments, but by mid-1863 "they were mustered directly into federal service."[12]) Many Union officers, including Thomas, had had reservations about employing black troops, but Thomas' doubts disappeared at the Battle of Nashville in December 1864, where he saw the bravery exhibited and the casualties suffered by the black troops serving under Steedman.

Granger had commanded some African-American soldiers in his 1864

Mobile campaign, and in 1865 his Thirteenth Corps included numerous USCT regiments. Granger had defended the interests of black prisoners of war, seeking to prevent their re-enslavement, in negotiations with Confederate General Maury in February and March. Then his black troops and others serving under Steele had performed well in the final Mobile campaign, showing particular courage in the storming of Fort Blakely. Now in Texas, black troops were occupying Galveston.

Granger exercised realistic political judgment on slavery and racial issues throughout the Civil War, and continued to do so in Texas. He was moving with and slightly ahead of the country, which was in the process of ratifying the 13th Amendment.

Abolitionists were a small, unpopular minority in 1861, when the antislavery Fremont, under whom Granger served, exceeded his orders in Missouri and had to be pulled back by Lincoln. Granger was no ideologue like Fremont, but a hard-bitten professional soldier. Yet four years of warfare had changed him and the nation. When Granger was not actually fighting the Confederates, he had often been grappling with issues of slavery and race relations. His policy changed with the president's, and Lincoln's Emancipation Proclamation at the beginning of 1863 was the clearest indication of that development. It had largely changed the meaning of the war, making it not just for preserving the Union but about the larger moral issue of extending freedom to slaves. Now, with the war over, Granger was trying to carry out the dead president's vision of a new birth of freedom in a rededicated nation, even in highly unreconstructed Texas. He was enforcing the end of the chattel system and pointing the way to a new era of race relations that the United States was compelled by the logic of events to adopt—albeit one that would be strenuously resisted for the next century. In Texas, "personal and vigilante violence were epidemic in the early postemancipation period,"[13] and white violence against blacks, often amounting to murder, would continue over the next few years.

Part of the white resistance was based on economics. With Granger's order, says historian Carl Moneyhon, "the labor system that had been the basis for the state's plantation economy disappeared, which raised critical questions about the economic and social future of Texas. Could landowners continue to grow profitable cotton crops without slave labor? If not, what would happen to the antebellum elites who depended on plantation wealth? In addition, what did freedom mean to a social hierarchy that had long placed blacks in subordination to whites?"[14]

Granger's orders threatened the continued economic dominance of major white landowners, most of whom doubted "an economic recovery could be managed with blacks as free laborers. Their racial views led them to believe that black laborers required coercion and had to be controlled. Granger threatened the implementation of any system of control when he indicated that the new relationship between masters and their former slaves would be one of employer and free laborer. Almost no white Texan could conceive of the freedmen working in such a relationship. . . . The general's action not only destabilized the state's economic future but also challenged the racial views of the community."[15]

Granger would soon be departing from Texas, after which the state went through the typical turmoil of Deep South Reconstruction. The Freedmen's Bureau arrived the month after Granger left, but ex-Confederates succeeded in blocking black voting rights and other progress. That led Republicans in Washington to impose a Radical government in Texas with the support of enfranchised blacks, but it did not last long. Blacks in Texas and much of the rest of the South wound up losing some of their new rights until the mid-20th century. Texas' record after the Civil War would be particularly problematic, as Granger would be one of the first to recognize in his 1866 report to President Andrew Johnson on conditions in the South. By then, though, Johnson was at odds with the Radicals, who also had no time for allies of the president such as Granger.

Nevertheless, Granger's famous order on June 19 is, with the exception of U.S. constitutional amendments, the most significant and influential statement of Radical principles in the postwar era. His orders that day showed the same vigorous, intelligent and productive independence he had demonstrated at Wilson's Creek, Chickamauga and other battlefields; and the same grasp of the changing realities and necessities governing slavery and race relations that he had shown throughout the war. He had been leery of abolition when it threatened to lose the border states and with them the war, but he embraced liberation now as the law of the land, the extirpation of the reason for rebellion, and the fulfillment of Lincoln's legacy.

That same day, June 19, Granger issued another general order declaring actions by the secession government illegitimate, requiring former Confederate soldiers and officials to report for parole and hand over public property to U.S. officers. Further, "All lawless persons committing acts of violence, such as banditti, guerrillas, jayhawkers, horse-thieves, &c., are hereby declared outlaws and enemies of the human race, and will be dealt with accordingly."[16] A third order sought to reopen and regulate the cotton trade through U.S. purchasing agents.

Granger also issued orders to Steele in south Texas, passing on Sheridan's instruction to demand the return of Confederate military supplies from Matamoras. Citing instructions from Grant, Granger also told Steele to establish posts on the Rio Grande as far inland as Roma, "to prevent robbers and plunderers passing with their spoils from Texas into Mexico. It is understood that extensive robberies are taking place in Texas, the property being conveyed into Mexico. The movement is supposed to be in the interests of the Imperialists [i.e. the French-backed government of Maximilian]."[17]

Through a staff officer, Granger also issued orders that day to the superintendent of the state penitentiary at Huntsville. The prison chief was to send to Granger's headquarters "all negroes now in your custody who have been placed there because of capture from the U.S. forces, or on account of the law of Texas under recent rule directing the imprisonment or assignment to master of all the free persons of color within the State. You will also send under proper escort all persons who are confined in the penitentiary solely on account of unfriendly disposition toward the late Confederate authority."[18] He was to submit a list of all prisoners with the reasons for their confinement.

Also on that busy June 19, Granger told Colonel F.W. Moore, commanding a brigade in the Second Division of the Thirteenth Corps, to occupy Houston with two regiments. "It is desirable that the troops leave as early as 6 o'clock tomorrow morning," the order read. The various actions taken by Granger on that extraordinary day demonstrate his substantial administrative ability as well as a realistic political vision to try to establish a just order in this vast and dangerously chaotic environment.

As commander of U.S. troops in Texas in the absence of civil authority, Granger was the military ruler of the state, but there weren't many soldiers to go around. While securing the coast, where supplies and reinforcements would be brought in, was a high priority, he also sent "small detachments to Austin, San Antonio, Tyler and Marshall."[19] On June 21 he ordered the collection of court records, and told an ex-Confederate court clerk to take a new oath enabling him to serve under the U.S. government. On June 29, he was directing a civilian, John Hancock, "to secure all public property, archives, records, &c., within the county of Travis, pertaining to the State and General Government"[20]—especially, he added, those of the land office, treasury and other executive departments.

On June 22 Granger ordered the occupation of Columbus, between

Houston and San Antonio, and Millikan, south of College Station. On June 30, he sent a lieutenant colonel to Indianola to expedite rebuilding the railroad and the wharves, and enforce the prior general orders. He was grappling with various problems, including the need for suitable boats to communicate with his coastal outposts, and a lack of forage for cavalry. On July 2 he told the president of the San Antonio and Mexican Gulf Railway that a line should be built to Victoria from Port Lavaca (near Indianola), and two days later ordered the 8th U.S. Colored Heavy Artillery to help do the work on it.

Texas was in economic crisis and public order was tenuous, with the former slaves particularly at risk. This led Granger and his staff to try to impose some restrictions on movements of freed backs while also seeking to establish humane employment contracts that recognized civil rights. So Provost Marshal Lt. Colonel Rankin Laughlin issued a June 26 order on Ganger's behalf, saying:

"All persons formerly slaves, are earnestly enjoined to remain with their former masters, under such contracts as may be made. For the present time, their own interests, as well as that of the former masters, or other parties requiring their services, render such a course necessary and of vital importance, until a permanent arrangement is made, under the auspices of the Freedmen's Bureau. It must be borne in mind in this connection, that cruel treatment, or improper use of employees will not be permitted, while both parties to the contract made, will be equally bound to fulfillment upon their part. No persons, formerly slaves, will be permitted to travel on the public thoroughfares without passes or permits from their employers, or to congregate in buildings or camps at or adjacent to any military post or town. They will not be subsisted in idleness, or in any way except as employees of the government, or in cases of extreme destitution or sickness; and in such case, the officer authorized to order issues shall be judge as to the justice of the claim for such subsistence. . . . humanity dictates that employment be furnished these people, while the commonwealth imperatively demands it, in order that the present crop may be secured."[21]

Laughlin's activities were reported in the Texas newspapers, which prompted a *New York Times* editorial, "The Negro Question in Texas." The *Times* praised Granger's General Order No. 3—"General Granger's order was right"—but added and concluded that he "will do well to see to it that proper obedience is rendered to his orders by his subordinates, as well as by the people of Texas."[22] This was, of course, easier said than done, and would remain so for the next century. The editorial implies that Laughlin was not properly obeying Granger's orders, which seems unlikely, and that Granger was not doing enough to enforce them—which was an easy criticism to make from a northern newspaper office. One of the motivations behind Laughlin's order was the protection of blacks, who were liable to be murderously attacked by ex-Confederates while travelling around Texas, and whom Granger did not have enough soldiers in the vast state to protect. Nor was the Freedmen's Bureau yet able to do anything to help the former slaves, since it did not establish a presence in Texas until September, a month after Granger's departure.

Meanwhile, says the historian Elizabeth Hayes Turner, "There is much evidence to suggest that southern whites—especially Confederate parolees—perpetrated more acts of violence against newly freed bondspeople in Texas than in other states."[23] According to another modern historian, Kenneth Howell, "By the late spring and summer of 1865, whites were beating, whipping and killing black Texans. Most of the freedpeople became victims of crimes because of their new status in society; they became victims of irrational racial hatred. In many cases the perpetrators were young men, most Confederate veterans. They hated the Yankees and the outcome of the war, and in their frustration they targeted freedpeople and white unionists."[24]

Granger tried to respond. On July 13, he told a brigade of the Fourth Corps at Indianola to move inland to Victoria and establish various outposts in the direction of San Antonio, "for the suppression of plundering, robbery, jayhawking, &c., throughout that section of the State."[25]

Although Granger was being reinforced, most of the new troops were being sent by his superiors to the Mexican border, not to protect freed slaves in the Texas interior. U.S. relations with Maximilian's imperial government of Mexico continued to be very tense as a result of the aggressive policy of Grant and Sheridan. The latter ordered Granger on July 5: "Get your troops on the Rio Grande in readiness for active service. Caution them, however, against provoking hostilities, and demand the surrender of all public property run across the Rio Grande since the first surrender. This will include batteries of artillery, means of transportation, cotton, &c. Make this demand, or cause it to be made at once, and furnish the reply to these headquarters promptly."[26] Sheridan remained on good terms with his new subordinate, addressing a routine order on July 6 to "My Dear Granger." The next day, Sheridan told him to occupy Sabine City, which Granger ordered done.

Grant had now turned his attention to Texas, which was not good news for Granger. A July 13 message from Grant to Sheridan reads in full: "I would like to go to the Rio Grande in person for a few days and manage affairs there according to your judgment. What you have done seems so well that I desire to change nothing. Do you not think it advisable to relieve Granger from command in Texas? If so, relieve him."[27] Grant here implicitly acknowledges that he has nothing to say against the management of Army affairs in Texas, but suggests relieving Granger anyway. Both Grant and Sheridan would become allies of the Radicals in the postwar struggle for black rights, yet at this time they removed the general who was most effectively pressing the Radical agenda. It is clear from Sheridan's memoirs that his main concern at this time was the situation in Mexico, not Texas, and he writes critically of the much less aggressive Mexican policy of the State Department under William H. Seward. Sheridan's headquarters for the Military Division of the Southwest was not in Texas, but the much more congenial location of New Orleans.

Mexico also was Grant's focus in the southwest. But the general-in-chief was increasingly aware that Texas was now a very important command, to which ever more U.S. troops were being sent, where they fell under the command of a man he disliked and in whom he had no confidence. Grant was well aware that Sheridan had served under Granger in the war, and probably wished to prevent any renewal of their previously close relations. The end of the war also had created a surplus of Army officers looking for employment, so there would be no difficulty coming up with a replacement.

Granger, meanwhile, continued to deploy his troops. He'd sent the First Division up the Red River, had the Second at Galveston, Houston, Millican and Columbus, and the Third with Steele in south Texas, mainly at Brazos de Santiago. In Houston, 50 miles northwest of Galveston, Granger "made himself accessible to all," says David Stanley, "listened with patience to every complaint, and lent counsel and assistance to the utmost in facilitating the transition from slave to free labor. That the critical period was passed without disturbance—the danger was at the outset—is due to the wisdom and prudence of his management."[28]

Earlier that year, Canby had defended Granger to Halleck by praising his administrative ability. Granger had demonstrated that ability in Texas, along with the clear and energetic approach demonstrated in his general orders. Three years previously, Granger had significantly aided the career of Sheridan, and the latter now expressed no objective reason to regret his decision to entrust the man he often called "My Dear Granger" with the command of Texas. However, Sheridan was also close to Grant, the still rising star, and had known since 1862 that Grant disliked Granger. He was not about to disregard the now clearly expressed preference of the commanding general.

So on July 15, Sheridan told Grant he would follow his suggestion: "I think it best that General Granger should be relieved. He never would have been where he is had it not been for General Canby and himself, who put his corps en route in a great hurry before I reached New Orleans. . . . I would suggest that he be ordered from Washington."[29] Grant sent a message back the same day ordering Granger's relief and suggesting as his replacement Horatio Wright, who got the job. (Wright, who ended the war as commander of the Army of the Potomac's Sixth Corps, had once been Granger's superior, working out of Cincinnati, when Granger led the Army of Kentucky.)

Accordingly, on July 19, a month to the day after "Juneteenth," Granger got two messages from staff officers of Sheridan. The key one was a general order saying: "In obedience to instructions from headquarters Armies of the United States Maj. Gen. Gordon Granger is hereby relieved from duty as commander of the District of Texas and will report by letter to the Adjutant-General of the Army for orders." A second message from Sheridan's chief of staff, Brig. General George Forsyth, purported to explain the order: "The major-general commanding directs me to inform you that information has been received at these headquarters from Washington that the Thirteenth Army Corps is to be consolidated and made into a division, which probably is the principal reason that directed the issue of the inclosed order."[30] The same day, Granger got a report that the wharf at Lavaca had been repaired and was ready to receive vessels. The work he had set in motion was ongoing.

As Granger continued in position for a transition period, he was able to transfer some of his responsibilities to a new civil authority in the person of Andrew J. Hamilton, the governor appointed by Johnson (and previously designated by Lincoln). Hamilton arrived at Galveston on July 2, and prepared to depart for Austin, the state capital. Granger, on Sheridan's orders, sent an escort and garrison with him. The stars and stripes were raised over Austin on July 25. Granger was also trying to collect former Confederate government property, only to find that much of it had been looted or lost. He continued to issue orders requiring collection of government records and their delivery to the new state government.

He left by ship for Mobile and New Orleans in early August.

The legacy of Granger's General Order No. 3, buttressed by the other orders he issued on that extraordinary day, has long endured. They enforced, reflected and prepared the way for a new framework of race relations. The reverberations have never ceased, which helps explain the strong roots and continued appeal of the Juneteenth holiday. Texas African-Americans celebrated it again on June 19, 1866, and, says Turner, "From the beginning, Freedom Day celebrations included church services in which preachers and educators reminded freedpeople of the sacred solemnity of the occasion, of their duty as emerging citizens, and of their profound right to the pursuit of legal equality. . . . Spirituals were the heart and soul of Juneteenth, including 'Free at Last,' 'Go Down Moses' and 'Many Thousands Gone,'" along with parades, picnics, speeches and sermons. Over the years, "It represented a public counter-demonstration to displays of Confederate glorification and a counter-memory to the valorization of the Lost Cause."[31]

This movement wasn't just feel-good fluff, but had real-world consequences. Texas' Juneteenth legacy of African-American empowerment was not lost after Reconstruction, in contrast to most of the South. "Indeed," says the modern historian Steven Hahn, "a far greater number of African-Americans held state and county offices in Texas after the collapse of Reconstruction than during it."[32]

Juneteenth became an official Texas holiday in 1979, and is now recognized to some extent by about 42 American states and the District of Columbia.

Presidents including George W. Bush mentioned Granger in Juneteenth proclamations. The pattern has been continued by the Unites States' first black president, Barack Obama, whose first such statement, in 2009, began: "On this day in 1865, more than two years after President Lincoln signed the Emancipation Proclamation, those who found themselves still enslaved in Galveston, Texas had their hopes realized and their prayers answered. Contrary to what others had told them, the rumors they had heard were indeed true. The Civil War had ended, and they were now free.

"General Gordon Granger issued the call . . ."[33]

Granger's name also can be found everywhere from the petition to make Juneteenth a "National Day of Reconciliation and Healing from the Legacy of Enslavement," to the letters of schoolchildren doing assignments. For all the official efforts and endorsements, Juneteenth remains a people's holiday, begun by freed slaves, and for the most part continued by their descendants.

The African-American writer Ralph Ellison, author of *Invisible Man*, spent the next four decades and more trying to complete a novel, *Juneteenth*, which was published after his death in the 1990s. The central character is a wise old preacher, Alonzo Hickman, whom Ellison's notes say comes out of "the betrayal of Reconstruction," and "foreshadows Martin Luther King."[34]

Juneteenth is celebrated, Hickman says, "Because we haven't forgot what it means. Even if sometimes folks try to make us believe it never happened or that it was a mistake if it ever did."[35] Later, he says: "Blood spilled in violence doesn't just dry and drift away in the wind, no! It cries out for restitution, redemption."[36]

Neither Granger nor, as it turned out, anyone else in the 19th century had the power to pacify Texas so as to guarantee the civil rights of African-Americans. But his bold stance in the brief time he was there in 1865 had permanent, significant and positive results.

NOTES

1. *OR,* Vol. 48, Pt. 2, 841.
2. Ibid., 866-67.
3. Quoted by Charles W. Ramsdell in *Texas From the Fall of the Confederacy to the Beginning of Reconstruction* in *The Quarterly of the Texas State Historical Association,* Vol. 11 (Austin, TX: 1908), 215.
4. *OR,* Vol. 48, Pt. 2, 902.
5. Randolph B. Campbell, *Gone to Texas: A History of the Lone Star State* (New York: Oxford University Press, 2003), 268.
6. David G. McComb, *Texas, a Modern History* (Austin: University of Texas Press, 2010), 75.
7. *OR,* Vol. 48, Pt. 2, 929.
8. Campbell, op. cit, 269.
9. Ibid.
10. Muriel Miller Branch, *Juneteenth: Freedom Day* (New York: Cobblehill, 1998), 16.
11. *The Civil War: A Book of Quotations,* ed. Blaisdell (Mineola, NY: Dover, 2004), 127.
12. Steven Hahn, *A Nation Under Our Feet: Black Political Struggles in the Rural South from Slavery to the Great Migration* (Belknap Press of Harvard University Press, 2003), 94.
13. Ibid., 394.
14. Carl H. Moneyhon, *Texas After the Civil War: The Struggle of Reconstruction* (Texas A&M: 2004), 8.
15. Ibid., 19.
16. *OR,* Vol. 48, Pt. 2, 929.
17. Ibid., 930.
18. *OR,* Series 2, Vol. 8, 659.
19. Smallwood, Crouch, Peacock; *Murder and Mayhem: the War of Reconstruction in Texas*

(Texas A&M: 2003), 10.

20. *OR,* Vol. 48, Pt. 2, 1026.
21. *The New York Times,* July 16, 1865.
22. Ibid., July 9.
23. Elizabeth Hayes Turner, *Juneteenth: Emancipation and Memory,* in *Lone Star Posts: Memory and History in Texas,* ed. Cantrell and Turner (Texas A&M Press, 2007), 147.
24. Kenneth W. Howell, *The Prolonged War,* in *Texans and War: New Interpretations of the State's Military History,* ed. Mendoza and Grear (Texas A&M Press, 2012), 199-200.
25. *OR,* Vol. 48, Pt. 2, 1075.
26. Ibid., 1050.
27. Ibid., 1075.
28. (David Stanley), *Society of the Army of the Cumberland, Fifteenth Reunion* (Cincinnati: Robert Clarke & Co., 1884), 224.
29. *OR,* Vol. 48, Pt. 2, 1081.
30. Ibid., 1093, for both messages.
31. Turner, op. cit., 152, 154, 145.
32. Hahn, op. cit., 394.
33. The White House Office of the Press Secretary.
34. Ralph Ellison, *Juneteenth.* Ed. John Callahan. (New York: Random House, 1999), 353, 356.
35. Ibid., 114.
36. Ibid., 271.

10

Postwar Service in the South and West

Soldiers, especially professional ones who survived the Civil War, recognized that it was highly unlikely anything they would do in the rest of their public lives would match the significance of their wartime service. For Granger, the opportunity for significant action extended into the summer of 1865. But eventually, for almost every officer who stayed in the Army, the drastically shrunken peacetime service would mean much reduced rank and prospects. That applied more than most to Granger, who was on bad terms with the army's commander, Grant, and by extension could expect little favor from his senior acolytes such as Sherman and Sheridan.

Yet the Army was what he knew, and his prospects were uncertain in the civilian world. Many soldiers would angle for political appointments, and Granger did try to make use of his connections to President Johnson, whom he had known as the wartime governor of Tennessee when the general helped protect the governor's family in the eastern part of the state. Many other Civil War commanders wrote their memoirs, and, in a highly literate age, Granger was one of those generals who had shown a talent for writing orders and reports. But Granger would not have wanted to write some anodyne autobiography skating over his conflicts with superiors such as Grant, and so it would make sense to postpone any book until after retirement, when it could not further damage his career prospects. He did not live long enough to retire, and thus there is no Granger memoir.

Granger's health, never strong, had not been improved by his wartime experiences. As it deteriorated, it gave him more reasons both to get out of the Army and to stay in it, where at least he had the option of taking sick leave with the possibility of returning to work. He also married late in life, and the support of his young family became the prime consideration of his later life, also tending to keep him in the Army.

In the immediate aftermath of the war and his service in Texas, Granger seems to have been somewhat adrift. *Cullum's Register* lists him as commander of the Department of Kentucky from Aug. 12, 1865, to Jan. 15, 1866, and a *New York Times* list says he was mustered out of the volunteer service from there, where he was serving under Major General John Palmer—but it does not appear to be the case that any of this purported service actually happened. Palmer, a volunteer who was the military commander of Kentucky, had served briefly under Granger in the war, commenting in his memoir: "I disliked Granger, and submitted to that part of the arrangement only as a matter of duty."[1] Palmer's book does not say anything about serving with Granger in 1865–66. Nor do there appear to be any records in U.S. Returns From Military Posts, or newspaper accounts, of him serving there at that time.

The *New York Herald* reported in September that Granger was likely to be appointed to succeed Palmer in Kentucky, but for whatever reason the change was not made.[2] In January 1866, the *Herald* reported Granger was going to resign, but he didn't. He was mustered out of the volunteer service that month, temporarily reverting to his 1861 rank of captain in the Regular Army, but he did not serve as such. Technically, the mustering out put him on the books of the Third Cavalry Regiment, successor to the Mounted Riflemen, which included him on its reports from posts in Arkansas and later New Mexico, but he was not serving there either.

From January to April 1866, he is listed in *Cullum's Register* as "awaiting orders." In these postwar years, with repeated reorganizations of the shrinking army, Granger often had to wait for a command—not perhaps an altogether uncongenial position for someone worn out by war who could now experience the pleasures of eastern society in New York, Washington, Saratoga Springs or elsewhere. Nor was it that unusual, especially during that period, for army officers to move in and out of active service.

Thomas J. Wood wrote: "On ordinary occasions, when nothing of special importance demanded immediate attention, Granger's indisposition to action amounted occasionally almost to indolence; but when the necessity was urgent, the exigency pressing, the danger great and imminent, he always rose to the dignity and importance of the occasion—became instinct with energy, ardor, and intrepidity, and martial daring, and was as fertile of resources as he was full of enterprise."[3] For better or worse, these years provided limited scope for urgent activity.

He was drifting into President Johnson's orbit, and would acquire the reputation of being what one hostile newspaper called "a political general." (As Reconstruction politics grew more bitter, so did the characterizations. A few years later a Radical paper referred to "the demoralizing influence of such half-rebel Generals as [Winfield Scott] Hancock, Gordon Granger, and [Alvan] Gillem."[4]) He must have met with Johnson in August and/or September 1865 to discuss Kentucky, and may have begun that fall to perform functions directly under the president's authority, as he would continue to do off and on for the rest of Johnson's term.

Granger's relationship with Johnson was based on personal loyalty to the man who had salvaged his career in 1864, and his continuing professional interest in finding a counterweight to Grant's hostility. In April 1866 he went on what *Cullum's Register* describes as a leave of absence, but in reality was a special mission on Johnson's instructions. The president, Granger wrote later that year, sent him on a journey "to examine carefully into the disposition of the people of the Southern States through which I might pass, toward the Government of the United States." In August Granger produced a report, *The Southern People*, which was published and attracted some notice in the newspapers.[5]

He was travelling just before the explosive growth of the Ku Klux Klan, and so was able to report he "found no sign or symptom of organized disloyalty." While his report was generally positive, he did note the existence of "an utterly irresponsible class, composed mainly of young men who were the 'bucks' of Southern society before the war, and chiefly spent their time in lounging around the courtrooms and bars, in chicken fighting and gambling." Those not killed in the war, Granger said, "are still disturbing elements in the community, and are doing much mischief. It is this class of men, and a number of the poor whites, who have formed gangs for horse-stealing. It is they who in some instances have made attacks on officers of the Freedmen's Bureau, and have ill-treated the freedmen."

He acknowledged that "cases of authentic outrage have occurred in the South," but said they are "few and far between." That may have been true at the time, when the South had not yet deteriorated into widespread white terrorism, but Granger may have been sugarcoating what he said to appease Johnson's prejudices. On the other hand, Grant had delivered a report to

Johnson the previous December—after a shorter Southern tour than Granger's—which said some of the same things, e.g. "the mass of thinking men in the South accept the present situation of affairs in good faith."[6]

Granger also was willing to criticize policies and actions of the U.S. government, which he said had contributed to Southern disaffection and lawlessness. Thus he cited "Treasury agents who, with their accomplices and imitators, fleeced the people right and left," and failed to send most of the proceeds to the government. The Freedmen's Bureau had agents, Granger said, who added "their quota of extortion and oppression. On every hand the people saw themselves robbed and wronged by agents and self-appointed agents professing to act under the sanction of the United States Government." Radical Republicans would have done well to take these criticisms seriously, because the laudable goals of Reconstruction were being undermined by the kinds of abuses Granger cited at the start of what would become a corrupt era, to be known as the Gilded Age, across many areas of American public life. Unfortunately, in the increasingly polarized political climate, and despite their shared outlook in Texas the previous year, the Radicals wrote Granger off as an ally of their enemy, the president.

Granger's report said that most Southern states, with the exceptions of Mississippi and Texas, had moved to protect civil rights. He closed by calling for "greater political, social and commercial freedom, more frequent intercourse, and a kinder appreciation of each other's peculiarities. The advantages to the country in its present financial stress of a reunion of heart and sentiment would be beyond enumeration. The broad lands of the fertile South are now lying almost in waste for want of means and capital to cultivate them, when every acre of the beneficent soil might be a gold mine to its possessor, were the political relations of the people better understood and acted upon."

The report is reasonably balanced, inclining more to the views of Johnson than his Radical Republican opponents, thus retreating a bit from the bold agenda of Juneteenth; but not endorsing the president's more extreme views such as opposition to black suffrage. Many soldiers who had fought for the Union shared Granger's desire for reconciliation with their former enemies, seeking to avoid lasting bitterness, enmity and conflict. Many of them, including both Granger and Grant, wanted to do this at the same time as they guaranteed and protected the rights of African-Americans in the South. Even as he became the Radicals' presidential candidate in 1868, Grant ran on the slogan, "Let Us Have Peace," a sentiment that could appeal to almost everyone. But in the tragic absence of Abraham Lincoln, those twin goals of true peace and civil rights proved impossible to reconcile. They were to remain so for almost another hundred years.

In September 1866, Granger and another former major general still in the Regular Army, George Armstrong Custer, helped organize a "soldiers' convention" in Cleveland to support the Johnson administration. The convention elected Granger its president. While in Johnson's camp, he was not then written off as a pawn of the U.S. president, who reportedly favored Generals John Wool or James Steedman, not Granger, as his candidate to lead the convention.[7]

Meanwhile, Granger had been named colonel of the 25th Infantry, effective July 28. This was a newly consolidated regiment, but its new colonel continued on leave of absence. Staying a good deal in New York City, he was lobbying Johnson for appointments such as naval officer of the port of New York, to succeed General John Dix, but he could not match the influence of Tammany Hall politicians. Earlier in the summer, he had been considered a likely "candidate for a mission to The Hague, when it becomes vacant,"[8] but like other potential presidential appointments, this one failed to materialize. In January of 1867 he suffered an attack of acute retinitis, an ailment that would by 1873 leave him blind in the left eye. He submitted a report to the army from a surgeon saying he could not leave New York for at least two months.

Congress was at odds with Johnson and already contemplating impeachment. The House Judiciary Committee summoned Granger in March, but his testimony did not create waves except among subsequent generations of anti-Masonic writers, since he confirmed in passing that Johnson was a freemason.

In April, he wrote to Johnson suggesting the president appoint a commission to examine militia changes in Europe, on which Granger hoped to serve. This proposal drew disapproval from Grant and a message from him to Stanton, saying Granger "has already received unusual and extraordinary indulgences"—and the general-in-chief had a point. Granger did seem to be avoiding service with his regiment. Granger, Grant further complained, "sends his application direct to the President instead of communicating through the regular military channel: a violation of the Army regulations which is inexcusable in an officer of his experience and length of service."[9] On August 8, a staffer writing on Grant's behalf moved to stop Granger's pay because of his "unauthorized absence."

There was also speculation that he would be named to head the Freedmen's Bureau to replace Oliver O. Howard, with one hostile newspaper complaining he "is only a Colonel in the regular service, who got up at the Johnson Soldiers' Convention at Cleveland last year, and who has ever since been revolving about the White House, and attending to politics, though ordered to join his regiment."[10]

Finally, on September 1, 1867, Granger did report for duty in his Regular Army assignment, leading the 25th Infantry Regiment as commander of the District of Memphis. He was again serving under his old wartime leader George Thomas, who headed the Department of the Cumberland with headquarters in Louisville, Kentucky.

Memphis was the home of Nathan Bedford Forrest, who by now had helped found the Ku Klux Klan. The city had been the scene of a bad race riot the year before, in which 46 blacks and two whites were killed and the army commander, George Stoneman, was criticized for his tardy response. But that hadn't stopped blacks from flocking to the city, where Granger and his soldiers were atop a potential tinder box—but one they did not permit to ignite on their watch. Granger's long experience with thorny racial issues in the South no doubt served him well, along with his good relationship with Thomas. Despite his Southern roots, Thomas had turned into a firm supporter of black rights in Reconstruction, and an opponent of the Klan. He also, like Granger but unlike Grant, remained on good terms with Johnson, which enabled him to avoid unwelcome presidential interference.

While Granger was carrying out Thomas' orders in Memphis, he also seems to have veered uncomfortably close to Johnson's racial agenda, sending the president a message on January 3, 1868 that read: "Memphis redeemed. [John] Leftwich elected Mayor. Peace, order and quiet prevail. Free white suffrage vindicated." The president telegraphed back enthusiastically the same day: "Thank you for the good news. Truth and justice must triumph. My faith in the people has not been diminished. The day is not distant when Tennessee will be redeemed."[11] Johnson was a more or less open racist, frankly opposed to black political participation including, in most cases, voting. His animus toward the Confederacy had been based largely on his hatred of the Southern upper class, but without corresponding affection for the region's downtrodden blacks.

While it may be that Johnson did not ultimately appoint Granger to head the Freedmen's Bureau or another sensitive position, or support him for president of the Cleveland convention, because they were not in full accord on crucial racial issues, the Memphis telegram makes clear that Granger was prepared to modify his Juneteenth-era racial radicalism. His reasons were not confined to playing politics in the hope of personal advantage. Like many war-weary Americans, including Republicans and ex-Union soldiers like Joshua Chamberlain,[12] he focused on reconciliation with the former Rebels, on moving from military government to restoring civilian rule and permanent peace—even if that meant not enforcing full civil rights for African-Americans. Still, it's likely that he sometimes disagreed with Johnson, and did not desist from a lifelong habit of forcibly expressing his opinions even when they conflicted with those of his superiors, which the president probably liked little more than Grant. But a time was fast approaching when Johnson would need all the help he could get, and would call on Granger for urgent assistance.

On January 25, 1868, Thomas telegraphed to Grant that Granger "absented himself from his Command early in this month without my knowledge or consent,"[13] and that his whereabouts were unknown. Granger apologized and offered an explanation to Thomas, who then recommended to Grant that the matter be dropped. On February 22, though, Grant was telegraphing Thomas asking why Granger was in Washington. Thomas replied the next day that Granger was on a 20-day leave, with permission to apply for an extension, "to attend to pressing private business."

That business involved the president of the United States, who saw to it that Granger's leave was extended. In April he was listed as the only Army officer on leave who was under the direct orders of Johnson. On May 1, Grant's office acknowledged Granger "is now absent with proper authority and entitled to draw his pay."[14]

Whatever Granger's differences with Johnson on racial or other issues, he was not about to desert the president at the crisis of his career: his impeachment by Congress. The Radical Republicans were trying to replace Johnson with one of their own, Senate President Pro Tempore Ben Wade, in what many Americans then and since regarded as a dangerous overreaction.

Johnson's presidency remains controversial. Indeed in the 21st century there is much less sympathy among historians and the public for his racial attitudes and policies, which foreshadowed the abandonment of Reconstruction in the 1870s and the establishment of Jim Crow laws discriminating against blacks throughout much of the South. But one of the president's strongest supporters in the impeachment crisis was the most distinguished American statesman of the day, Secretary of State William H. Seward, a lifelong opponent of slavery, founder of the Republican Party, and Lincoln's closest political ally in the war. Many historians, including amateurs such as John F. Kennedy, have taken the position that whatever Johnson's failings he did not deserve impeachment, and that his conviction would have damaged the American system of constitutional government. A participant in the event, Kansas Senator Edmund G. Ross, who was lauded in Kennedy's book *Profiles in Courage*, wrote: "It would have practically revolutionized our splendid political fabric into a partisan Congressional autocracy."[15]

Granger was brought to Washington by Johnson for advice and assistance in this political emergency. The House voted to impeach on February 24, and, after a trial, the Senate acquitted the president—by the narrowest of margins, with Ross a key player—in votes on May 16 and May 26.

Moorfield Storey, an aide to Massachusetts Senator Charles Sumner, wrote to his sister on March 28 that Johnson had put Granger "in command of Washington," which "is as yet not public." This purported appointment, and another of Gen. Winfield Scott Hancock (a Democrat) to command the Division of the Atlantic, headquartered in Washington, "make this movement almost a menace of force, and it cannot fail to have an influence in hastening the trial," Storey wrote.[16] There was also newspaper speculation about Granger succeeding Brig. General William Emory as commander of the Department (formerly District) of Washington.[17]

However, while the Hancock appointment was made, Granger's was not. Storey may have been equally inaccurate in the same letter when he referred to Granger's "notoriously bad character"—or his remark may have been motivated by political malice, since Sumner was one of the staunchest Radical Republicans and determined to secure Johnson's conviction.

To the extent there was any truth in the slur, it probably related to a strict view of sexual morality taken by Storey, a descendant of Massachusetts Puritans who was writing in the high Victorian era. Back in 1862, Granger had forbidden "laundresses"—whom his order implied did more than laundry—from traveling with the 2nd Michigan Regiment, but his concern had been wartime military discipline. Now, this middle-aged bachelor had become a habitue of East Coast society, and may have held somewhat laxer views than young Storey. If so, or if rumors were circulating to that effect, it would have been one more reason for the uxorious Grant to disdain him.

Some lines from a light poem of this era, *Hurrah for Gordon Granger*, reinforce the image of him as a still dashing ladies' man:

His manly grace of form and face
Made women bless our stalwart ranger;
Her sparkling eyes, her tenderest sighs
Were all for Gordon Granger.

Each rebel lass, to see him pass,
To loyalty the sight would change her.
For "Union" she would henceforth be
With winsome Gordon Granger.[18]

Johnson's political enemies tried to find out what the president was up to with Granger and Hancock, drawing them into the impeachment proceedings. On March 23, the two officers were called "before the impeachment managers this morning, and were questioned as to what transpired between them and the president in recent interviews. . . . General Granger was interrogated at great length. The facts elicited by the examination failed to substantiate what the managers sought to prove."[19] The Radicals were trying to indict Johnson for plotting a military coup or other extraconstitutional measures to resist impeachment. But the testimony of Granger and other officers including Emory helped to exculpate Johnson of this charge and build momentum toward acquittal.

While most of what Granger was doing on Johnson's behalf during the impeachment trial is not known, he must have advised the president regarding the appointment of a new Secretary of War. One was needed to resolve an absurd standoff that had developed in the War Department, which continued to be run by Stanton who was supported by Congress, although Johnson had appointed Brig. General Lorenzo Thomas to the same job Stanton still claimed to hold. At one point Stanton even had Thomas arrested, then released him after sharing a drink.

The Radicals claimed Johnson's attempt to fire Stanton was a violation of the new Tenure of Office Act, and made it one of the counts against him in the impeachment trial. But it looked like Congressional overreach into the Cabinet, breaching the Constitution's separation of powers, even to many of those who agreed with the Radicals on Reconstruction policy—where they had a much better case.

According to an anonymous but credible newspaper account written 20 years later, Granger himself was under consideration to head the War Department. But Johnson's nomination of General John Schofield to the post in late April was widely seen as a conciliatory gesture that helped win him support in the impeachment crisis. The key factor was Schofield's acceptability as Secretary of War to the Radicals' ally, Grant—whereas Granger himself would obviously have been unacceptable. Grant soon changed his mind and asked Schofield not to take the position, but by then it was too late because he had already agreed to serve. If Granger advised Johnson to appoint Schofield, then he did play a significant role in helping the president appease Congress and avoid conviction. The Senate confirmed Schofield's nomination after Johnson's acquittal, and Stanton vacated the office.

According to the newspaper account, "Granger had incurred the enmity of Stanton, and almost daily an order would reach him to join his regiment, somewhere in the South [i.e. Memphis], but in an hour the order would be revoked by the President and Granger ordered to remain."[20]

There is no evidence of Granger engaging in bribery on Johnson's behalf as some others apparently did, but he was probably conveying assurances about the president's future conduct while lobbying senators for acquittal. Whether or not this was proper behavior for a serving officer, Grant, too, was engaged in lobbying, on the other side. Now they were both "political generals"—although Granger's actual current rank remained colonel.

An Ohio politician, William Groesbeck, later wrote to the president recommending he name Granger as a major general in the Regular Army to replace Joseph Hooker, who had retired. Nothing came of it. Groesbeck had been one of Johnson's most effective counsels in the impeachment trial, and probably worked with Granger in advancing the president's cause. *The Nation* magazine reported speculation that Johnson might name Granger to succeed George Thomas as commander of the Department of the Cumberland, but in the end he got no special appointment from his presidential friend.

Running the hurdle of confirmation in the Republican Senate was one drawback to presidential patronage. Granger may have figured by now that there was little Johnson could offer him that could not soon be reversed by the next occupant of the White House—and the odds-on favorite in the 1868 presidential campaign was Ulysses S. Grant. Granger's friend William Rosecrans, also disdained by Grant, had accepted an appointment from Johnson as minister to Mexico, but only got to serve five months before being replaced by the new president. It was certainly not unusual for Civil War generals to angle for such appointments, often in the diplomatic corps, including much more obscure officers than Granger. Among Grant's appointments would be C.C. Andrews, who had served as a brigadier under

Granger at Mobile, as minister to Sweden and Norway.

Ready at last to return to ordinary army life, on October 6 Granger arrived back in Memphis. In Thomas' absence at a court of inquiry in Washington, Granger was put in temporary command of the Department of the Cumberland.[21] But he would only serve there a few more months. Johnson had survived impeachment but was on his way out of office, to be succeeded by Grant. The Army was again reorganized and reduced, with the result that Granger's 25th Infantry was subsumed into another regiment and another 25th Infantry Regiment was formed, to be commanded not by him but by Colonel Joseph Mower. (Mower had been a major general under Sherman during the war, and served under Granger in Texas.) Later that year, a local newspaper paid tribute to Granger, "so well and favorably known to the Memphis public, and who, as a Federal soldier in our midst, completely won not only the respect and esteem, but the affection of our people."[22]

Once again, he found himself awaiting orders, but now with no friend in the White House to provide him with extracurricular duties. Still, if he did not resign from the Army it would be hard to get rid of him, and eventually its commanders would find him something to do.

He now had ample time for romance and family life. Granger had not had much success in romance before the war, but in more recent years his fame and dash made him a more eligible, if aging, bachelor. He ceased to be one on July 14, 1869, at St. Paul's Episcopal Church in Evansville, Indiana, where he made a late first marriage to Maria Letcher, daughter of Dr. Joseph Letcher from Lexington, Kentucky. Large photographic portraits of Granger and his bride now in the possession of their great-grandson, Gordon Granger IV, show a good-looking, genteel couple. Gone are the full beard and fierce expression of Granger's Civil War days. In the later photo there is no beard but a full moustache and an Attilio or imperial—a patch of facial hair below the upper lip—and less hair on his head, too.

The middle-aged Granger was obviously a changed man, looking much milder, more content and civilized, under a wife's benign influence. It was a long time since 1845, when fellow army officer Friend Palmer had called him "the roughest specimen of a West Point graduate I, or anyone else, ever saw." However, a less charitable interpretation is that Granger had softened up in his easy postwar lifestyle, which would leave his fragile health vulnerable when he returned to the rigors of active service.

Maria Letcher was born in Lancaster, Kentucky, south of Lexington, in 1842, making her over 20 years younger than her husband and about 27 at the time of their marriage. A great many young men of her own generation in Kentucky had died on one side or the other during the Civil War. Granger may have met her when he was stationed in Lexington during the war, or in East Coast society during the postwar years. She lived as a young woman, and again as a widow, in Evansville, Indiana, and after her death in 1887 was described with extravagant praise by the Evansville *Courier:*

"There were such charms about her as are rarely given to mortals. . . . Her beauty of form and face was statuesque and would sometimes have seemed cold in its refinement had it not been for the warm heart in her bosom, the geniality and ingenuousness of which expressed itself in every act and word. Her smile gave a radiance to her face . . . and when this broke into laughter it was like the rippling music of a waterfall on a June night."

She was highly intelligent, too, the obituary said, and an ornament to society: "Whether in the brilliant circles of the National Capital, at Saratoga in the season, or in the salons of New York or Paris, Maria Letcher was always the center of the most brilliant circles . . . a wit of whose flashes were all the more admirable because they never gave pain but only pleasure."[23]

Those "brilliant circles" imply expensive tastes that could have presented problems for a couple living on an army salary. Within a month of the marriage, there were newspaper reports of them attending balls in the highly fashionable summer resort of Saratoga Springs in upstate New York, where the August horse racing probably appealed to the experienced cavalryman.[24] Later in the year, they moved to New York City, where "Mrs. Gen. Gordon Granger it is understood will frequently entertain in this city during the winter."[25]

But Maria may have had useful connections. She was, according to a *New York Times* story, a relative of perhaps the richest man in America, steamboat and railroad baron "Commodore" Cornelius Vanderbilt.[26] While the *Times* report, may, in fact, have been erroneous, Maria still was a social asset to her new husband, including in their dealings with Vanderbilt, whether or not there was a family connection to him.

Vanderbilt, too, had married in 1869, to a much younger second wife from Mobile with the unlikely name of Frank Crawford. According to his biographer T.J. Stiles, "When [Granger] called on the newly-weds, he warmly remarked that he remembered when he had first met Frank. It seems that he had shown particular courtesy to the Crawfords during the occupation, and it proved to be a source of lasting gratitude from the Commodore."[27] In August 1869, the month after Granger's marriage, he and Maria were staying at the ritzy Clarendon Hotel in Saratoga Springs, where the Vanderbilts also were guests, and no doubt they also spent time together that winter in New York City.

Granger probably knew Vanderbilt independently of Maria, having become acquainted during his years of under-employment, presidential connections and society hobnobbing after the war. Vanderbilt befriended Granger as he did another cantankerous former Civil War general, Granger's old foe Braxton Bragg. What Stiles says about Vanderbilt and the onetime Confederate Bragg could also have applied to his relationship with Granger: "What he probably liked most about the general was the fact that so few others liked him, especially in the North."[28]

Granger, the *Courier* said, "was a fitting mate" for Maria, and "They lived a life of ideal happiness. . . . A truer man and woman never plighted their vows at the sacred altar. His was the strength and courage of the cavalier."[29]

His unassigned status gave him leisure to attend the funeral of George Thomas, who died on duty in San Francisco on March 28, 1870. Thomas' Virginian family, especially his two sisters, had disowned him for sticking with the Union, and accordingly the funeral was held in his wife's hometown of Troy, New York. As many as 10,000 people were in the procession from St. Paul's Episcopal Church in downtown Troy to Oakwood Cemetery north of the small city. While Thomas, like Rosecrans, Canby and Granger, had fallen afoul of Grant during the war, the president and his Cabinet were among the mourners. Granger was one of the pall-bearers.

The Grangers were living in Lexington in 1870, according to the U.S. Census taken July 29, and their son was born there that year on October 22. The boy grew up to be another Gordon Granger, but in his childhood and adolescence was at least nicknamed Commodore, after Vanderbilt.

At last, Granger's enforced leisure came to an end. In December 1870, Wood writes, "he was assigned to the 14th Infantry. Five days thereafter he was transferred to the 15th Infantry, then stationed in New Mexico. He immediately joined his new regiment. The 8th Cavalry was also stationed in New Mexico; Granger being the senior in the Territory, the command of it devolved on him, with headquarters at Santa Fe."[30]

New Mexico only became part of the United States after the Mexican War, in which Granger had served. But it was not new territory for him. He had been stationed there from 1858 to 1860, with assignments at Fort Craig and in escorting the district commander, the post which now was his own.

It is fortunate that Granger had experience in the area of his new command, because the New Mexico Territory was no quiet backwater when he took it over, and although no longer including Arizona, was nonetheless a large responsibility—and an unruly one. Three years earlier, John Slough, chief justice of the New Mexico Supreme Court and a former Civil War general, had been shot to death in Santa Fe by a member of the Territorial Legislative Council.

But it was relations with the Apache Indians that would dominate Granger's concerns there. The Apache were relative newcomers to the Southwest, having moved down from northern Canada at about the same time the Spaniards were moving north from Mexico in the 16th century. Even 300 years later they operated mainly as hunter-gatherers, with the raiding of stock and other items from Mexicans, Pueblo Indians and Anglo-Americans an essential part of their economy. Relations were peaceful at this time between the Army and the Pueblo; however, there continued to be conflict in neighboring Texas with the Comanches, which would effect Granger in New Mexico in a campaign against the Comancheros.

The Apache, says historian Gordon C. Baldwin, "was one of the first of the American Indians to fight back against the invading Europeans, and he was the last to give up the struggle." Of all American Indians, many U.S. Army officers regarded the Apache as "the greatest all-around fighters."[31]

The Apache, according to Baldwin, regarded all outsiders as "enemies" who "could be preyed upon without scruple." The descendants of Europeans were equally implacable in their hostility, and the warfare was embittered by both sides' atrocities. Apaches sometimes tortured their captives to death, while in the 1830s two Mexican states offered a bounty for Apache scalps, including those of women and children. Some Anglo-Americans and Comanche Indians sought to collect the bounties.

Cochise, chief of the Chiricahua Apache, had been fighting the U.S. Army for about a decade before Granger's arrival. In the early1870s, most of the Apache warfare was in the Arizona Territory, commanded by Lt. Colonel George Crook, who earned a reputation later in his career as being a friend of the Indians but at this time was a hard-liner toward the Apache and especially Cochise. On April 30, 1871, there was a massacre of more than one hundred Apaches, mostly women and children, at Camp Grant east of Tucson, by a band of Mexican, Anglo-American and Indian civilians.

Granger did direct military operations against the Apaches shortly after his arrival in New Mexico that spring. But soon he would be a participant in the Grant administration's "peace policy" with the Western Indians. The president sent a peace commissioner to the Apaches in the summer of 1871. The commissioner, Vincent Colyer, was regarded with hostility by many white settlers who were implacably opposed to the Indians. Nevertheless, Colyer established reservations and reported that he was "received with cordiality by General Granger (commander in New Mexico), General Crook, and all the officers of the army in New Mexico and Arizona, and there was at no time any discord of action."[32]

Despite the hostility of the settlers toward Cochise, the military under Granger's direction "resisted taking punitive action against him, and tried desperately to get him to cooperate,"[33] according to a 21st-century report for the National Park Service. There were plenty of senior military officers who did not share that attitude, including Crook and at least to some extent his superiors Schofield, Sheridan and Sherman. But Granger was one of the most important Army officers seeking to implement the peace policy, which also was supported by his superior, John Pope, and sincerely advocated by the commander-in-chief, Grant. (Crook and Granger were in different military divisions, and so reported to different commanders.)

Granger helped to establish a safe haven for Mescalero Apache and other Indians near Fort Stanton in south-central New Mexico, where almost 2,000 were reported living in 1872.[34] The numbers continued to grow and a reservation was founded there in 1873, which continues to exist in expanded form today. But he was reluctant to enforce deadlines advocated by settlers for forcing the Apache to relocate.

Apache attacks and raids on settlers continued, mainly in Arizona, where the Army responded, and in Mexico. This prompted Cochise to escape Crook's forces by moving to New Mexico, a move which was also in accord with U.S. policy (pushed by Indian agent Orlando Piper and others) that he go with other Chiricahuas to Canada Alamosa. This was a temporary reservation established by Colyer, near Monticello in southern New Mexico. U.S. policy was to induce him to move again, westward within New Mexico to the new reservation at Tularosa, and to remove the Apaches there by force if they declined to cooperate. Authorities also wanted Cochise and other Apache leaders to visit Washington, D.C. to negotiate with the Federal government.

Granger, according to Cochise's biographer Edwin R. Sweeney, "realized it would not be practical to relocate the Indians before spring [1872]. . . . Granger decided to delay the entire relocation until April 1, 1872, with the actual transfer to take place on May 1. His superior, Brig. General Pope, concurred and the date was established."[35]

According to Sweeney, Mexican traders induced many Apaches at Canada Alamosa to exchange their rations for whiskey, leaving them destitute that December. Piper requested help from Fort McRae, an army post in Granger's jurisdiction, which sent soldiers to help him distribute blankets and discourage trading.

Crook, meanwhile, blamed Cochise for continued Apache raids in Arizona, including the killing of three mail carriers in January 1872 near Fort Bowie in Apache Pass, in the southeastern part of the state near the borders of New Mexico and Mexico.

Granger arranged to meet Cochise, arriving for that purpose near Canada Alamosa on March 17, and summoning patience to wait for two days until Cochise showed up at the rendezvous. The leading Apache chief here met the most senior representative of the U.S. government he had so far encountered.

Granger tried to persuade him to visit Washington, D.C., assuring him he would not be harmed, and to move his people to the Tularosa reservation. Cochise, suspicious of white men and their leaders, did not commit to either, and made an eloquent speech about the Apaches' plight and the injustices done to them. Despite the chief's refusal to comply with U.S. policy, Granger gave him permission to leave Canada Alamosa, rightly concluding that his influence with other Apaches would be positive and peaceful. The conference ended on March 20.

The meeting was criticized in a long, scornful article in an Arizona newspaper which mocked Cochise. The newspaper criticized Granger for his conciliatory attitude, comparing him unfavorably to Crook.[36] While a few hundred Apache did go to Tularosa, Cochise headed to Mexico and then Arizona, where Apache attacks continued, although not under his direction. Grant appointed a new peace commissioner with enhanced authority, Brig. General Oliver O. Howard.

Howard was not immediately able to meet with Cochise, but did take a delegation of Indians to Washington that summer, where they met with Grant. Howard passed through New Mexico and Santa Fe on both his way east and on the way back, and must have conferred with Granger about Cochise and the Apaches. He does not, however, mention Granger or the groundbreaking meeting with Cochise in March in his memoir *My Life and Experiences Among Our Hostile Indians,* although he does note Crook's skepticism about the peace process. Perhaps Howard did not want to share any credit with Granger for making peace with the Apache, because of lingering resentment over Granger's 1866 criticism of abuses in the Freedmen's Bureau in his report to Johnson. At that time Howard had headed the Freedmen's Bureau.

Howard was able to meet with and make peace with Cochise in October 1872, permitting a reservation at Apache Pass in southeastern Arizona. It was an achievement which Granger had contributed to earlier that year. But the Yavapai and Tonto Apache continued to resist in Arizona, and were defeated by Crook that winter and in spring 1873. Granger was more willing to implement the peace policy than Crook, and more successful at doing so.

Yet he also engaged in warfare in 1872, with the Comancheros, Mexican-Indian traders with the Comanche who provided weapons and other supplies in exchange for slaves who had been captured in raids. The campaign on the high, dry Llano Estacado (staked plain) of eastern New Mexico was in coordination with an Army offensive against the Comanches in Texas which, after Granger's departure, finally defeated the tribe and drove its survivors into life on a reservation at Fort Sill in what is now Oklahoma.

But it was Granger's campaign that crushed the Comancheros. He "kept his troops in the field through 1872. Ranging across the llano from the Canadian River to the Rio Hondo, the troops arrested Comancheros, broke up trading camps, and slaughtered stolen livestock. Short of men, Granger ordered surplus arms to be distributed to a group of more than ninety Texas cattlemen who set out in the summer of 1872 to recover stolen stock. The Texans spent three months on the Llano Estacado and in eastern New Mexico intimidating livestock buyers and terrorizing ranches and villages that owned Comanchero cattle. These actions all but destroyed the Comanchero trade."[37]

Granger turned 51 that November of 1872, and his life might have seemed content at last—happy with his new family, and back on track in the army doing useful work in his own sphere of influence. But that happiness was undermined by serious health issues, in fact a slow-motion health collapse from which he never really recovered.

In March 1872—the same month he met Cochise—Granger was with his troops in the New Mexico desert when they encountered a heavy dust storm, and he "developed a severe cough with hemorrhage," says Welsh. "By September he had chronic bronchitis with occasional hemoptysis. He was granted a thirty days' leave of absence on certificate of disability on December 6, 1872, but did not avail himself of the privilege."[38]

Says Wood: "For several years Granger had been a great sufferer from asthma and bronchitis; his lungs were also weak; the great altitude of most of the posts in New Mexico caused him much suffering, and finally brought on a hemorrhage from the lungs, in September, 1872. In the month of December, 1872, he lost the sight of his left eye entirely, by a bursting of a blood vessel on the retina. During the winter of 1872–73, he suffered much from repeated hemorrhages of the lungs; but though much prostrated by these attacks, he continued to attend faithfully to his duties."[39]

Says Welsh: "On May 2, 1873, an ophthalmoscopic examination of his left eye revealed retinitis and extensive hemorrhage into the retina from the choroidal vessels. . . . There was almost total loss of vision in the left eye. . . . He also had consolidation of a portion of his left lung, associated with intermittent episodes of hemorrhage. The surgeon recommended he go to a better climate and a lower altitude. On May 19, 1873, he was granted a sick leave."[40]

NOTES

1. *Personal Recollections of John M. Palmer* (Cincinnati: Robert Clarke Co., 1901), 191.
2. Quoted in *The Cleveland Leader*, Sept. 30, 1865.
3. T.J. Wood, *Seventh Annual Reunion of the Association of the Graduates of the United States Military Academy* (New York: A.S. Barnes & Co., 1876), 58.
4. *White Cloud Kansas Chief*, April 8, 1869.
5. The report was published in *The Proceedings of the National Union Convention Held at Philadelphia* (Washington: 1866), and in many newspapers, including the Aug 28, 1866, *New York Times* and the Sept. 1 editions of *The Daily Phoenix* of Columbia, S.C., and the *Army and Navy Journal*.
6. Grant quoted in Josiah Bunting III's *Ulysses S. Grant* (Macmillan, The American Presidents Series, 2004), 76.
7. *New York Tribune*, Sept. 19, 1866.
8. *Philadelphia Evening Telegraph*, July 2, 1866.
9. *The Papers of Ulysses S. Grant*, Vol. 17, ed. John Y. Simon (Southern Illinois University Press, 1991), 140.
10. *The Evening Telegraph*, Aug. 27, 1867, Philadelphia.
11. *The Bolivar Bulletin*, Jan. 11, 1868, Bolivar, TN. Also *Nashville Union and Dispatch*, Jan. 7, 1868.
12. Chamberlain's conservative views on Reconstruction are quoted in his biography by Alice Rains Trulock, *In the Hands of Providence: Joshua L. Chamberlain and the American Civil War* (Chapel Hill, NC: University of North Carolina Press, 1992), 351–4.
13. *The Papers of Ulysses S. Grant*, op. cit., 141.
14. Ibid., 142.
15. Edmund G. Ross, *History of the Impeachment of Andrew Johnson* (Teddington, England:

Echo Library, 2007. First published 1896), 148.

16. Mark Antony De Wolfe Howe, *Moorfield Storey, Portrait of an Independent, 1845–1929*, 85.

17. As reported in the Cincinnati Chronicle, reprinted in the April 2, 1868, *Gallipolis Journal* of Gallipolis, Ohio. See also *New-York Tribune*, Feb. 24, 1868.

18. Charles G. Halpine (aka Miles O'Reilly), *Poetical Works* (New York: Harper, 1869), 81.

19. *The Baltimore Sun*, Washington correspondent, March 23, 1868, reprinted in the *Charleston (S.C.) Daily News*, March 27, 1868.

20. *New York Evening Telegram*, June 16, 1888.

21. *The Evening Telegraph*, Oct. 1, 1868, Philadelphia.

22. *Memphis Daily Appeal*, July 18, 1869.

23. *Evansville Courier*, reprinted in *Semi-Weekly Interior Journal* of Stanford, KY, Dec. 9. 1887.

24. *New York Evening Telegram*, Aug. 11 and 14, 1869.

25. Ibid., Nov. 6, 1869.

26. *The New York Times*, Dec. 30, 1878.

27. T.J. Stiles, *The First Tycoon: The Epic Life of Cornelius Vanderbilt* (New York: Vintage Books, 2010), 491.

28. Ibid., 489.

29. *Evansville Courier*, op. cit.

30. T.J. Wood, *Seventh Annual Reunion of the Association of the Graduates of the United States Military Academy* (New York: A.S. Barnes & Co., 1876), 65.

31. Gordon C. Baldwin, *The Apache Indians: Raiders of the Southwest* (New York: Four Winds Press, 1978).

32. Vincent Colyer, *Peace With the Apaches of New Mexico and Arizona* (Washington: Government Printing Office, 1871/72), 3.

33. Sanchez, Gurule, Larrichio and Miller, *Fort Union National Monument Ethnographic Overview and Assessment* (National Park Service, 2006), 48.

34. Morris and Catherine Opler, *Mescalero Apache History in the Southwest*, in *New Mexico Historical Review*, Vol. 25, Jan. 1950, 23.

35. Edwin R. Sweeney, *Cochise, Chiricahua Apache Chief* (University of Oklahoma Press, 1991, 1995), 333.

36. *The Citizen*, Tucson, April 13, 1872.

37. Pekka Hamalainen, *The Comanche Empire*, New Haven, Yale University Press, 2008), 35.

38. Jack D. Welsh, *Medical Histories of Union Generals* (Kent, Ohio, Kent State University Press, 1996), 136.

39. Wood, op. cit.

40. Welsh, op. cit.

11

Final Tour

For some time, things went as well as could be expected. The Granger family moved around a good deal on what turned out to be a very long sick leave. They spent the winters of 1873–74 and 1874–75 in Florida, where Granger was a founding member of the St. Augustine Yacht Club and was elected its commodore. This was not purely a place for diversion, as the club's charter, according to its website, "issued by the United States War Department gave it the express responsibility of defending St. Augustine and blockading the St. Augustine inlet in times of war." Granger's military expertise obviously would have been helpful in that regard.

The Grangers' son Gordon, or Commodore, had been born with a foot problem, in his heel or Achilles tendon, which caused him to limp and required a special type of shoe and some kind of repeated stretching medical treatments in New York City.[1]

Upstate New York was a pleasant place to spend summer and early fall, either Saratoga Springs or Clifton Springs, the latter being another, much smaller resort where people took the waters, this one closer to Granger's relatives in the west-central part of the state. The couple was keeping a lower profile in these years, probably for reasons of frugality as they settled in to family life. They were less likely to be seen in society columns than had been the case early in the marriage. On September 23, 1874, the *Geneva Courier* did report in its "Local Affairs" column that Granger was "at Clifton Springs with his family." (A post of the Grand Army of the Republic, the principal Union veterans organization, would be named after Granger in Clifton Springs in 1878.)

Two days later, on September 25, 1874, Maria gave birth to their second child, a daughter named Ellen Gordon Granger. A couple of weeks after that, on October 9, Granger was in New York City with a group including his fellow Union general and postwar political ally, Winfield Scott Hancock, and a former Confederate general and current congressman, Pierce M.B. Young. They "inspected the fortifications and torpedo systems in this harbor,"[2] a newspaper reported. But for Granger it appears to have been more politicking than official duty, since his sick leave continued.

Ellen was not baptized until the following summer in Saratoga Springs. The July 19 baptism may have been scheduled then because her health was poor. Ellen Granger died on Aug. 2, 1875, in Saratoga, at 10 months old. Her funeral was held the next day, at Bethesda Episcopal Church,[3] and she was temporarily interred at Green Ridge Cemetery in Saratoga Springs.

Granger's own health had failed to improve. "In June 1875," says Welsh, "he had daily hemorrhage from his lungs and the last of the month had lost a gill (¼ pint) or more of blood."[4]

He was in no condition to go back on active duty, especially in the hard service and high altitude of a frontier territory, yet could not stay on leave indefinitely. Sherman's 1875 memoir contains a passage indicating impatience with Granger's purported leave request in 1864, which probably reflects Sherman's state of mind regarding Granger's much-extended leave from 1873 to 1875, at the time the book was published. Sherman was still head of the army, and unsympathetic to Granger. He was not about to give him a cushy desk job. If Granger aimed to stay in the service, he would have to return to his post in New Mexico.

The alternative to active duty was resigning his commission, which presented practical problems. He thought himself too young and impecunious to retire, with marriage turning out to be an expensive proposition. But was he well enough to work? If so, it was questionable whether he would be able to find any, given that the country had fallen into an economic depression in 1873 in which it still remained. He had been a soldier all his life and it was his only demonstrable skill—unless one counts, as Granger probably did not, a couple of years of teaching as a teenager. In retrospect, it seems he should have opted to retire from the Army, which might have extended his life for years. But he didn't.

Granger decided to go back to Santa Fe and resume command of the District of New Mexico. Maria and young Gordon stayed in New York City. His family had been with him for most of his previous tour in Santa Fe, but the boy's foot required continued medical attention, and Maria was planning to supervise the removal of Ellen's remains from the grave site in Saratoga Springs to a family plot in Lexington, Kentucky. His daughter's death was probably one of the things spurring Granger back to military activity, as a distraction from the grief he would allude to in letters home.

Granger travelled west in October 1875 through Leavenworth, Kansas, where he conferred with his superior General Pope and "found them glad to see me" at division headquarters, as he wrote to Maria from the Planter's Hotel. A collection of Granger's letters now in the possession of his great-grandson, Gordon Granger IV, sheds light on these last months of his life.[5]

"My Darling Wife," he wrote from Leavenworth on October 16, "I arrived here yesterday and tried to write you last night but I was so fatigued and half sick that I had to go to bed and take some rest. While I did not feel tired traveling, the moment I stopped I found myself very nervous and entirely used up.... I am lost and blue away from you and Commodore. Oh! hon, I miss his sweet prating voice and accents and you my better half. It is impossible for me to exist without your endearing caresses. Yet I feel my course was the only proper one for me to pursue and I must make every effort to endure it without complaint.... Be of good cheer my darling, be contented and keep in good health and be ready to come to me next spring."

Travelling west a day out of Leavenworth he sent a postcard: "... every pain except my hand has left me, also the hemorrhages seem to be fast disappearing."

Granger arrived at Santa Fe on October 31. Things had not improved in his absence of almost two-and-a-half years. Cochise died in 1874, and there had been raiding and violent incidents between Apaches and settlers. The Federal government had embarked on a misguided "concentration" policy of putting the Apache and other Indians in the San Carlos reservation in Arizona—a policy which would bear bitter fruit after Granger's death in the renewed warfare with Apaches led by Victorio and Geronimo.

"I'm nearly worked to death getting things in shape," he wrote to Maria on November 2. A week later he sent another letter saying, "I am yet very busy." But this time it wasn't Indians he was mainly concerned with.

"There is a civil war raging at Cimarron," wrote Granger in a November 9 letter, "a party of cut throats here (Texans) have taken forcible possession of the town and I am sending troops to suppress violence and maintain law and order." This "Colfax County War" in northeastern New Mexico was between settlers and agents of a land grant company, with both sides implicated in murder. It would flare up at intervals over the next dozen years, costing about 200 lives. Like the killing of John Slough in 1867, and the "Salt War" after Granger's death, it is a reminder to modern readers that it was by no means only Indians who threatened the peace and disrupted law and order in the territory, and kept putting more demands on hard-pressed Army units.

Wood says that "For some time previous to his death General Granger had been a devoted and consistent member of the Protestant Episcopal Church,"[6] and Stanley's SAC memorial says, "In his later years General Granger became a communicant of the Protestant Episcopal church, and of a very serious turn of mind."[7] His letters to Maria also provide evidence of his turn to religion at this time.

"I just returned from church," Granger wrote on November 14, "you[r] favorite one the Presbyterian, where I listened to a most excellent discourse from Rom[ans] 11th and 33rd which opened my poor blind reason to points of belief which have hitherto been obscure and doubtful." He had "not yet attended our own church [i.e. the Episcopal] as the pastor has been absent," but said "the thought came over me that I must remember the Sabbath day and keep it holy and abstain from all worldly occupations and keep our mind on heavenly affairs, looking and hoping for eternal life in that happier and better place to come."

He wrote about the death of their daughter, whose remains Maria was arranging to be reburied in Lexington Cemetery. In this context, the letter slightly misquotes a verse from an Isaac Watts hymn, saying the burial site is "where her 'flesh shall slumber in the ground till the last trump of joyful sound.'" The same line, as earlier noted, appears on the grave stone by Lake Ontario of Granger's own mother, who died in 1825 when he was three years old.

His son also was on his mind. He worried about the cold in Kentucky provoking asthma, and suggested a trip south, while acknowledging, "It may become necessary at any time for you to take Commodore back to NY."

But it was Granger's own health that now collapsed. Says Welsh: "Granger had a stroke on November 19, 1875, which involved his left arm and left leg. He recovered sufficiently to attend to duty some weeks prior to his last illness."[8] Wood says the stroke "entirely paralyzed his left side."[9] The letters bear witness to that recovery and those duties. "The doctors "& everybody," he told Maria on November 30, "are astonished at my speedy recovery." Their surprise was doubtless genuine.[10]

According to Welsh, a surgeon in Santa Fe had told Granger in 1873 that he needed a better climate and a lower altitude. Yet he had now convinced himself otherwise, or, more likely, had determined to talk up the health benefits of where he was so as to reassure his absent wife. Doctors had told him, he wrote, that leaving "the dry, mild climate" of Santa Fe in mid-winter would be too risky. "I could not live one more week in either Kentucky or New York so great would be the change.

"I am now almost well of hemorrhages," he continued, "and hope soon to be entirely over them." But the next sentence shows his focus was not just on his own health. "What I suggest is you take Commodore to New York and have everything necessary attended to there and then return . . . to Santa Fe. . . . Get our Dear Boy fixed up and we will have a delightful summer here next year."

Granger suggested Maria and young Commodore (or Gordon) could stay with Vanderbilt in New York. Saving money was probably on his mind, as in the same letter he asks Maria to collect an $82 debt due from the sale of a horse.

His next letter was apparently written the following day, in response to one he had just received from Maria. "I have been here one month today and have been very much occupied in fitting out the 8th Cavalry for Texas, in organizing 100 men to build the telegraph line from here to Arizona, in receiving and assigning 150 recruits to our regiment in preparing for the survey of Indian reservations, in hiring transportation and making preparations of the coming regiment of Colonel T———, with a thousand other botherations. . . . Don't run any risk by keeping Commodore too long away from Dr. Taylor. You are with him and know what is for the best."

He wrote a cheerful postcard on December 14 to "My Dear Son," urging him to "Tell Mama to give you plenty of oysters in NY and you must eat much for Papa."

A December 16 letter returns to a religious theme, beginning with prayer and thanks "to the great Jehovah for his manifold mercies and blessing toward us in watching over and caring for our welfare. Oh how my heart yearns to be with him, to have a taste of those immortal joys promised to all those who truly love and obey their loving Redeemer. . . . It will be one month tomorrow since I was struck down with a fatal malady from which few if any recover. And already the lord has come to my rescue and I am almost in my usual health with every hope and prospect of my total recovery."

He says he trusts Maria and their son have arrived in New York, hoping "that this may be the last visit we shall be compelled to make to Dr. Taylor to insure his ultimate recovery. Did you succeed in accomplishing the final interment of his darling sister before leaving Lexington? If so, I am really happy."

While he urges Maria to visit Vanderbilt, whose help in providing for the treatment of their son is noted and appreciated, she was not staying with him, and Granger expressed doubts about her lodging: "Don't like Mrs. Balah's upper room," he writes, preferring "one lower down if it costs twice as much. The third story is too high for you."

Writing on Sunday December 19, Granger says he has already attended church and plans to go again that evening "and pray for greater strength to be drawn nearer to Him in all that pertains to Eternal Salvation."

Continuing the letter the next day, he indicates he did go to the evening service and heard a sermon which "explained many things in Revelation I never understood."

Also on his mind was his immediate future, and he reveals a moment of weakness: "I never felt so much like retiring from the Service as I do at this time but if I do we have no home and as for living around in hotels and boarding houses I can not endure it. I do wish Com. V. would take compassion on us and let us have a house. I would work hard Economics and try to pay him back at an early day."

In these last weeks of Granger's life, there is yet another parallel with Grant, who would die nine-and-a-half years later having lost all his money and heavily in debt to Vanderbilt's son William. As the dying Granger did his duty on active service, earning a living for his family, so the cancer-stricken Grant, although retired from public life, would struggle to finish his memoirs so as to provide for his widow.

Granger's letter continues: "Congress is moving every day to cut the Army down to 10,000 men which will undoubtedly leave us out in the cold. So much for the gratitude of Republics."

His health, he says, is getting better, but his description of improvement must have been small comfort: ". . . the paralysis has nearly left my left side, except the left hand and arm." He expresses concern for the health of his wife and son, hoping they "will be very careful and not take bad colds. The climate of NY you must remember at this season of the year is very treacherous and trying."

A letter on the 26th of December has the usual religious notes, and promised to "send you some money" and suggests Maria might leave Mrs. Balah's lodging: "I think you had better try and find a better place."

The next day he responds to a telegram of Maria's, in which she had suggested dispatching their son to Kentucky and herself coming out to New Mexico. He opposes the plan, saying his health is improving. "Now try and comfort yourself and trust in our Heavenly Father's kind mercy and protecting care and all will be for the best. I know you could not stand the cold hard trip, neither is it necessary. The roads are almost impassable and it is too late for an ambulance to meet you and the stage would kill you in half a day." The railroad had not yet come to mountainous Santa Fe.

A January 7, 1876, letter expresses approval for Maria's plan to bring their son back to Kentucky on February 1, adding "I have long since thought that the doctors have done everything possible for him . . . and that providence and time for the future must do the rest. Honey you keep asking me if I won't come home. Quit and settle down. Why I have told you many times it is not possible for me to do before warm weather sets in. I could not endure the hardship and exposure of the trip, and if I could the terrible cold and changeable climate of the North would be more than I could stand. . . . it would be death for me to go anywhere except with a warmer climate."

His last letter to Maria was written January 8, and is here quoted in full:
"My dearest loving Darling,

"I was telling you yesterday some of the reasons why I could not return to the States at this time. You know we have no abiding place there while here we have a most comfortable home and everything necessary to make life agreeable. I do hope and pray that Commodore will be well enough to come in the Spring. I believe this climate will do him great good and lend restoration of his health. However as tis impossible for you [to] come here or for me to go East before Spring there is yet some 3 months to make our plans for the future. So do try and be more contented and rely of God's goodness and mercy for protection, and happiness. Maybe it is [the] key which alone can bring to the mercy seat and fill you[r] soul with joy and gladness, and lighten all your sorrows and turn your discomfort into bliss eternal.

"The doctors all say I am slowly but surely being restored to my former good health. If careful living and regular habits combined with hope and trust in the goodness of our Dear Heavenly Father will rescue me, no effort on my part will be spared to be a comfort for you for many years. Give my love to all our friends. Be thankful and prayerful. Keep your mind on heavenly things and all will be well with your own, Gordon."

According to family lore, after Granger's death one of his sisters criticized the widow for not being with him at the end.[11] While Granger's January 7 letter did start off complaining about the "horrible bad humor" of a recent letter of hers, the correspondence as a whole seems to vindicate Maria.

Granger in his last days had some faint hope of soldiering on at Santa Fe, with his family joining him there. That would have enabled him to save a little money, maybe enough to buy a house in St. Augustine. He may have hoped to hold on until the Democratic candidate won that year's presidential election, which might open up a patronage job. Or perhaps Vanderbilt would come through with something. But the letters also contain a strong undercurrent of awareness, often expressed in religious terms, that he is on the verge of death.

On January 9, Granger had an unpleasant interview with Lt. Frederick E. Phelps, who had failed to report to Santa Fe in a timely fashion because of a conflicting order from department headquarters dispatching him to Texas.

Phelps says in his memoir that Granger "was a very distinguished soldier, but arbitrary and overbearing. . . . I knew what was behind all this anger on his part. General Granger, though a fine officer in some respects, was a foul mouthed brute in conversation and a hard drinker; a great many ladies declined to have anything to do with him. He had been to my station the year previous on an inspection tour; my wife had declined to meet him and he was very sore on that subject. He informed me that if I would apologize to him personally for my wife's refusal to meet him he would overlook the matter. Of course I promptly refused, and he informed me that I would be tried by court martial for disobedience of orders. . . . although I expected to be put in irons, I was not, for some reason, and was ordered to remain at Santa Fe until a court could be ordered."[12]

No doubt Granger's anger would soon have abated, as it almost always did in similar circumstances. Before he could back down, however, he had what Welsh calls "an attack of apoplexy" on January 10, 1876.

According to a newspaper account: "The General had visited several of his friends during the day and was at military headquarters [in Santa Fe] until after two o'clock. After returning home and about three p.m., he had a paralytic stroke on the left side. Dr. McParlin was immediately called and the proper remedies applied but without effect. At the first arrival of the Doctor, the General was able to explain his situation intelligently, but his voice soon thickened, when the Doctor advised him not to talk but to rest quietly. He gradually sank and expired seemingly without pain and without a struggle at six o'clock."[13]

Granger's life, even up to its end, had demonstrated his flawed temper (which may have contributed to his death). His postwar politicking is certainly open to criticism. Nevertheless, these words of Thomas Wood, his West Point classmate and wartime comrade, ring true: "Thus—his work well and faithfully done, at his post of duty, and with his harness on, did this gallant soldier sink to his last rest."[14]

NOTES

1. Interview with Gordon Granger IV. General Granger's letters also discuss the boy's medical treatment, one referring to a brace.
2. The *National Republican,* Oc. 10, 1874.
3. This information is recorded at the church office.
4. Jack D. Welsh, *Medical Histories of Union Generals* (Kent, Ohio: Kent State University Press, 1996), 136.
5. The letters quoted in this chapter are used by permission of Gordon Granger IV.
6. T.J. Wood, *Seventh Annual Reunion of the Association of the Graduates of the United States Military Academy* (A.S. Barnes & Co., 1876), 66.
7. (David Stanley), *Reunion of the Society of the Army of the Cumberland,* Vol. 15 (Cincinnati, Robert Clarke & Co., 1884), 225.
8. Welsh, op. cit.
9. Wood, op. cit., 65.
10. Wood, op. cit., 65.
11. 2012 interview with Gordon Granger IV.
12. Frederick Phelps, *A Soldier's Memoirs (New Mexico Historical Review,* Vol. 25, July, 1950), 196–7.
13. From a contemporary newspaper in the collection of Gordon Granger IV. The title and date of the paper are not preserved with the clip, but it appears to be from *The Dispatch* in January 1876. The *Dispatch* was published several days a week in Lexington, KY, between 1874 and 1876.
14. Wood, op. cit., 65.

Epilogue

A villain now takes center stage, in the form of Lt. Thomas Blair, a member of Granger's staff. Granger had written to Maria that he held Blair in high regard, that since he became ill Blair "cares for me like a brother." But according to Phelps, Blair's real feelings were hostile.

Blair, whom Phelps described as "an intimate personal friend of mine," showed up at 9 a.m. on January 10, "and, slapping me on the shoulder, said, 'Old man, the Lord is certainly on your side. General Granger fell dead in his office an hour ago.' Pulling a bundle of papers out of his pocket, he grinned as he said, 'Allow me to present to you the charges he had preferred against you, and which were lying on his desk awaiting his signature when the devil got him.' I have never forgotten in all these years the look of satisfaction on Blair's face, for he, like all the other officers, utterly despised General Granger."[1]

No doubt Blair did disdain Granger, but his credibility regarding the feelings of the other officers is low, as he was later proven to be a liar about the most serious matters. Meanwhile, the officers and soldiers of the regiment raised the money to send Granger's body to Lexington, Kentucky (which the U.S. government declined to pay for). Nor is the Blair-Phelps account of the time of Granger's death consistent with newspaper accounts.

Blair had met Maria when she was in New Mexico during Granger's previous tour. He now renewed their acquaintance, for it was he who accompanied the body back to Lexington, having previously taken it to be embalmed at Fort Union, New Mexico.

The funeral on January 28 was held in Lexington's Christ Church, which later became (and still is) the cathedral of the Episcopal diocese. "The attendance was large," said the Lexington *Dispatch*, "including a considerable number of ladies, the civil and military, and members of the Legislative Assembly; a sympathetic feeling was generally manifest."[2] It "drew out an immense crowd," said the Louisville *Courier-Journal*. They closed the service by singing "Nearer My God to Thee."

The procession to Lexington Cemetery was "escorted by two companies of the 16th Infantry, U.S.A., with their regimental band and the cadets of the University," according to another newspaper account. It "was a singularly impressive sight. The police, forming a hollow square, kept the crowd from the military and the streets clear. The dirge was as beautiful and solemn as could be. At the grave the usual military honors were shown the dead chief."

The senior officer in attendance was Irvin McDowell, now commander of the Department of the South and a major general. His Civil War record was no match for Granger's, being distinguished only by defeat. Lt. Blair, an immigrant from Scotland who had joined the U.S. Army in 1865 and missed the Civil War entirely, was one of the pall-bearers.

An impressive monument, a stone obelisk with a star, was erected over Granger's grave, with inscriptions of four sides. One tells of his two brevets from the Mexican War, and another of his five in the Civil War "in battles of Wilson's Creek, Mo. Chickamauga, Ga. Chattanooga, Tenn. Mobile and Forts Gaines and Morgan, Ala." Another side records his wartime commands, and the other tells of his birth and death. His wife and daughter are in adjacent graves, young Ellen's marked with a small stone cross on which are finely carved a dove, perched on top, and laurel leaves.

There are more famous Americans buried at Lexington Cemetery, including U.S. Senator Henry Clay, the "Great Compromiser," whose statue stands there atop a 120-foot Corinthian column. The former U.S. vice president and Confederate general John Breckinridge is there, as is another of Granger's Civil War enemies, General John Hunt Morgan. Granger's section of the cemetery, near a central lake, even has a Confederate war memorial. But in a nearby section, just across a path, there is a small National Cemetery which includes some Union soldiers, including United States Colored Troops. The National Cemetery section has long been filled up, but the larger cemetery is still used for burials, and it is all well tended, still a quiet, pleasant, scenic place.

Cornelius Vanderbilt died on January 4, 1877, and according to a December 30, 1878, *New York Times* article, left Maria $20,000—although the

Granger family tradition is that he left her $2,000 per year. She settled in Washington, D.C., where Blair may have seen her on sick leave in 1877. Now a captain, in December 1877 Blair played a notably uncourageous role in the El Paso "Salt War." Blair's "efforts to relieve the besieged Texas Rangers were something less than gallant," according to a 20th century account.[3]

Nevertheless, Blair married—or seemed to marry—Maria Granger in Kentucky on September 17, 1878, and she moved back to New Mexico. It soon turned out, however, that a Scottish woman claimed Blair was still married to her and was the father of their two children. Newspapers relished the scandal. Blair went east with Maria to defend himself, but Sherman had him arrested in January 1879. He was convicted the next month in a military court of bigamy and forgery, having been abandoned by Maria as the overwhelming evidence against him came out. Dismissed from the army, he fled the country.

Maria retired to Indiana, where her health soon deteriorated. She was only 45 when she died, on November 17, 1887. It may be she had cancer, which is the opinion of her great-grandson, Gordon Granger IV. The *Evansville Courier* obituary described: "With what fortitude and resignation she carried on the struggle, without complaint or murmurings, with always a sweet, cheery disposition that made the inevitable decree of nature the more intensely sad to those who loved her, there are those in Evansville who know too well, and to them the news of her death came not as a surprise, hardly as a regret, because it was an assurance at least of her release from pain."[4]

Her step-brother, W.T. Price, wrote that she died with Christian resignation, surrounded by family including her son. They "received her last beams of fondness."[5] Maria was buried in Lexington, next to Granger and their infant daughter.

Gordon Granger II (or Commodore), their son, had just turned 17, and went to live with one of Maria's sisters. He attended Princeton and then the University of Virginia at Charlottesville, in which area his family has mostly remained. All, or almost all, his American descendants live in the former Confederacy.

When he was 21, in 1892, Gordon Granger II married a 19-year-old Charlottesville girl, Lucy Champe Maury. She was apparently a distant relative of another Virginian Maury, Dabney, who spent three years at West Point with Gordon Granger, and served in the same regiment with him in Mexico and on the frontier. In the Civil War's Mobile campaign, Granger and Dabney Maury were major generals on opposite sides, often dealing with each other. Another distinguished Virginia relative of Lucy's was Matthew Fontaine Maury, the scientist and officer in the U.S. and Confederate navies. (Confusingly, Lucy's father was a different Matthew Fontaine Maury.)

Gordon Granger II and Lucy had three children, but the marriage did not last.

The 1900 Census shows Gordon living in an El Paso lodging house, listed as an unemployed miner. He soon moved south of the Mexican border, living in Oaxaca from 1902 to 1911, and then in Mexico City for two years. In 1917 he was in Empalme, working for the Southern Pacific Railroad of Mexico as a "section man," responsible for a section of track.[6] That would have been no easy task in those days of Mexican revolution. (In one last parallel, Grant also had close connections with Mexico.) Gordon Granger IV thinks his grandfather also did some journalism in Washington, D.C.

The only one of his American children to have children of their own was another Gordon Granger, the III, who flew Army transport planes to the front in France during World War I. Back in the United Sates, he worked for a construction company, then became a contractor, house builder and developer, mostly in the Charlottesville area. One of his five children, Gordon Granger IV, as an infant met his grandfather just once, in 1928. The grandfather, Gordon Granger II, was then in his late 50s and on his way back from Europe, having travelled on the ocean liner *Leviathan*. He was going by train to Mexico City, which his father had fought hard to capture in 1847.

If General Granger liked a drink, so it seems did his son, as he died in 1938 from cirrhosis of the liver in Monterrey, in the north of Mexico, according to a U.S. consular document. Senora Concepcion Hernandez, described as a "friend" who lived in Monterrey, took custody of the body and had it buried there. Gordon Granger II left two surviving children, according to the consulate, one being Gordon Granger (III) in Charlottesville. The other was a daughter, a Mexican lady named Senora Guillermina Granger de Soto, of Mexico City. Some years later, according to Gordon Granger IV, after his father's death in an accident in 1944, the Mexican side of the family contacted the American, proposing a visit, but his mother did not follow up on the idea. Still, it seems likely that in addition to the considerable number of Granger descendants in the old Confederacy, there is another branch of the family in old Mexico.

NOTES

1. Frederick Phelps, *A Soldier's Memoirs (New Mexico Historical Review*, Vol. 25, July 1950), 197.

2. The Jan. 30, 1876, clip from the *Dispatch,* and the other newspapers here quoted, are in the personal collection of Gordon Granger IV.

3. Philip J. Rasch, *The Men at Fort Stanton* (Brand Book, April 1961, Volume 3, Number 3, Publication No. 68). (The English Westerners' Society Web site)

4. *Evansville Courier,* reprinted in *Semi-Weekly Interior Journal* of Stanford, KY, Dec. 9. 1887.

5. *Semi-Weekly Interior Journal,* Jan. 10 (written Jan. 3), 1888.

6. Documents from U.S. Census and passport application, along with other information in this chapter, were accessed through ancestry.com.

Bibliography

This is not meant to be an exhaustive list. It does not include contemporary newspaper articles, which are cited in the notes; nor the many standard works which have formed my understanding of the period but are not quoted from, such as Shelby Foote's three-volume *The Civil War: A Narrative*.

Andrews, C.C. *History of the Campaign of Mobile*. 2nd ed. New York: Van Nostrand, 1889.

Aten, Henry J. *History of the Eighty-Fifth Regiment, Illinois Volunteer Infantry*. Hiawatha, Kansas, 1901.

Atkinson, William F. *The Rock of Chickamauga*, in *War Papers Read Before The Michigan Commandery of the Military Order of the Loyal Legion of the United States*. Vol. 2. Detroit, Mich: Winn & Hammond, 1898 (first delivered 1893).

Baldwin, Gordon C. *The Apache Indians: Raiders of the Southwest*. New York: Four Winds Press, 1978.

Bauer, K. Jack. *The Mexican War*. New York: Macmillan Publishing, 1974.

Beard, Michael F. *The Battle of Mobile Bay and Mobile: The Overland Campaign*. civilwaralbum.com

Bergeron, Arthur W. *Confederate Mobile*. University Press of Mississippi, 1991.

Berlin, Ira, et al., eds. *Freedom, a Documentary History of Emancipation, 1861–1867*, Vol. 1. Cambridge University Press, 1985.

Bierce, Ambrose. *A Sole Survivor: Bits of Autobiography*. Ed. Joshi and Schultz. Knoxville: University of Tennessee Press, 1998.

Black, Robert W. *Cavalry Raids of the Civil War*. Mechanicsburg, PA: Stackpole Books, 2004.

Blackford, Robert W. *The Civil War Service of General Gordon Granger, U.S.A.* Unpublished master's thesis. Edwardsville, Illinois: Southern Illinois University, 1990.

Boynton, H.V., *Chattanooga and Chickamauga: reprint of Gen. H.V. Boynton's letters to the Cincinnati Commercial Gazette, August 1888.* Washington, DC: G.R. Gray, 1891, 1888.

Boynton, Henry V. *Annual Address Delivered at the Twenty-third Reunion of the Society of the Army of the Cumberland.* Cincinnati: R. Clarke, 1892.

Branch, Muriel Miller. *Juneteenth: Freedom Day.* New York: Cobblehill, 1998.

Brewer, Richard. *The Tullahoma Campaign: Operational Insights.* Master's thesis. Fort Leavenworth, Kansas: U.S. Army Staff College, 1991.

Bunting III, Josiah. *Ulysses S. Grant.* New York: Macmillan, The American Presidents Series, 2004.

Burr, Frank A. and Hinton, Richard Josiah. *'Little Phil' and His Troopers: The Life of Gen. Philip H. Sheridan.* Providence, RI. Reid, 1888.

Cadwallader, Sylvanus. *Three Years With Grant.* New York: Knopf, 1956. University of Nebraska Press, 1996.

Carter, Arthur B. *The Tarnished Cavalier: Major General Earl Van Dorn, C.S.A.* Knoxville: University of Tennessee Press, 1999.

Catton, Bruce. *Grant Takes Command.* Boston: Little, Brown and Company, 1968.

Cist, Henry M. *The Army of The Cumberland.* (First published 1882.) Edison, NJ: Castle Books, 2002.

Colyer, Vincent. *Peace With the Apaches of New Mexico and Arizona.* Washington: Government Printing Office, 1871/72.

Cobb, Stephen A. *The Siege of Mobile.* Beloit, WI: Beloit College Archives. http://www.beloit.edu/archives/documents/archival_collections/civil_war/reminiscence_cobb/

Cool, Paul. *Salt Warriors: Insurgency on the Rio Grande.* College Station, Texas: Texas A&M University Press, 2008.

Cooling, Benjamin Franklin. *A War Anything but Civil, The Legacies of Forts Henry and Donelson.* Hallowed Ground Magazine, Winter 2011.

Cox, Dale A. *The Battle of Marianna, Florida.* Bascom, FL, 2011.

Cowles, George, ed. *Landmarks of Wayne County, New York.* Syracuse, NY: D. Mason, 1895.

Cozzens, Peter. *General John Pope: a Life for the Nation.* Champaign: University of Illinois Press, 2000.

Cozzens, Peter. *The Shipwreck of Their Hopes: The Battles for Chattanooga.* Urbana: University of Illinois Press, 1994.

Cozzens, Peter. *This Terrible Sound, The Battle of Chickamauga.* Chicago. University of Illinois Press, 1992.

Cullum, George. *Biographical Register of the Officers and Graduates of the United States Military Academy.* Vol. 2. Boston: Houghton Mifflin, Third Ed., 1891.

Dana, Charles Anderson. *Recollections of the Civil War.* New York: D. Appleton & Co., 1909.

Davies, Henry Eugene. *General Sheridan.* New York: D. Appleton, 1895.

De Forest, John William. *Miss Ravenel's Conversion from Secession to Loyalty.* New York: Harper, 1867.

Dobak, William A. *Freedom by the Sword: The U.S. Colored Troops, 1862–1867.* Army Historical Series. Government Printing Office. 2011.

D'Orleans, Louis-Philippe-Albert. *History of the Civil War in America.* Philadelphia: J. Coates, 1875, 1888.

Duffy, James P. *Lincoln's Admiral: The Civil War Campaigns of David Farragut.* New York: John Wiley & Sons, 1997.

Eckenrode, H.J. and Conrad, Bryan. *George B. McClellan: The Man Who Saved The Union.* Chapel Hill, NC. University of North Carolina Press, 1941.

Einolf, Christopher J. *George Thomas, Virginian for the Union.* Norman, OK: University of Oklahoma Press, 2007.

Eisenhower, John S.D. *Agent of Destiny: the Life and Times of General Winfield Scott.* New York: The Free Press, 1997.

Ellison, Ralph. *Juneteenth.* Ed. John Callahan. New York: Random House, 1999.

Faust, Patricia, et al., eds. *Historical Times Illustrated Encyclopedia of the Civil War.* New York: Harper, 1986.

Fellman, Michael. *Citizen Sherman.* New York: Random House, 1995.

Fitch, John. *Annals of the Army of the Cumberland.* Philadelphia: J.B. Lippincott, 1864.

Forman, Sidney, and Morton, William, *Cadet Life Before the Mexican War, West Point Library Bulletin No. 1.* West Point, NY: U.S. Military Academy Printing Office, 1945.

Fort Granger's History signage, adapted by Civil War Landscapes Association.

Fullerton, J.S. *The Reserve Corps at Chickamauga,* in *The Century Magazine,* April 1887. New York: The Century Company, Vol. 23, New Series Vol. 11 (Nov. 1886 to April 1887), 1887.

Fullerton, J.S. *The Army of the Cumberland at Chattanooga,* in *Battles and Leaders of the Civil War,* ed. Johnson and Buel, Vol. 3. New York: The Century Co., 1884, 1888.

Gordon, George H. *A War Diary of Events in the War of the Great Rebellion.* Boston: James R. Osgood, 1882.

Gracie, Archibald. *The Truth About Chickamauga.* Boston: Houghton Mifflin, 1911.

Graf, LeRoy P., Bergeron, Paul H., and Haskins, Ralph W., eds. *The Papers of Andrew Johnson.* University of Tennessee Press.

Grant, Ulysses S. *Personal Memoirs of U.S. Grant.* Vol. 2. New York: Charles L. Webster & Co., 1886.

Hahn, Steven. *A Nation Under Our Feet: Black Political Struggles in the Rural South from Slavery to the Great Migration.* Cambridge, Mass.: Belknap Press of Harvard University Press, 2003.

Halpine, Charles G. (aka Miles O'Reilly). *Poetical Works.* New York: Harper, 1869.

Hamalainen, Pekka. *The Comanche Empire.* New Haven: Yale University Press, 2008. Harris, Elisha. *American Medical Times.*

Hartje, Robert G. *Van Dorn: The Life and Times of a Confederate General.* Nashville: Vanderbilt Press, 1967.

Hazen, William. *A Narrative of Military Service.* Boston: Ticknor, 1885.

Henry, Robert Selph. *The Story of the Mexican War.* New York: Frederick Ungar Publishing, 1950.

Holmes, J.T. *Then and Now.* Columbus, Ohio: Berlin Printing Co., 1898.

Howard, O.O. *Chattanooga,* in *The Atlantic Monthly,* Vol. 38. Boston: H.O. Houghton and Co., 1876.

Howard, O.O. *Autobiography of Oliver Otis Howard.* New York: Baker & Taylor, 1907.

Howe, Mark Antony De Wolfe. *Moorfield Storey, Portrait of an Independent, 1845–1929.* Boston: Houghton Mifflin, 1932.

Howell, Kenneth W. *The Prolonged War,* in *Texans and War: New Interpretations of the State's Military History,* ed. Mendoza and Grear. College Station: Texas A&M University Press, 2012.

Kinsley, Rufus. Ed. David C. Rankin. *Diary of a Christian Soldier.* Cambridge University Press, 2004.

Lane, W. B. *The Regiment of Mounted Riflemen, or From Puebla to the City of Mexico,* in *United Service: A Monthly Review of Military and Naval Affairs,* Vol. 1. Philadelphia: L.R. Hamersly & Co., 1895.

Lee, Dan. *Thomas J. Wood: A Biography of the Union General in the Civil War.* Jefferson, NC: McFarland & Co.

Lewis, Lloyd. *Captain Sam Grant.* Boston: Little, Brown, 1950.

Lockley, Fred. *The Mounted Riflemen of the North-West Territory* in *The Overland Monthly,* Vol. 72, Second Series, July–Dec. 1918.

Longstreet, James. *From Manassas to Appomattox.* 2nd Ed. Philadelphia: J.B. Lippincott, 1908.

Mathes, J. Harvey. *General Forrest.* New York: D. Appleton, 1902.

McClellan, George. *McClellan's Own Story.* New York: C.L. Webster, 1887.

McComb, David G. *Texas, a Modern History.* Austin: University of Texas Press, 2010.

Moore, Frank, ed. *The Rebellion Record: A Diary of American Events, with Documents, Narratives, Illustrative Incidents, Poetry, etc . . .* 12 volumes. New York: G.P. Putnam, 1861–68. Washington: Government Printing Office.

Morton, Charles. *The Third Regiment of Cavalry*, in *The Army of the United States.* Ed. Rodenbough and Haskin, New York: Maynard, Merrill & Co., 1896.

The Official Records (abbreviated as *OR* in most references). *The War of the Rebellion: a Compilation of the Official Records of the Union and Confederate Armies.* Multiple volumes. Washington: Government Printing Office, 1880–1901. (See Preface.)

Opdycke, Emerson. *Notes on the Chickamauga Campaign* in *Battles and Leaders of the Civil War,* Vol. 3., ed. Johnson and Buel. New York: The Century Co., 1884, 1888.

Opler, Morris and Catherine. *Mescalero Apache History in the Southwest,* in *New Mexico Historical Review*, Vol. 25, Jan. 1950.

Palmer, Friend. *Early Days in Detroit.* Detroit: Hunt & June, 1906).

Palmer, John M. *Personal Recollections of John M. Palmer: The Story of an Earnest Life.* Cincinnati: Robert Clarke Co., 1901.

Parker, Foxhall A. *The Battle of Mobile Bay and the Capture of Forts Powell, Gaines and Morgan.* Boston: A. Williams & Co., 1878.

Phelps, Frederick. *A Soldier's Memoirs,* in *New Mexico Historical Review*, Vol. 25, July 1950. First published in *New York Herald*, March 12, 1893.

Piston, William Garrett. *Carter's Raid: An Episode of the Civil War in East Tennessee.* Johnson City, TN: The Overmountain Press, 1977.

Pope, John. *The Military Memoirs of General John Pope.* Ed. Cozzens and Girardi. Chapel Hill, NC: University of North Carolina Press, 1998.

Ramage, James A. *Rebel Raider: the Life of General John Hunt Morgan.* University Press of Kentucky, 1995.

Rister, Carl Coke. *The Southwestern Frontier.* Cleveland: Arthur H. Clark Co., 1928.

Ramsdell, Charles W. *Texas From the Fall of the Confederacy to the Beginning of Reconstruction,* in *The Quarterly of the Texas State Historical Association*, Vol. 11. Austin, Texas: 1908.

Rasch, Philip J. *The Men at Fort Stanton.* Brand Book, April 1961. (The English Westerners' Society.)

Roberts, David. *Once They Moved Like the Wind: Cochise, Geronimo and the Apache Wars.* New York: Touchstone, 1994.

Robertson, William Glen, et al., Combat Studies Institute, *Staff Ride Handbook for the Battle of Chickamauga.* Fort Leavenworth, Kansas: U.S. Army Command and General Staff College, 1992.

Ross, Edmund G. *History of the Impeachment of Andrew Johnson.* Teddington, England: Echo Library, 2007. First published 1896.

Ross, D. Reid. *Lincoln's Veteran Volunteers Win The War.* Albany, NY: SUNY Press, 2008.

Rowland, Thomas J. *George B. McClellan and Civil War History.* Ohio: Kent State University Press, 1998.

Sanchez, Gurule, Larrichio and Miller. *Fort Union National Monument Ethnographic Overview and Assessment.* National Park Service, 2006.

Seventy-eighth Illinois Infantry Regiment History, adjutant-general's report, per The Illinois USGenWeb Project.

Shanks, William F.G. *Personal Recollections of Distinguished Generals.* New York: Harper, 1866).

Sheridan, Philip. *Personal Memoirs of P.H. Sheridan.* Vol. 1. New York: Charles Webster & Co., 1888.

Sherman, William T. *Memoirs of General William T. Sherman.* New York: D. Appleton, 1875.

Simon, John Y., ed. *The Papers of Ulysses S. Grant,* Vol.10. Southern Illinois University Press, 1982.

Simpson, Brooks. *Ulysses S. Grant, Triumph over Adversity, 1822–1865.* New York: Houghton Mifflin, 2000.

Smallwood, Crouch, Peacock. *Murder and Mayhem: the War of Reconstruction in Texas.* College Station: Texas A&M University Press, 2003.

Smith, George and Judah, Charles, eds. *Chronicles of the Gringos.* University of New Mexico Press, 1968.

Stanley, David S., ed. Samuel Fordyce. *An American General, The Memoirs of David Sloan Stanley.* Santa Barbara, Calif.: The Narrative Press, 2003.

(Stanley, David S.) *Society of the Army of the Cumberland, Fifteenth Reunion.* Vol. 15. Cincinnati: Robert Clarke & Co., 1884. (See note 8 to Chapter 1.)

Starr, Stephen Z. *The Union Cavalry in the Civil War.* 3 volumes. Baton Rouge: LSU Press, 1979, 1981, 1985.

Stuart, Reginald Charles. *The Role of Cavalry in the Western Theatre of the American Civil War From the Battle of Shiloh to the Tullahoma Campaign.* Master's thesis in history. University of British Columbia, 1968.

Stewart, David O. *Impeached: The Trial of President Andrew Johnson and the Fight for Lincoln's Legacy.* New York: Simon & Schuster, 2009.

Stevens, Joseph E. *1863: The Rebirth of a Nation.* New York: Random House, 2000.

Stiles, T.J. *The First Tycoon: The Epic Life of Cornelius Vanderbilt.* New York: Vintage Books, 2010.

Sweeney, Edwin R. *Cochise, Chiricahua Apache Chief.* University of Oklahoma Press, 1991, 1995.

Taylor, Col. Samuel. *Granger Saves the Federal Right at Chickamauga,* in *About North Georgia,* http://ngeorgia.com/history/granger.html).

Thatcher, Marshall P. *A Hundred Battles in the West: St. Louis to Atlanta, 1861–65. The Second Michigan Cavalry.* Detroit: Published by the author, 1884.

Third Cavalry Museum staff, *Blood and Steel!* (regimental history). Fort Hood, Texas: 2008.

Turner, Elizabeth Hayes, *Juneteenth: Emancipation and Memory*, in *Lone Star Posts: Memory and History in Texas*. Ed. Cantrell and Turner. College Station: Texas A&M University Press, 2007.

Trulock, Alice Rains. *In the Hands of Providence, Joshua L. Chamberlain and the American Civil War*. Chapel Hill, NC: University of North Carolina Press, 1992.

Van Derveer, Ferdinand., report in *Minnesota in the Civil and Indian Wars, 1861–1865*. St. Paul, Minnesota: Pioneer Press, 2nd ed., 1891.

Welsh, Jack D. *Medical Histories of Union Generals*. Kent, Ohio: Kent State University Press, 1996.

Williams, Kenneth P. *Grant Rises in the West: From Iuka to Vicksburg, 1862–1863*. University of Nebraska Press, Bison Books, 1956, 1997.

Wilson, Ephraim. *Memoirs of the War*. Cleveland: W.M. Bayne Printing Co., 1893.

Wilson, James H. *Under the Old Flag*, Vol. 1. New York: D. Appleton and Co., 1912.

Wood, Thomas J. *The Battle of Missionary Ridge*, in *Sketches of War History, 1861–65*, Ed. Chamberlain. Cincinnati: Robert Clarke Company, 1896.

Wood, T.J., in *Seventh Annual Reunion of the Association of the Graduates of the United States Military Academy*. New York: A.S. Barnes & Co., 1876.

Wyeth, John Allan. *That Devil Forrest: The Life of General Nathan Bedford Forrest*. First published in New York: Harper, 1899. Revised edition, LSU Press, 1959.

Index

Farragut, Admiral David D., 1, 33, 151–
154, 156–157, 161, 176
First Baptist Society of Sodus, 12
Forrest, Gen. Nathan B., 7, 51, 64, 71–73,
75, 77, 88, 96–97, 99, 109, 144, 162,
170, 195
Forsyth, Gen. George, 186
Fort Alexis, 167
Fort Barrancas, Florida, 160
Fort Blakely, Alabama, 163, 166, 168, 170,
180
Fort Bowie, 205
Fort Craig, 30, 202
Fort Defiance, 30
Fort Donelson, 48, 70
Fort Ewell, 28
Fort Gaines, Alabama, 153–154, 156, 158,
160–161, 166
Fort Granger, 73
Fort Inge, 28
Fort Leavenworth, Kansas, 29, 35, 211
Fort McIntosh, 28
Fort McRae, 205
Fort Merrill, 28
Fort Morgan, Alabama, 154, 156, 160,
164–166, 175
Fort Powell, Alabama, 154, 156
Fort Sill, 206
Fort Stanton, 204
Fort Wayne, Michigan, 20
Foster, Gen. John, 132, 139–140, 142–
143, 145
Fosterville, Tennessee, 77
Frankfort, Kentucky, 57, 61, 67
Franklin, Tennessee, 71, 73
Freedmen's Bureau, 181, 184, 193–195,
206
Fremont, Gen. John C., 36, 40, 65, 180
Fullerton, Lt. Col. Joseph, 6, 89, 95, 98,
100, 104, 106, 118, 125, 132, 140

Galveston, Texas, 176, 178–179
Garfield, Gen. James, 71, 79–80, 85, 87,
100–103, 151

Garland, Louise, 20
General Order No. 3, 177, 183–184, 186
Geneva Courier, 209
German, Lt. Obadiah, 127
Gilbert, Gen. Charles, 71
Gilded Age, 193
Gillem, Gen. Alvan, 192
Gillmore, Gen. Quincy A., 66–67, 70
Gordon, Gen. George H., 157
Gracie III, Gen. Archibald, 33
Gracie IV, Gen. Archibald, 103–104,
106–108
Granger, Catherine, 10
Granger, Elihu, 13
Granger, Emeline, 10
Granger, Gaius, 9–10, 12–15
Granger, Gen. Gordon, 4–5, 47, 57, 69,
72, 74, 79, 87–89, 105, 135, 163, 177,
194, 212, 218; AAG to Sturgis, 36;
adrift after Texas, 191; advance on
Spring Hill, 72; Andrew Johnson, 181;
antagonism with Grant, 16, 190;
appointed colonel of 2nd Michigan
Cavalry, 6, 40–41; appointed
commander of the District of West
Florida and Southern Alabama, 158;
appointed commander of the Reserve
Corps, 75–76; argumentative, 2;
arrives in Kentucky, 58; assigned to
14th Infantry, 202; assigned to 15th
Infantry, 202; assumes command of
Fourth Corps, 114–115; attends
Thomas' funeral, 202; bad terms with
Sheridan, 190; birth of daughter, 210;
Booneville, 51; brevet promotions to
brigadier general and major general,
160; brevetted captain, 25; brevetted
first lieutenant, 24; brevetted
lieutenant colonel, 114; brevetted
major, 40; brevetted second lieutenant,
20; Bridgeport, 85; brought to
Washington to advise Johnson, 197–
199; brutal honesty, 2; burial of, 219;
buried in Lexington, Kentucky, 68;